FUNDAMENTALS
OF
SPIRITISM

Jon Aizpúrua

ISBN: 1484101634
ISBN 13: 9781484101636

Dedicated to the memory of my dear friend Juan Albino Serrano.

FORWARD

This book is an English translation and updated edition of *Los Fundamentos del Espiritismo (Fundamentals of Spiritism) (Ediciones C.I.M.A., 2000)* written by Jon Aizpúrua, a professor of psychology. It has had wide circulation in Spanish-speaking countries.

Jon Aizpúrua was born in Caracas, Venezuela. He was trained in many disciplines and works as a clinical psychologist, economist, producer, and radio broadcaster. He has had a brilliant career as author and scholar. A University professor for over 30 years, Jon currently is the Professors' Counsel Representative at the University of Venezuela, Caracas. In addition, Jon was president of the Spiritist Cultural Movement (C.I.M.A.) in Venezuela and the Spiritist Pan-American Confederation (CEPA) during the years 1993 to 2000. He is the vice – president of the Circle for Writers of Venezuela (2012 to 2014). As a author, Jon's major books are*: Tratado Espiritista (Spiritist Treatis) (Edicomunicacion, S.A, 1991), Espiritismo y La Creación Poética (Spiritism and Poétic Creation) (Ediciones C.I.M.A., 1993), Historia de la Parasicología (History of Parapsychology) (Editora Cultural Espirita Leon Denis C.A., 1995), Los Fundamentos del Espiritismo (Fundamentals of Spiritism) (Ediciones C.I.M.A., 2000), and Arquitectos de la Libertad Americana (Architects of American Liberty) (Casa Editora Ex-Libris, 2006), and Razón y Passión de la Novela (Reason and Passion for a novel) (Editorial Universidad Central de Venezuela, 2009).*

Jon Aizpúrua is a captivating and talented orator. He has offered conferences and seminars at universities and cultural institutions throughout Europe and America. He presently acts as cultural supervisor for the History Channel International for Latin America.

He has produced 94 audio-book disks on history, literature, art and philosophy. His radio programs are well known: "Values of the Spirit" and "Great Biographies". These are transmitted weekly since the year 2000 to Venezuela and the world by Union Radio – AM–1090 and 90.3– FM – Caracas. His website is: www.valoresdelespiritu.com.

Fundamentals of Spiritism (Epsilon Book S.R.L., 2000), offers a critical and rational analysis of the differences and similarities between spiritual tendencies through the prism of Spiritism. It describes Spiritist views on the soul, the purpose of material life, the afterlife, and reincarnation. What makes it even more valuable is that it takes a textbook form, which facilitates reading and study; this makes it ideal for group learning. This book is a practical resource for independent readers, health and behavioral health clinicians and researchers who wish to better understand Spiritism from a logical, reasoned, naturalistic and non- dogmatic perspective.

The author clarifies the many mysteries behind the study of the soul, as well as spirituality, and its relation to religion and science. Other significant topics are ESP, ghosts, psychokinesis, poltergists, near death experience, reincarnation, mediumship/channelers, spirit release therapies, mental healings, and paranormal phenomena and their inter-relationships. In the final sections, the book presents a workshop with specifics on techniques and requirements toward development as an effective psychic, medium, healer, spiritual person and/or researcher into these phenomena. He offers recommendations for the healthy development and use of mediumship and relationships to paranormal phenomena.

The study and understanding of Spiritism as an ethnomedical practice continues to be important since distressed persons of various social strata and nationalities seek help and solace from Spiritist mediums. One attraction of Spiritist healing is that it avoids the stigma of psychiatric illness; it is also person-centered and empathic. It deals with spiritual crises without being dogmatic; supplicants feel supported and understood. Study of Spiritism as an ethnomedical system illuminates one kind of spirituality that can act as a reference for health and mental health clinicians.

Fundamentals of Spiritism explains how Spiritism seeks answers guided by science and philosophy. The role of science here is to objectively confirm Spiritist observations; philosophy facilitates an understanding of the moral and social consequences of such findings. The book's purpose is to satisfy those persons who want to fulfill their inner need for evidence of the survival of consciousness, providing a new perspective that has implications applicable to all dimensions of life.

San Juan, Puerto Rico
Jesús Soto Espinosa, Ph.D.

ENDORSEMENT:

Endorsement for the Fundamentals of Spiritism
Spiritism, a philosophical –ethical movement, has been popular in all of the social strata in Latin America since the late 19th century. Jon Aizpúrua's book, Fundamentals of Spiritism (2009), is a well written, systematic explanation of Spiritism in a detailed form which encompasses not only the history and philosophy of this movement but also the practices of mediumship, a complex and new world view that includes spirits, and a rational, science-based perspective on the elements that make up this world. I highly recommend it as a comprehensive introductory text for the English speaking world.

Joan Koss, Ph.D.

NOTE OF ACKNOWLEDGEMENT:

I would like to express my sincerest gratitude to the following people: Yvonne Crespo Limoges, Tania Nanfra, Jesus Soto-Espinosa, Juan Albino Serrano and Maria Gabriela Cuzcó for their moral support and suggestions, especially valuable were Carmen Diéguez's ideas and technical guidance.

Again, I am particularly thankful to Yvonne Crespo Limoges who offered advice on bringing the book up-to-date and editing the entire book.

My warmest gratitude is extended to the Spiritist organization Ciencia Espiritista Kardeciana in Miami that held a conference in 2006 where fruition for the idea for the publishing of this book began.

CONTENTS

Chapter One

BASIC PRINCIPLES OF SPIRITISM

"Spiritism is both an observational science and a philosophical doctrine. As a practical science, it consists of the interactions that can be established with spirits; as a philosophical doctrine, it comprehends all the moral consequences derived from such a relationship."

***Allan Kardec* – Codifier of Spiritism**

The essential principles which support, are studied, and revealed by the Spiritist doctrine have been well known since remote epochs of time and have been expressed in various forms in every cultural, artistic, mythological, religious, and philosophical manifestation that has accompanied humanity's evolutionary process. Therefore, it is not an original doctrine in its basic ideas regarding the existence of God, immortality of the soul, spirit communication, or reincarnation since these ideas were already part of accepted beliefs amongst a majority of people. Nevertheless, Spiritism differentiates itself because it views this knowledge through a completely different prism that comes from a rationalist and naturalist perspective in its approach and explanation of these concepts.

From a strictly historical sense, Spiritism arose from the tremendous theoretical and experimental work accomplished in the mid-nineteenth century by the French educator Hippolyte Léon Denizard Rivail, more widely known by his *nom de plume* ALLAN KARDEC, who elaborated on the definition of these concepts, framed them within a doctrine, and noted their consequences. Spiritism founded, systematized and codified by Kardec is a truly scientific, philosophical and moral cosmic vision completely capable of offering humanity a new comprehension of the Creator, of the laws that govern the material and spiritual substances of the universe and its evolutionary processes and of the eternal transcendence of Being and of Life. Its chief work is *The Spirits' Book* which contains the primary principles of the Spiritist Doctrine and is part of a whole work in which its parts are integrated into several books that constitute the Codification. They are: *The Mediums' Book*, *The Gospel According to Spiritism*, *Heaven and Hell*, *Genesis*, *What is Spiritism?*, *Posthumous Works*, and other smaller works, as well as the twelve volumes of the newsletters of the S*pirite Revue*.

LÉON DENIS, Kardec's greatest philosophical disseminator and an illustrious writer of Spiritism, proclaimed, that upon reflecting on the wide-ranging implications of the Spiritist Doctrine, it would most certainly reunite and fuse within a grandiose synthesis all the schools of thought and of the sciences.

A profile of the Spiritist Doctrine can be formed by the following basic concepts:

THE EXISTENCE OF A CREATOR

"One should adore God by the practice of love and goodness, and for that there is no need of temples or priests; the best altar is the heart of a virtuous being, and the best cult is an irreproachable morality. God does not demand that a man follow a specific religion, but that he be humble and above all else that he love others as he does himself."

Amalia Domingo Soler
Spiritist Writer and Poet from Spain (1832-1912)

The Spiritist Doctrine sets as its first major principle the existence of a Creator, acknowledging it as Supreme Intelligence and First Cause of all things. Taking into consideration intuition, in synthesis with proper philosophical deduction that effects are proportional to the forces that generated them, this presents a Creator as a necessary and efficient cause that allows understanding of the majesty of the universe and its harmonious unfoldment, from the minuscule subatomic particles up to the immensity of the cosmos.

Realizing the limitations of thought and language derived from a rational and logical perspective, Spiritism, nevertheless, tries to approach a cosmic vision of the Divinity, affirming that by definition and nature, the Creator is eternal, infinite, immutable, immaterial, unique, omnipotent, supremely just and good, since if any of these attributes were not present it would cease to be the Creator.

Eminent contemporary scientists have pronounced themselves in favor of the existence of a Creator in its cosmic plenitude, as an intelligent force, creator of everything that exists, as a natural corollary of their investigations into the intricacies of matter and the complexities of life. This is how the British physicist JAMES JEAN expressed it in an eloquent phrase that unites poetry with quantum physics:

"Each day scientists perceive the universe less as a machine and more as a system of thought."

That is why the Spiritist concept of the Creator distances itself radically from anthropomorphic ideas which attribute to a God, human forms and attributes as characterized in religious doctrines from various civilizations and cultures all over the planet. Therefore, God is not conceived as a personal being, a patriarchal entity, or as a severe and capricious judge that applies harsh punishments or distributes prizes and compensations.

Spiritism explains that the law of adoration is fulfilled elevating one's thought towards the Creator and conducting life in a dignified, honest and loving way, dispensing with all intermediaries, as well as any types of cults, rituals, or sacramental formulas.

No one progresses morally and spiritually by the simple act of believing a certain religious or spiritualist belief or by participating in specific cults or mystical ceremonies. Real progress is the result of personal effort manifested in the moral and integral transformation that each human being demonstrates in its thoughts and actions. In conformance with the superior moral teachings of JESUS, the law of adoration is summarized within these universal principles: Love God in spirit and truth; love your neighbor as yourself, and do not do to others what you would not want done to yourself. In short, Spiritism, echoing the simple yet at the same time profound message of the brilliant Master of Nazareth, states that: God is Love.

PREEXISTENCE AND SURVIVAL OF THE SPIRIT

"The cradle has a yesterday, and the grave a tomorrow."

Victor Hugo
Renowned French Author (1802-1895)

The spirit is the intelligent principle of the universe. All that has life has a spirit. We existed before we were born and we will continue to live after death. Regarding life as a continuum and from an existential viewpoint we can affirm that we were, are and will be, and, from a more amplified spiritual perspective we may uphold that we preexist, exist, coexist and subsist.

All human beings are imbued with an immortal psychic entity. In the vegetable kingdom it manifests itself through their sensitivity to stimuli. In animals, this rudimentary soul expresses itself mainly through instinct and reasoning at an elemental level. In human beings, it is the seat of a superior individuality and manifests itself through its cognitive expressions, desires and conduct progressing in alternating phases of successive incarnations and reincarnations. The fundamental attributes of the spirit are: individuality, intelligence, conscience, will power and free will. Spirits are the intelligent beings that populate the universe in its incarnated and disincarnated aspects. Using Spiritist terminology, a soul is an incarnated spirit and spirits are souls that are disincarnated.

Therefore, one should not say that we have a spirit because in reality we are a spirit, but with a body. The physical organism is not the true individual but its external representation. We are a spirit with a body that we utilize and conduct according to our intellectual and moral level of evolution. And between them both, defined and called the *perispirit* by Kardec, is a subtle fluidic body that envelopes the spirit. The perispirit plays a series of functions of great importance and acts rather as a force field uniting the dense particles of matter that constitute the biological organism. In this way, the Spiritist vision of an incarnate being is as an individual having a spirit with its perispirit and physical body, perfectly attuned with the current holistic concept which presents an Integral Human with a four dimensional perspective as a biological-intellectual-social-spiritual entity.

Surmounting apparent and sensory illusions, the majority of men and women in all ages have felt germinate the wonderful idea of continuous survival as a profound and intimate claim of the essential principle that vibrates within each and everyone: one's immortal spirit. Many of these beings have found support for this ideal through faith and others by speculative theorizing. Now, thanks to Spiritism, humanity can attain certainty through research and experimental verification. The continuous existence of a spirit entity regarding the state that awaits all human beings after death is no longer a metaphysical abstraction or an article of religious faith, but instead a positive and specific fact demonstrated through the study of psychic phenomena and mediumship by way of Spiritism. +NDEs + hypnotic LBL plenl news,

Theologians of all religions have characterized the soul as such an intangible idea, that in truth, this has equaled to almost a denial of it. In reaction to this absurd conception, intellectual materialists thinking they could cut this Gordian knot, decreed the extinction of the soul or spirit and transferred all of its properties to the physical body. Although DESCARTES brilliantly expressed in his time the dualistic idea that addresses all of spiritualism at its essence by calling *res extensa* (the material substance) and *res cogitans* (the spiritual element). It is Spiritism, although a scientific spiritualism, that has established the real, concrete, and the objective existence of the spirit. And, it was precisely the discovery of the perispirit (because of its plasticity and mediatory action) that could resolve the great metaphysical problem of the incompatibility of both substances due to their essential differences. Supported by the Spiritist thesis, countless experiments, and much research, the eminent French physician GUSTAVE GELEY presented a coherent system of philosophy, yet at the same time scientific, idealistic, and dialectic, supported on two capital propositions:

1) Whatever is essential in the Universe and in the individual, is a unique dynamic psychism, primitively unconscious, containing within, all its potentialities. The diverse and innumerable appearances of things are nothing more than their representations.

2) The essential dynamic psychism and creation passes, by evolution, from the unconscious to the conscious. [1]

of IRREDUCIBLE MIND

Today, both propositions are sustained by facts that can be objects of precise verification, first in the individual, and then later, by vast induction within the Universe.

Spiritism liberates men from its anguish over death, giving meaning to immortality by bringing out with crystal clarity the authentic reality of human destiny after the physical state of disintegration. This situation completely differs from the sanctimonious heavens and gloomy hells of all religious mythologies. In reality, the soul's state of consciousness after physical death, whether agreeable or unpleasant, satisfying or unhappy, are the acquired consequences of our own acts within transitory stages that have to be overcome by our own efforts through new opportunities.

---

[1] GUSTAVE GELEY. *Del Inconsciente al Consciente* [*From the Unconscious to the Conscious*]. CIMA, Caracas, 1995, p.204. (Geley used his term "dynamic psychism" as a synonym for the word "spirit.").

REINCARNATION

> *"With reincarnation, one can no longer say, 'it's not my fault to have been born within these terrible times!' You helped prepare this period during a previous existence. Endeavor to make the world of tomorrow much better; more just, more enlightened, because you will surely return to it, and you will reap what you have sown. In the course of some centuries, perhaps you may rest under the shade of this centennial oak tree you planted today."*

> **Amado Nervo**
> **Journalist, Diplomat and Poet from Mexico**
> **(1895-1919)**

To reincarnate is literally, to return to the flesh. It is a return of the spirit to the corporeal life within a different body in each existence, formed and constituted in accordance with the prevailing psychical and biological characteristics at that stage of its evolutionary course.

The spirit will utilize diverse biological organisms along its millennial trajectory, obtaining new knowledge and experiences within multiple successive lives. In this manner, the past and the present are linked into a causal relationship that frames the perfecting of every being's development and the creation of its own future. Earthly life is nothing more than an episode of an extensive drama in which each death (as well as when we are sleeping) is an intermission. In between the cradle and the grave, the being accumulates new intellectual and moral data that is incorporated within the spirit and taken to the spirit world in transit to the frontiers of the beyond. Material life is a school, and as such, there are grade levels permitting those who have gotten behind in their studies to repeat a course that was missed. Life is short; as short as one year of school, in order to acquire all knowledge. Death arrives and the human being, after spending a period of life in space, is born again within an organism that is adequate to its conditions, in accordance with its progress, and the type of life it needs for its continued improvement.

There is no going back in evolution. Spirits may remain temporarily stationary, but they do not regress. Reincarnation, understood and explained with full precision through Spiritism, excludes the erroneous concept of metempsychosis that pretends the transmigration of the soul of a human being into inferior animal states, respective of levels already superseded within the stages of the phylogenetic scale.

The spiritual progress acquired in past existences is never lost, even though we do not remember the details of those former experiences with our cerebral consciousness. The unconscious, subliminal or extra cerebral memory stores all that information that can emerge and manifest during certain modified and amplified states of consciousness. It can be obtained through procedures like hypnotic induction, holotropic breathing or deep meditation. This demonstrates that human beings possess reserves of superior psychic faculties that does not explicitly appear in everyday life, but implicitly is known within intuitive knowledge or in early precocious talents as child prodigies or as creative genius manifesting in the arts or sciences. Reincarnation insures learning continuity, and is therefore an indispensable mechanism to guarantee the moral and physical evolution of mankind. It explains in a form most rationally and satisfactorily the material, social, intellectual and moral differences among humans, and the reparation and the personal recovering of committed wrongs, creating paths of progress for all

The doctrine of reincarnation, also known as palingenesis, is self-evident due to its logic and rationality. Belief in reincarnation has been widespread among many peoples' traditions and has been reflected upon by numerous great intellectuals around the world, in ages past up until this modern age. One can assert that it is one of the most universally accepted concepts of human existence and its destiny, in all epochs around the world. Humanity will have reached a milestone in its evolution when it completely understands that to be born, to die, and to be reborn, are the same terms in the equation equal to: LIFE.

UNIVERSAL EVOLUTION

"The law of development is the law of succession.

The law of succession is the law of perfectibility.

The law of perfectibility is the law of progress.

Every degree of development implies a mode of manifestation.

Every manifestation implies a different organic form.

Every determined form implies a manner of life distinct from others.

The germ of spiritual potential, in the fulfillment of its forced progress, must indispensably go through each and every level, through all manifestations, through every form and genres of known life, and it must complete its full realization in its infinite potential, in its infinite possibility and in its infinite time, going through infinite forms, manifestations and types of life unknown, which it synthesizes into absolute perfection."

Manuel Gonzalez Soriano
Spiritist Author from Spain (1837-1885)

The fundamental law that rules the Universe is evolution, from which all the others are subsidiary and complementary. From micro particles to the immense stellar systems, from the initial cosmic explosions to its actual configurations; all that exists, vibrates, transforms and evolves to the compass of the dynamic impulses of evolution. Energy, matter, life, spirit, consciousness, mankind, society; everything is interrelated within an infinite process of evolutionary transformations.

Spiritual evolution occurs parallel to material evolution. At the initial steps of planetary formation, the spiritual principle essays in a rudimentary form as a cohesive force that associates with molecular bodies. In later and higher stages, there are present characteristics of vital elements prepared to ascend a non-stop path towards the complete achievement of its potentiality. It goes through progressive complex phases on a superior evolutionary course, through the vegetal and animal kingdoms until it reaches the humanoid state wherein the soul acquires the consciousness of its own reality. Now, man not only is, but he knows that he is; turning himself into a historic subject, at the same time being protagonist, witness and author of his own existence. Experience, training, learning gave stronger wings to thought and reason, progressively turning it into the beautiful and powerful tool manifested into an actual human. Ideas originally transmitted orally and later through the written word, linked individuals and laid the foundations for the formation of social, economic and political organizations, and its expression through the most various forms of knowledge in its magical, mythological, pre-logic, religious, artistic, philosophical, scientific, judiciary and ethical aspects.

The Spiritist Doctrine perfectly reconciles with the notion of a Creator, as Supreme Intelligence and First Cause of all things, within the general dynamic of evolution and when it discovers an intentionality that guides the process that originates and transforms all that exists. It secures its feeling and destiny, covered in the following stages: **Cosmogenesis** (origin and evolution of all universal reality), **Spirit genesis** (creation and progress of spirits fulfilling the laws of reincarnation), **Biogenesis** (life's emergence and species' successive transformations), **Anthropogenesis** (appearance of man, ontogenetic and phylogenetic development), **Psychogenesis** (beginning and progressive psychic complexity until acquisition of the reflexive consciousness), and **Socio genesis** (formation and expansion of mankind's collective life within the process of civilization.).

The evolutionary vision was clearly embraced by Kardec in all his works, sanctioned by the spirits that advised him in the grand codification of Spiritism. In the major work of the Spiritist Doctrine, *The Spirits' Book*, its first edition appearing in Paris on April 18 of 1857, spiritual guides precisely answered every question posed by the French educator:

-Since animals have an intelligence that gives them a degree of free action, do they have a principle independent of matter? "Yes, and it survives their bodies." (Question 597)

-The intelligence of man and of the animals emanates, then, from one and the same principle? "Undoubtedly, but in the human it has received an elaboration that elevates it above that which animates the brute." (Question 606)

-You have stated that the soul of man, at its origin, is in a state analogous to that of human infancy, that its intelligence is only beginning to unfold itself, and that it is essaying to live; where does the soul accomplish this earliest phase of its career? "In a series of existences, which precedes the period of development you call humanity." (Question 607) [2]

Later, in his book *Genesis* published in 1868, Kardec reiterates and elaborates this, supported by rigorous scientific arguments and in light of new information obtained by spirit communications through mediums, his convictions about the biological and spiritual evolution that links all living forms:

"Although one can observe the scale of living beings at an organic point of view, one can see from the lichen to the tree and from the zoophyte to man, there is a continuous elevating hierarchy without interruption and maintaining a relationship linking the chains altogether. Following step by step the series of beings,

---

[2] ALLAN KARDEC. *El Libros de los Espíritus* [*The Spirits' Book*]. Lake, Sao Paulo, Book II, Ch. XI, p. 267.

one can say that each species is an improvement, a transforma-tion of the species immediately below it. Since the same chemical and constitutional conditions are identical in the body of a man, and is born, dies, and lives in the same manner, he must have been formed in the same manner." (Answer to question 28)

"Although it may be humbling, man must resign himself to the fact that his material body is the last step in the animal pro-gression upon the earth. The argument in favor of this concep-tion is inevitable and valid." (Answer to question 29) [3]

By the light of Spiritism, the evolutionary concept is funda-mentally supported by the thesis of the plurality of existences, resolv-ing doubts and difficulties that were not possible to explain solely from a biological or materialistic perspective. Completely reason-able, this assisted GUSTAVE GELEY to affirm that the law of rein-carnation was a logical corollary to the law of evolution. The distin-guished French metaphysicist and Spiritist in his brilliantly written book *From the Unconscious to the Conscious*, the so-called classical factors are impotent in the demonstration in the origins of the species, incapable to explain the sudden creative transformations of new spe-cies, as well as to solve the philosophical difficulty related to evolu-tion that the complex would arise from the simple, that is, from the less to the more, without the factor of a spiritual continuity.

In short, Spiritism helps us understand both aspects of the evolutionary process, energy and matter, body and spirit, and that the entire phenomena can only be grasped when, aside from the physi-cal description of things, one looks also at the interior of things as well, that is to say, taking into consideration the essential psycho-dynamic factor, the spiritual force that resides in every living being that transcends the death of the physical organism, remaining identi-cal in essence, in spite of experiencing constant modifications and

---

[3] ALLAN KARDEC. Génesis [*Genesis*].CIMA, Caracas, 1995, Ch. X, No. 28 & 29.

continuous improvements. Man is not an accidental caprice of nature or the uncertain results of trial and error. It is a part of a vast cosmic theological plan, which is demonstrated within the dynamic of its spirit, emerging from the abyss of life, advancing, step by step, until it converts into a superior spirit. This concept is synthesized within this masterful phrase of superior spirituality with what question Item 540 closes with, in *The Spirits' Book*:

"In this manner, everything in nature is linked together, from the primitive atom to the archangel, for it began as an atom."

MEDIUMSHIP

"Mediumship is a delicate flower that must be cultivated with care and love."

Léon Denis
French Author, Lecturer, and Disseminator of
Spiritism (1846-1927)

The faculty of mediumship has always existed and mediums have always had the capability to act as intermediaries between the incarnated and the disincarnated, or as some say, between the living and the dead. This last phrase is a totally inappropriate expression as no one is really dead and we are all definitively alive. History records the presence of mediumship manifestations in all epochs and in all civilizations, accompanying the human being in its evolutionary process. Nevertheless, the universality of mediumship phenomena does not coincide with the diverse interpretations that have been given for it covering a considerable range that extends to ideas ranging from the magical, mythological, demonic, celestial, mystical, esoteric to the psychological or psychiatric concepts that try to reduce it to an unconscious mental expression of a suggestive or pathological nature.

Fortunately, in these modern times, Spiritism emerges in order for us to know, understand, and explain the mechanisms of the process of mediumship which acts in a mode as intermediary by which both the visible and the invisible worlds, incarnate and disincarnate beings, may relate in a diverse and permanent way. Mediumship is one thing and Spiritism is another. Mediumship is the phenomena. Spiritism is the doctrine that studies the phenomena. The Spiritist Doctrine reveals that mediumship is a natural human faculty that we all have in different degrees, independently of race, nationality or beliefs. Spiritism acknowledges and studies two types of extrasensory phenomena: mediumship and psychic. In the first, **a disincarnate spirit** produces the intellectual or physical manifestations through the intellectual and physical resources within the medium. In psychic manifestations, **the person's own spirit**, having acquired a certain degree of emancipation in relation to its physical body may produce similar effects, but in reality the spirit has only temporarily recovered a certain freedom. These are identified as paranormal phenomena of extra sensory perception and psychokinesis.

Through mediumship, the immortality of the soul is scientifically proven. This rectifies the false ideas of heaven and hell, the devil and eternal punishment, because we can now make contact with our loved ones and receive important information from diverse spiritual sources. A well developed and utilized mediumship can offer significant contributions for the explanation of many situations and conflicts, involving the individual, or of a familial, social, or of an organic and psychological nature. When studied and practiced within the technical, cultural, and moral parameters taught by the Spiritist Doctrine, mediumship is an effective instrument in aiding us in the process of our own personal and moral growth, as well as in self-knowledge. Mediumship activity, from the Spiritist viewpoint, should not be considered as a profession but solely as a service for the good of humanity. Therefore, no remuneration or profit is permitted nor is it to be used for any frivolous or wicked purposes. Spiritist mediumship is inconsistent and unconnected to any combination of different beliefs or to any ritualistic, ceremonial, or mystical practices, or any superstitious beliefs. Spiritist mediumship consecrates itself exclusively to Goodness, Truth, and Love.

PLURALITY OF WORLDS

"The idea of the plurality of inhabited worlds affirms and arises within men's spirit through the study of the Cosmos."

Camille Flammarion
French Astronomer and Author (1842-1925)

In the early stages, when Kardec established the foundations of the Spiritist Doctrine, included within its basic principles was the existence of life and intelligence beyond the earth. Logical arguments in favor of this thesis, derived from a coherent rational deduction, were amply corroborated by information provided by responses from the spirit world. Among the studious Spiritists that collaborated with Allan Kardec there was the famous French astronomer CAMILLE FLAMMARION who published various works about this topic; one among them would reach wide circulation entitled *Plurality of Inhabited Worlds* first published in 1862. In modern times, the American Pulitzer Prize winning author, advisor to NASA and eminent scientist of astronomy, CARL SAGAN (1934-1996), wrote profusely about and greatly promoted the search for intelligent life outside of our world.

Life is not an accident, a coincidence or an exceptional event produced on earth as a result of a combination of organic elements preceded by an infinite sequence of trials and errors. No; life obeys a cosmic plan and it is a universal constant. We are not alone in the universe. Our planet is not the only one inhabited by intelligent beings.

It should be taken into account that the astronomical dimensions, mathematical figures, and statistical calculations demonstrate the improbability of the earth being the only one with life. Our planet does not possess any particular privilege within the universe. It is just one more planet within a particular solar system that is part of a galaxy, the Milky Way, in which there are well over 200,000 billion suns. Recent technology has already allowed us to discover planetary systems outside our own. It has been demonstrated that in the area of the universe that we have observed there are more nebulas of amazing magnitudes than stars within our own Milky Way galaxy! Could we be the only living beings within a cosmos of such proportions? Only the anthropocentric prejudices, similar to the old geocentric prejudices, could allow humans to believe that WE are the geographic, biologic and spiritual center of the Universe.

Spiritism teaches that the diverse worlds that constitute space are differentiated in their physical formation and structure as well as in the level of the progression of its inhabitants. In relation to the inhabitants on earth, some are more advanced and others more inferior. Spirits, at their starting point being one of simplicity and ignorance, reincarnate into different worlds, fulfilling their evolutionary cycles in each one, as needed. The spirits that have been reincarnating on our planet are not eternally tied to it, and will pass on to others more advanced as they reach the appropriate levels of progress. In the same manner, spirits inhabiting more morally, socially and intellectually advanced worlds may reincarnate on Earth to contribute to its progress fulfilling noble missions based on Truth and Love.

Plurality of existences within the plurality of inhabited worlds is a basic thesis of Spiritism that gives us a global comprehension of the cosmic and spiritual process of evolution.

SPIRITISM IS AN EXPERIMENTAL SCIENCE

"Spiritism is the science to which its end is the experimental demonstration of the existence of the soul and its immortality by means of communication with those who inappropriately have been called the dead."

Gabriel Delanne
French Paranormal Researcher (1857-1926)

Spiritism is a field of study of integral knowledge. As a science, it is supported by facts that are investigated, verified and explained. As a philosophy, the derivation taken from such actions establishes the consequences for comprehension of the whole of reality. As a moral doctrine, it proposes the transformation of human beings by means of education of its sentiments and through the practice of love. From the experimental scientific perspective, Spiritism presents incontestable evidence regarding the existence of a spirit animating life, the spirit's continuity beyond the death of the physical body, its existence in another dimension preserving its individual attributes and characteristics, its capability to establish interaction with the material world and its return to the physical plane in new existences. It is not about chasing chimeras or about illusions or about theories more or less probable solely achieved by intuition or philosophical reasoning, but by solidly supported evidence of the facts. If science has not officially proclaimed its existence as of yet, each day the number of the wise acknowledging these as being positive truths increases.

Science is a systematic and organized body of knowledge relating to certain categories of facts, objects, or phenomena. All disciplines, to be recognized as science must comply with three fundamental prerequisites: possess an appropriate object of study, establish adequate methods to prove your objective, and, be able to state general laws or principles in relation to the phenomena of study. Based on these conditions, Spiritism is a Science; and every definition elaborated upon by Kardec points towards the recognition of this:

> *"Spiritism is the science that studies the nature, origin and destiny of the spirits and their relationship with the corporeal world."* [4]

"Strictly speaking, the object of science is the study of the laws of the material principle, inasmuch as the object of Spiritism is the knowledge of the laws of the spiritual principle; but since this last principle is one of the forces of Nature and acts continuously upon the material principle, and vice versa, the result is that knowledge of one cannot be complete without the other. Consequently, Spiritism and science are mutually complementary." [5]

Regarding methodology, Spiritism applies the procedures and outlines formally accepted within scientific fields to investigate and experiment:

> *"As a means of elaboration, Spiritism exactly use the same approach as the positive sciences, that is to say, it applies the experimental method. Some facts of a new order present themselves that cannot be explained by known laws; Spiritism observes, compares, and analyzes it, and from the effect it advances to the cause, and from that to the law that governs*

[4] ALLAN KARDEC. *Qué es el Espiritismo [What is Spiritism?]*.CIMA. Caracas, 1994, p.10.
[5] ALLAN KARDEC. Genesis [*Génesis*]. CIMA. Caracas, 1995, C. I, No. 16, p.19.

it. Later, it deduces the consequences and looks for useful applications. It does not establish any **preconceived** *theories, which is the reason why it has not formulated a hypothesis about the existence or intervention of the spirits, neither of the perispirit, reincarnation, nor any other principles of the doctrine; it ends up accepting the existence of the spirits when it is evident through the observation of the acts, and in the same way it handles its other principles. The proofs did not come to confirm the theory, but it is the theory that came later that has come to explain and summarize these proofs. Therefore, it is rigorously exact to declare that Spiritism is a science of observation, and not the product of the imagination."* [6]

In tune with his scientific nature, Kardec always insisted that Spiritism must always adjust to the facts, be open to criticism, be ready for revision and be brought up to date whenever new discoveries arose. On many occasions he warned that "Spiritism, on pain of suicide, should never close its doors by any means to progress." The sense of evolution and progress of the Spiritist Doctrine is an essential component of its scientific condition:

"One must bear in mind that the ultimate distinctive stroke of the Spiritist revelation, which is drawn from the conditions in which it was realized, and it is that, leaning upon the facts, its character is essentially progressive, like all the sciences based on observation...

Spiritism, marching in rhythm with progress, will never be overthrown because if new discoveries should demonstrate that it is in error upon a point, it would modify itself in regard to it or if a new truth is revealed, it would make a correction." [7]

While demonstrating that it is possible to apply scientific investigation in the spiritual field, Spiritism surmounts the old theological conceptions that impeded the purpose of spirit and its manifestations; it also tears

---

[6] ALLAN KARDEC. Ibid. C. I., No. 14, p.18.

[7] ALLAN KARDEC. *Génesis* [Genesis]. CIMA. Caracas, 1995, Ch. I, No. 55, pp. 36-37.

down previous concepts relating it to magic, mystery and superstition. It has opened the way, as well, for other disciplines to emerge whose purpose is the study of mediumship and paranormal manifestations from different perspectives, with their own appropriate nomenclatures and methodologies, like investigation of consciousness, metaphysics or parapsychology which, by the way, always derive their own basic principles and conclusions. It is impossible not to comprehend the decisive contribution offered by the science of Spiritism in the theoretical and experimental development of these studies. It should be more than enough to mention the names of some important researchers in this related field such as: GABRIEL DELANNE, GUSTAVE GELEY. ERNESTO BOZZANO, WILLIAM CROOKES, FEDERICK MYERS,WILLIAM JACKSON CRAWFORD, OLIVER LODGE, KARL DU PREL, JOHANN Z0LLNER, ALEXANDER AKSAKOF, JOSE S. FERNANDEZ, ANDRE DUMAS, CARLOS IMBASSAHY, JORGE ANDREA, HENRIQUE RODRIGUES, and HERNANI GUIMARAES ANDRADE. The day when science acknowledges the principles set forth by Spiritism, it will create a veritable epistemological revolution, and its investigations, that nowadays are limited to knowledge of the material world, will extend to the spiritual, opening a new era for humanity in which it will finally fulfill the eternal desire to unite intellectual advancement with moral regeneration.

SPIRITISM IS A PROGRESSIVE PHILOSOPHY

"The Spiritist philosophy synthesizes within its ample and dynamic conceptualization, all the actual conquests of traditional philosophy, and at the same time initiates a new dialectic cycle in view of modern civilization."

Jose Herculano Pires
Brazilian Philosopher, Author and
Spiritist (1914-1979)

Etymologically, the term "philosophy" means "lover of wisdom," and in effect, the essential finality of philosophy is the conquest of truth. The history of philosophy encompasses an intense and permanent effort achieved by the human being to understand the universe and the role it plays in it. In consequence, the main topics in philosophy have always revolved around three areas: the study of Being or in the study of everything that exists which establishes an ontological approach; the study of Knowledge or the epistemological approach; and, the study of Man, in its individual as well as social dimensions, that is known as an anthropological problem.

In its cosmic vision, Spiritism approaches the study of the universe in its double constitutional aspects, the material and the spiritual, as well as its integral evolution, and presents a perfectly coherent theory of knowledge that leads to an understanding and comprehension of that reality. By its particular characteristics, one can establish that Spiritism is:

- a deist philosophy, because it acknowledges the existence of a Creator as the intelligent force, primary cause of everything, as Supreme Logos, reason from which all exists.

- a spiritualist philosophy, because it affirms the existence of the spirit as a principle independent from matter, as well as its survival after death.

- an evolutionary philosophy, because it acknowledges that evolution is the law which rules the universe, presiding over all its transformations, both in the physical and spiritual orders. Cosmic evolution, biological evolution, spiritual evolution, social evolution, everything is in permanent transformation towards new stages or phases.

- a scientific philosophy, because it establishes as part of universal facts that: there have been spirit manifestations at all times and in all places and catalogues these as natural phenomena, accessible to experimental verification, and, from the study of such phenomena one can develop a concept regarding its being, a sense of its existence and the reason of its destiny.

- a rationalist philosophy, because it does not impose any dogma or belief whatsoever, but invites the study and rational analysis of all its principles. Spiritism is based on knowledge of the facts not just a belief. To know, one must doubt, investigate, research, verify and many times rectify. A belief implies an act of blind faith in that one accepts the reality of something that has not been confirmed.

- a humanist philosophy, because it places the human being and its needs within the center of its attention. The Spiritist doctrine is a tool so that man can evolve morally and intellectually from a comprehension of himself and his evolutionary process. And, he will solely know himself when he recognizes that he is a spirit that transforms, through states of incarnation and disincarnation, by erring, modifying, learning and developing towards the attainment of a superior destiny.

Within *The Spirits'Book*, we can find expressed in a most precisely instructive and comprehensive manner the fundamental theses that join within the Spiritist philosophy. These may be grouped within the following classical categories of philosophical knowledge: Metaphysics- reason and the existence of a Creator, Origin – the nature and destiny of the soul, Cosmology- the universe and its laws, Anthropology- a study of mankind in all aspects. In addition, there can be found answers relating to biology, psychology, practical philosophy (society and ethics), as well information about Divine or natural laws. In conclusion, the Spiritist Doctrine in light of First Causes (the reason why of existence) and Final Causes (the reason for existence) is an authentic philosophic body of knowledge, being of a rational and progressive nature, as well as supported by a solid scientific base that has immense consequences for the moral and social transformation of the world.

SPIRITISM DOES NOT CONTAIN SUPERSTITION

"Spiritism is characterized by its complete absence of ritual as its doctrine is based on natural laws; it rationally excludes the idea of the supernatural, miracles, and the powers of the fetish, talisman, or amulet".

Deolindo Amorim
Brazilian Spiritist Journalist, Author, and
Lecturer (1908-1984)

Within Spiritism, there are no African or indigenous practices or types of rituals, or religious or folkloric syncretism (ex. Santeria, voodoo, etc.). There is no ritualized prayer, herbal baths, or any vice-related practices or ceremonies that may include the use of alcohol, tobacco, other drugs or other related substances. Spiritism does not consist of pseudo-medicinal practices, divination, or the casting of curses or magical spells. All of the above corresponds to an underworld of beliefs and practices based on superstitions, ignorance, and fraud that has nothing to do with the Spiritist Doctrine.

There are many who are called Spiritists that are not deserving of that honorable name for their practices are ignorant and crude as well as openly repulsive to reason and commonsense. This damages the image of Spiritism as well as provides a cause for ridicule among serious people. Its ideological adversaries then believe they have found the primary reason for Spiritism's purpose which is that of certain individuals, in bad faith, presenting themselves falsely as mediums at the expense of the ignorant and gullible, to exploit them with the ulterior motive of monetary gain.

Those who have read its main tenets comprehend that Spiritism is a scientific and philosophic study that rejects witchcraft, shamanism and all acts of medicinal quackery or fortunetelling due to the ignorance inherent in these, as well as the desire for profit that encourages those that promote these practices, together with the deceitful and unscrupulous spirits surrounding them. There are those that superstitiously attribute their adversities to magical or supernatural causes, believing that when things go wrong at work or at home, in love, or if they get sick, it is due to some curse or magical spell. They turn to a shaman or witch in an attempt to secure some remedy to counteract it. Most of the time, the anguish they are experiencing or the illnesses that they have brought upon themselves are the consequence of their imagination, moral weaknesses and fixed or obsessive thoughts creating psychosomatic disturbances.

Spiritism, with its elevated principles, explains that the best remedy (for these inappropriately called "works of witchcraft" that have no effect on people) consists in living a dignified, honest, and moral life, in addition to refusing to participate in such dubious gatherings that partake in such unhealthy practices, as well as adopting a positive and optimistic mental attitude that keeps them far from those spheres of influence that provides for a loss of all fear and thus even generating amusement at any and all supposed types of spells. Assuming this manner, no psychic vibrations with perverse intentions can reach them, since a pure and clear mind generates a force field that repels them. Those with the intent of harming others by projecting despicable thoughts will only be hurt by them in return, due to a rebound effect because of their own vibratory affinity and these will permeate their own psychic structures, suffering then the same harm they were trying to cause in others. Many of these unfortunate persons, known as witches or shamans, do not end up well; with some going to jail, mental hospitals, or losing everything, and this does not include the effects that their actions will have had on their future existences.

It is true, that Spiritism has revealed in its studies, within the fields of mediumship, psychic phenomena, the powers of the mind and magnetism indications that in some practices of witchcraft or those involving cults with a combination of different practices, diverse psychic energies are mobilized by means of invocations, mental forces, and trances in which some disincarnate entities cooperate, vibrating at the same level of their participants. It happens then that a complex and disorganized phenomena is created that is utilized with the most diverse of purposes within a scenario where all types of superstitions and atavistic beliefs prevail. Nevertheless, what is most certain is that none of the acting participants, whatever the powers they presume to have, or whatever association they may have with spirits of a perverse nature, cannot have an effect upon the soul of a noble, loving person since their own goodness places him or her out of range of any evil action, shielded from this psychic venom, if we can call it such. In the final reckoning, hatred and evil always come from below, but never rises above. Goodness always conquers evil. Hatred, in all instances, is inferior to love; for nothing is so beneficial than doing good.

Those who believe they are "bewitched" must become clear-minded, strong, and optimistic. They must overcome their mental habits and conduct, develop a psychic armor created by their own thoughts, one of peace and goodness, and this will confer upon them immunity from these psychic attacks. Those who do not desire ill will onto others, base their relationships on respect and dignity, and conduct their personal, family and social lives with solidarity and fraternity among their fellow human beings, may rest assured and relaxed that no kind of "curse" or "spell" may reach or hurt them. Naturally, there is always, in extreme cases, the recourse of obtaining assistance at a Spiritist Center genuinely oriented under Spiritist principles, to receive the practical aid that may be needed, given efficiently and with abnegation.

For this reason, the Spiritist doctrine makes a firm appeal for an individual's efforts towards moral improvement and henceforth to live an honest, productive, creative, and content life. Therefore, in regard to our moral life, the fastest way for the spiritual evolution of a spirit is found in following a life of rectitude.

SPIRITISM IS NOT A RELIGION OR A
PSEUDO-RELIGIOUS SECT

> *"By stating that Spiritism is a religion, our ideology absolutely does not advance and nothing is gained; for it will lose its scientific conceptions and the consideration of educated men that have given, and will give it, positive value and the only ones who can elevate it with the support of their investigations and with their higher level reasoning. Meanwhile, the label of religion takes away its credibility and prestige without adding one whit to its content."*

Manuel S. Porteiro
Spiritist Author and Activist of
Argentina (1881-1936)

In light of all the definitions Allan Kardec gave to Spiritism, it is imperative that it be acknowledged that it is a philosophy that is fundamentally based on science that results in moral consequences. This is why the epistemological characterization of the Spiritist Doctrine as a Science, Philosophy, and one of Moral principles completely corresponds with its founder and the codifier's reasoning and helps to precisely place it without ambiguity within the world of contemporary culture.

Below are some of his definitions:
"Spiritism is both a science of observation and a philosophical doctrine. As a practical science, it consists in the relationship that can be established with spirits; as a philosophical doctrine, it comprehends all the moral consequences that come from such relationships.

It can be defined like this:

Spiritism is a science that deals with the nature, origin, and destiny of the spirits and their relationship with the corporeal world." [8]

"All science is solely acquired through study and time; so it is then with Spiritism that touches on all the most profound questions of philosophy; all the branches of social order, that embraces both the material man and the moral man, is by itself all science and all philosophy that cannot be learned in a few hours, the same as it occurs with any other science." [9]

"Spiritism presents itself with three different aspects: the facts of the manifestations, the philosophy and the moral principles derived from them, and the application of those same principles. From these three classes, or better, from these three levels, so are its adepts; first, are those who believe in the manifestations and limit themselves in verifying them. For them, Spiritism is an experimental science. Secondly, are those that understand its moral consequences, and third, those that practice or make the effort to put this morality into practice." [10]

Within the spiritualist doctrines, Spiritism coincides with religions regarding its basic principles such as the ideas of a Creator, the soul, and life after death, but it differs from all of them regarding the manner in which it believes, defines, understands and interprets them. Religions belong to a dogmatic spiritualism meanwhile Spiritism is a scientific spiritualism. In the religious version, especially in Judeo-Christian theology, men live only once, and are marked with original sin from

---

[8] ALLAN KARDEC. *Qué es el Espiritismo* [*What is Spiritism?*]. Ediciones CIMA. Caracas, 1994, Prologue, p. 10.

[9] ALLAN KARDEC. *El Libro de los Médiums* [*The Mediums'Book*]. Ediciones CIMA. Caracas, 1994, First part. Ch. II, No. 13, p. 25.

[10] ALLAN KARDEC. *El Libro de los Espíritus* [*The Spirits'Book*]. Ediciones CIMA. Caracas, 1992, Fourth Book, Conclusion, p. 38.

which they can only be freed or saved by means of the granting of divine grace. Spiritism is an evolutionist doctrine that does not agree with such ideas as "sin," "salvation," "divine rewards or punishments," "eternal penalties," "heaven" or "hell," and presents the law of reincarnation as the most practical instrument for individual and collective progress, teaching man that he is responsible for his evolutionary progress and the architect of his own destiny over the course of successive existences.

Every religion is supported by dogmas, that is, in absolute principles taken as indisputable truths. Every religion accepts mystery and the supernatural. Faith is preferential as the supreme path in the acquisition of knowledge, and priests, etc. in their temples and churches practice the most diverse rituals, liturgies, and cults. Nothing like this exists within Spiritism; there are no dogmas or sacred books. The entire contents of its doctrine are constantly submitted to free and critical analysis. Reasoning is recognized as the fountain of knowledge, and when speaking about faith it is made clear that it is a rational faith, that is, conviction that is proportionate to current knowledge. In Spiritism, there are no practices or ceremonies such as baptisms, communions, confirmations, or marriages. In addition, there exist no altars, churches, or ecclesiastical structures. Spiritist institutions are cultural associations of a civic character, dedicated to the study and dissemination of the doctrine, with community service and social work oriented by its moral and spiritual guidance. Foreseeing there could be confusion regarding this issue, and in fact, it has occurred where Spiritism inaccurately has been classified as a religion, Allan Kardec left well established criteria on many occasions and opportunities, in the writings of his books and in the *Revue Sprite* as well as in the various lectures he gave. As a cultured and studious professor, well-versed in philosophy and pedagogy, he knew precisely that the Spiritist doctrine constituted a superior synthesis that was able to surmount within the dialectics of knowledge the everlasting contradiction between the religious thesis and materialistic antithesis. It is not possible to have declared it any more categorically than when he stated below:

"The true character of Spiritism is one of a science and not that of a religion." [11]

On November 1, 1868, the same date of the so-called "Day of the Dead," as was customary, the codifier Kardec gave his well known "opening address" at the annual meeting of the *Paris Society of Spiritist Studies*. His topic was presented in the form of a question: "Is Spiritism a Religion?" He was only five months away from disincarnating, and would here again declare his opinion regarding this issue. After conducting an extensive analysis of the term "religion" and considering it in its true etymology, it should be understood as "a bond that unites men within a community of feelings, principles, and beliefs" and solely in the philosophical sense could it be said that Spiritism is a religion, he arrived at the following conclusion:

"Why then, do we declare that Spiritism is not a religion? Because there is not one word to express two different ideas, and because, in the general opinion, the word religion is inseparable from sect, and only awakes an idea of a form that Spiritism is not. If Spiritism was to be taken as a religion, people would only see it as a new edition, or one can say, a new variety of absolute principles that are a matter of faith; as a priestly social order with its hierarchal entourage, one of ceremonies and privileges; it could not be separated from the ideas of mysticism and the abuses which so many times the public opinion has risen against. Spiritism, not having any religious character in the usual acceptance of the term, it could not or should not present itself with a title whose equivalent inevitably would be wrong. That is why it is simply: a moral and philosophic doctrine." [12]

In light of its most important and authoritative voice, that of its founder, the one who codified and systematized it, that is what Spiritism truly is. It is an experimental and observational SCIENCE, a rational and progressive PHILOSOPHY and a MORAL doctrine that inspires in

[11] ALLAN KARDEC. *Qué es el Espiritismo* [*What is Spiritism?*]. Ediciones CIMA. Caracas, 1994, Ch. Third Dialogue. P. 83.

[12] ALLAN KARDEC. *Revue Spirite*. EDICEL. Sao Paulo, December 1868, p. 357

men with the highest sentiments of love of the Creator and our fellow beings, consecrated to goodness, the practice of all virtues, a passion for truth, and devotion to a morally upright, dignified, and happy life.

SPIRITISM IS A DOCTRINE OF PROFOUND MORAL AND SOCIAL CONSECUENCES

"Spiritists have an aphorism that faithfully symbolizes the ideals that we pursue;

where love prevails, all laws are superfluous. And this is the ideal that guides us; that it be love that unites all men and all peoples into an indissoluble bond and that the sentiment of solidarity extends throughout the world, just as solidarity regarding material interests has. In short, that is the thought behind the simple words of Jesus: Love one another; because solely within that resides all the law."

Cosme Mariño
Humanitarian, Journalist and Spiritist Author from
Argentina (1847-1927)

Spiritist science and philosophy receives its complement within Spiritist ethics. It is not sufficient to be knowledgeable about Spiritism's principles, it is essential that they be internalized and integrated within our lives, within a process that compels us towards a permanent moral transformation in all areas of our intimate and personal life, as well as with family and society.

The fact is that the beauty of the moral postulates of Spiritism and its philosophic principles should be supported by the reality of convincing scientific verification so that there can never be disdain from intellectual or academic attitudes arising from any of the elements of the doctrine, but on the contrary, they should reinforce them. The three characteristics inherent within Spiritism as a science, a philosophy and with its moral principles integrated into a marvelous synthesis in the process of knowledge with its transforming action, is a denial of those that believe that the disciplines that promote reasoning do so at the cost of the annihilation of the sentiments. It is always appropriate to keep in mind that human intellect achieved the technology to produce nuclear fission, as well as the atom bomb and biological weapons. Without love, intelligence can become a scourge upon humanity.

Charity - per Kardec?

Spiritism is a science with a plethora of sentiments because is the science of the soul, as defined by the distinguished Italian meta-physicist and Spiritist ERNEST BOZZANO. Hence, a love of science should be nurtured within the science of love.

The morality of the Spiritist doctrine is radically distinct from conventional morality. It is not formulistic. It is also not con-cerned with external appearances, sanctimony, false humility or mystical devotion. Spiritism emphasizes authenticity, honesty, dig-nity, solidarity, and fraternity, and, this is encompassed within one word – LOVE.

but- not Christ. Kardec was certainly correct when he equated Spiritist morality with the teachings of Jesus, inasmuch as they form a true treasure of spirituality. They are a certain guide for the complete transformation of humanity; to liberate it from hate, revenge, lies, selfishness, pride and the immoral passions. They guide humanity down the path of love, forgiveness, truth, altruism and humility that impels it toward the conquest of new phases on the infinite road of its spiritual evolution.

The inward changes promoted by the moral principles of Spiritism translates into a practical conduct directed towards the transformation of society and consequently towards a more humane world, that is more just, free, equal, fraternal, and united in solidarity. That is why personal inner reformation accompanies external and social reform. Being humanist, the Spiritist doctrine offers a rational, liberated, optimistic and progressive vision concerning man and its alternative phases as an incarnate and disincarnate being, responding to his doubts and expectations, as well as opening up a universe of hope that motivates his evolutionary process towards the superior destiny that is reserved for him.

We will find the essence of the Spiritist moral doctrine contained in the third part of *The Spirits' Book*, submitted as ten basic laws, called by KARDEC, Divine or Natural Laws. They are named: Adoration, Work, Reproduction, Conservation, Destruction, Society, Progress, Equality, Liberty, and crowning that monument of moral ethics, the Law of Justice, Love, and Charity. The knowledge, comprehension, and practice of these will enlighten humanity and conduct it toward the conquest of a new time and a new era - **Era of the Spirit**.

Chapter Two

SPIRITUALISM AND SPIRITISM

"True spiritualism should be supported by the Kardecian method, for all spiritualism that hails from traditions and legends that are chaotically mixed within it, will never reach the degree of necessary veracity and will not amount to anything but a spiritual thought that is but a weak hybrid.

Always predominant within ancient spiritualism, no matter how advanced it presented itself, the ecclesiastic and ritualistic methods predominated because of its adherence to the past. In contrast, Spiritist spiritualism is the end result of the mental and spiritual evolution of mankind; that is why the Kardecian method takes us from Spiritualism to Spiritism, revealing to us that the latter is much more adequate a spiritual conception in order to penetrate into knowledge of the spirit."

Humberto Mariotti
Spiritist Poet, Journalist, Author and Lecturer from
Argentina (1908-1984)

The history of thought is marked by man's perseverance to grasp and understand the reality around him and to give it some sort of satisfactory explanation. The central question of the existence of the soul in the human being has been and continues to be very much debated, having been approached from diverse points of view, with greater or lesser depth. And, the disparity in opinions is found not only between those who deny its existence and those who acknowledge it, but among the latter, there is a great variety of opinion with respect to its nature and attributes. It is within this scenario where the opposing tendencies of materialism and spiritualism have waged a tough battle, wielding their best arguments to defend the validity of their respective theories.

The diverse philosophical systems that have been conceived throughout the ages as general reflections regarding a Creator and the universe, about matter and spirit, of life and death, about man and society, can only be summarized and placed within two fundamental concepts paying attention to the definitions attributed to each one of those categories: **materialist philosophy**, which considers matter as the only reality, rejects the existence of a Creator or of any creating force of the universe, assumes that thought and all psychic manifestations are expressions of a material/physical nature, and therefore, denies that living beings may be animated by some spiritual principle or that such a principle may live on after death; and, the **spiritualist philosophy**, which assumes the participation of two different elements in the constitution of the universe: matter and spirit (spirit being the intelligent, active, and superior principle). It also attempts to establish the premise of the existence of a Creator and of spiritual immortality. Spiritualism, therefore, is the opposite of materialism.

It is evident that the term *spiritualism*, because of its scope and generality, becomes rather ambiguous and is subject to be understood and utilized in many different ways depending on the definitions that each of the spiritualist tendencies gives to the predicate, "the spiritual." Here we are acknowledging as spiritualist doctrines, be they of a philosophical or religious nature, all of the ancient or contemporary doctrines that have a dualistic spiritual-material focus in their explanation of a universal reality; those that are deist in that they accept the existence, omnipresence and omnipotence of a Creator, that affirm the supremacy of the spirit in the explanation of psychic phenomena, and, that accept the continuity of the spiritual principle after physical death. These propositions are common to all spiritualistic tendencies, notwithstanding the many varied definitions and interpretations that each of them presents.

For being such a generic, extensive and widespread notion, spiritualism is not restricted to a defined school of thought, but is rather the common denomination of all beliefs, religions, philosophies or doctrines that accept some mode of the existence of a spiritual factor. It is for that reason, within the particular context of its own doctrine, the following can be included: those beliefs ranging from the Vedic traditions to Egyptian Hermeticism, from the profound philosophical works of the Greco-Roman civilization to the Neo-Platonic syntheses, from the Hebrew Kabala and the speculations of Christian academics, the dualism of Cartesian metaphysics, Spinoza's pantheism, Berkeleian absolute idealism, Kant's critical philosophy, Hegelian idealist dialectics, Bergsonian intuitionism, Teilhardian Christian evolutionism, the modern versions of the vitalists, the teleologists, and the holistics, including the inclinations of the esoterics, the initiation-oriented and the occultists.

Spiritualism, therefore, includes the entirety of religious and philosophical systems that accept the existence of a spiritual substance as the foundation of all reality, as opposed to, materialism. In that sense, all religions are variations of spiritualism, as are those philosophical principles that give the spirit an ontological category and give it preeminence over matter. In that manner, one can speak perfectly of a religious spiritualism or of a philosophical spiritualism, about dogmatic spiritualism or about rational spiritualism, about a mystical spiritualism or scientific spiritualism. Those that belong to religious or theological spiritualism are Brahmanism, Buddhism, Taoism, Islam, Judaism, Christianity in all of its versions, and many other religions that are not as common or widespread. Although all of them are spiritual doctrines, they differ, however, in their dogmas and in their explanations concerning the origin, attributes, and the destiny of the soul. Those that form a part of philosophical spiritualism are all of those that, in spite of presenting various approaches and diverse terminologies, maintain as essential principles the acknowledgement of a Creator and the existence of an immortal soul, independent from the physical body, that lives on after death, and, they make great efforts in explaining or demonstrating these concepts through logical and rational arguments.

It is well-known that all present day religions and those that have existed from remote times teach that a human being is not composed of a physical body alone, but that it possesses something immaterial and immortal, in other words, a soul; that universality is an historical and cultural factor of great importance. Furthermore, even before the formal establishment of religions, the idea of the soul was already present in primitive human groups, as it can be inferred from numerous anthropological findings that provide information about the beliefs and customs that characterized the ancient inhabitants of the planet, and was expressed in their myths and legends, in rites of worship, in adoration of their deities, and in their funeral ceremonies.

HISTORICAL OVERVIEW

In the first religious beliefs of India, the concept is found that all living beings, vegetables, animals, and humans are animated by a breath emanating from Brahma, this word being used to refer to a Universal Spirit. The *atma*, or human spiritual principle, needs to reincarnate multiple times until it reaches divine perfection. In the doctrine of the *Upanishads*, which are philosophical treatises of a high level of spirituality that arose at the end of the Vedic era, the teaching of *karma* appeared well-defined. For them, karma meant that all earthly existences are interconnected in relation to cause and effect, a link having been established between a personal spiritual reality and a cosmic reality, which brings about experiences and knowledge that place man in direct contact with the basic notion of his being, of conscience, universal life, personal destiny and a superior transcendence. From Vedism, the principal philosophic and religious systems that prevailed in East Asian cultures like Brahmanism, Buddhism, Lamaism, Tantrism, Shintoism or Taoism, took form.

Among the Egyptians there also was a widespread belief in a universal, divine spirit that filled every living thing, and from which was derived the spiritual spark that animates each being and which lives on after death. They accepted that every human being was made up of three entities: the physical body, the soul (*ba*), and a fluidic double similar to the body but made of less dense matter they named the *ka*. This idea of survival is connected to their funerary rites, the practice of mummification, and provided an explanation of the degree of development they had attained in medicine and architecture. The cult of the sun (*Ra*) was the representation of their adoration of a God, among those that considered it the fountain of life. Upon death, the soul of each person was subjected to a trial before the tribunal of Osiris, and depending on the deeds that the person had carried out in life, thus would be the rewards or punishments that the person would experience in future existences. Alongside the popular cults of the religious beliefs of the great masses, there also developed in Egypt an esoteric spiritualism by way of the mystery religions. These were reserved for a select group of initiates that were rewarded with the comprehension of great truths, such as the existence of one God, the immortality of the soul, the consequences of their deeds in future lives, and the participation in psychic tests and exercises that would allow them to reach superior levels of spirituality.

From the dawn of Hellenic thought through to its moments of greatest splendor, the cutting edge of spiritualist ideas captivated the great majority of its artists, poets, writers, philosophers, and men of science. Already in the times of the Homeric poems and during the mythological and philosophical periods, the Greeks acknowledged that man was of a dual nature, with his perceptible body and his invisible representation or *psyche*, which assured spiritual continuity after death, although such beliefs became confused and denaturalized within a polytheistic, anthropomorphic and superstitious culture.

In a work outstanding for its scholarship and historical accuracy, a product of EUGENE BONNEMAIRE, this remarkable French writer considers that the first teachings that explicitly introduced Greek antiquity to a system of spiritualistic thought appears in association with the legendary figure of the poet and musician ORPHEUS, in whose name numerous cults would later be established:

> *"ORPHEUS was the one who perhaps formed the body of a doctrine out of what hitherto had been no more than an accumulation of isolated superstitions. He acknowledged an active principle, God; and, from that chaos or a shapeless nature, was a passive principle. They were united and had existed eternally. God confined within Him how much He had been, is and will be: heaven, earth, the stars, the sun, the moon, the gods, the goddesses all were his works, and the poet taught that man should worship God the creator, initiator, incomprehensible and infinite. In conclusion, from the bosom of that unbridled polytheism, began to arise the true idea of the only God, and the same Fathers of the Church confirm that ORPHEUS initiated the Greeks regarding the dogma of the oneness of God."* [13]

The birth of classical Greek philosophy can be found in the sixth century before the Christian era, with that brilliant group of thinkers that flourished in Ionia on the coast of Asia Minor headed by THALES OF MILETUS (640-545 B.C.E.), ANAXIMANDER (610-547 B.C.E.) and ANAXIMENES (588-524 B.C.E.). They undertook the examination of reality from a rational rather than a mythological perspective until arriving at a theory that would explain the relationship between universal macrocosms and human microcosms by their common essen-

---

[13] EUGÉNE BONNEMÉRE, *El Alma y sus manifestaciones a través de la Historia* [*The Soul and its Manifestations throughout History*]. Editorial Victor Hugo, Buenos Aires, 1946, p.80.

tial principles, parting from the theory of the four basic elements: water, air, earth and fire. The philosophy that they spread was closely related to physics and cosmology, focused on finding the initial cause of all things and it was saturated with a vision that there is life in all things and the world is animated and filled with spirits.

In general, the successors of those that followed the Ionic school of thought continued with this spiritualistic trend. Nevertheless, the following can be considered representatives of the materialist thought: DEMOCRITUS (460-370 B.C.E.) and LEUCIPUS (500-440 B.C.E.), who were the founders of atomism, and subsequently, the hedonist EPICURIUS (341-270 B.C.E.).

Eminent thinkers like ANAXAGORAS (499-428 B.C.E.) and EMPEDOCLES (483-430 B.C.E.) argued in favor of a clearly dualistic position that distinguished between spirit and matter or, in other words, between that which is animate and inanimate. Anaxagoras also postulated *nous* (spirit or mind) as the author and director of the human organization and first principle of the cosmic forces.

For HERACLITUS (530-470 B.C.E.), reality is essentially mobile and fluidic. *"We cannot bathe twice in the same river,"* is the phrase that best reflects his thinking. From this stems a dialectic system of reasoning where activity is everywhere and rest nowhere, within a universal dynamism. He conceives the origin of reality as an eternal fire, from which everything comes from and goes to. This divine fire, that he sometimes calls "living fire" and other times "intelligent fire," is the supreme activity of the being, and whose visible force is movement. He applied his dialectic reasoning to support his belief in spirit by arguing that everything passes from one state to another, from death to life and from life to death, thereby implying that there is no extinction, only transformation.

The spiritualist thinking of PYTHAGORAS (570-496 B.C.E.) has such great importance due to the grandeur and elevation of his ideas in the philosophical arena, such as his immense contribution to the development of science and art. In the school that he founded and directed at Croton, his disciples were taught a global doctrine for the purification of the spirit through the development of pure reasoning, comprehension of science (especially mathematics, geometry, astronomy and physics), the cultivation of music and the exercise of living a just and austere life in accordance with the highest ethical and hygienic standards. They adopted as a basic premise that the essence of things is found in numbers and in mathematical relationships. The renowned scholar and critic of ancient philosophy, EDOUARD SCHURÉ, with good reason affirmed that "PYTHAGORAS was the Master of laic Greece, as ORPHEUS was of the sacerdotal one." [14]

The teachings of Pythagoras absorbed and perfected Egyptian, Babylonian and Hindustani spiritual traditions, and divulged with singular mastery and beauty, knowledge of God, the soul, its immortality and its constant reincarnation.

From SOCRATES (469-399 B.C.E.), we have received the precious legacy of his teachings which reunite and summarize a genuine knowledge of the cosmos, of life and of Being, and establishes the foundations of philosophical anthropology, for it places first the necessity for intimate self-knowledge before any external knowledge, thus putting into effect the GNOTHI SAUTON (Know thyself) at the Temple of Delphi. Being opposed to the rhetoric of the sophists which brought about states of uncertainty, hopelessness and skepticism, Socrates preached non-utilitarian eudemonism that proclaims happiness as an ultimate superior goal, but which is indissolubly tied to virtue and the practice of goodness. For Socrates, the existence of God was confirmed through reason by proofs that were evident upon examining the order and finality of the world; the human soul is of a divine and an immortal nature, pre-existing birth and surviving death, and it improves itself in successive incarnations. The world is inhabited by spirits that manifest themselves to humans in multiple ways: in dreams or by way of voices that guide or warn them, as it happened to Socrates throughout his life with his *daimon* or familiar spirit.

---

[14] EDUARD SCHURÉ, *Los grandes iniciados*[*The Great Initiates*]. Editorial Continental, Buenos Aires 1943, p. 237

PLATO (427-347 B.C.E.), the most brilliant and loyal among the disciples of Socrates, took philosophy to the highest summit achieved by his universal thinking, since his reasoning has served as an inspiration and a model for development that came afterwards. His teachings are so broad that they encompass all of the fundamental themes that are of interest to philosophical knowledge: cosmology and anthropology, ontology and epistemology, ethics and politics, and psychology and metaphysics.

Following a well-defined dualistic criterion, for Plato there are two main regions of what is real: the understandable world of ideas, and the world perceived by the senses. Starting from a radical separation between the spiritual world and the physical plane, he considers that ideas are eternal and immutable, that the Being is in the Ideas, pre-existing archetypes from which physical things are merely their representation or imitation. Ideas are eternal and unchangeable, possess a permanent and real existence; meanwhile, things revealed by the senses are changeable, are born, perish and are illusory. The originating spirit of the world of Ideas is immortal and eternal. The material body that belongs to the physical plane is perishable and transitory.

Platonic spiritualism presents a God not only as Intelligent Principle, but as Love. It studies the soul in its state as a force that governs the body and distinguishes within it two functions: a rational soul wherein intelligence originates and an irrational soul wherein emotions and instincts arise. Platonic spiritualism teaches that souls or spirits exist independently from physical life, pre-exist birth, and since they have come from heaven or a spiritual dwelling to successively animate diverse organisms, they go back there and later return in subsequent lives continuing along a path towards perfection. At each rebirth the soul forgets its origins even though that memory is intimately safeguarded, otherwise every new intellectual conquest would be nothing more than newly acquired knowledge, a reminiscence of what it already once knew because of having contemplated them in the world of ideas. From there, comes Plato's well-known and often misunderstood affirmation, "to learn is to remember."

Not unlike Plato, ARISTOTLE (384-322 B.C.E.) was openly a deist and a spiritualist, while he did separate himself from his teacher in numerous conceptual and methodological ways, such as his rejection of theories concerning innate ideas and reminiscences. He explains reality by distinguishing four fundamental causes: material (the substance of which a thing is made), formal (its innermost essence or design), efficient (the reasoning that justifies it), and final (its purpose or function). God is the prime mover, the unmoved mover. God is pure action and form without matter. The world of nature depended on the divine. Aristotle believed in the existence of a vegetative soul that is found in plants, a sensitive soul that is present in animals, and an intellectual soul exclusive only to human beings giving them their superior abilities to reason, and which is independent of the body and is immortal.

Like the Greeks, their masters, the great Roman thinkers adopted the basic philosophical references that brought much renown to their nation. In Roman culture, the ideas concerning God and immortality constituted the main fundamental beliefs, and if not unanimously, the majority accepted the plurality of existences and spirit communication, as it is confirmed in the writings of CICERO (106-43 B.C.E.), VIRGIL (70-19 B.C.E.), OVID (43 B.C.E.-17 B.C.E.), SENECA (2 B.C.E. - 65 C.E.), and APULEIUS (125-180 C.E.).

Neo-Platonism established a vigorous philosophical movement, contemporaneous to the nascent Christianity, which proposed to gather and merge the best religious traditions and the initiative traditions of the ancient world. By adopting an eclectic attitude, neo-Platonists combined the ideas of Eastern mysticism with dogmas and precepts from the Hebrew Kabala and of Christianity, together with the Greek doctrines that were linked to the Pythagorean and Platonic schools of thought. Continuing in this direction, schools were founded in Asia, Europe, and North Africa, bordering the Mediterranean Basin in cities like Rome, Athens, Antioch and Pergamum, with Alexandria being the most flourishing center. Among its outstanding representatives were: PHILO (25 B.C.E.-50 C.E.), AMMONIUS SACCAS (175-242 C.E.), PORPHYRY (232-304 C.E.), PLOTINUS (205-270 C.E.), IAMBLICHUS (260-330 C.E.), HYPATIA (370-415 E.C.) and PROCLUS (410-485 C.E.).

They taught that the human soul, an emanation from the Universal Soul, came before and survived the physical body, and as such is a superior and independent principle. They taught and practiced the evocation of spirits or souls of the dead that can be found in varying conditions and can appear and manifest themselves in many ways. They believed in reincarnation and in the plurality of inhabited worlds.

Neo-Platonism exercised a considerable influence on early Christian thinking, especially among some of the Fathers of the Church such as ORIGEN (185-250), CLEMENT OF ALEXANDRIA (130-217), and SAINT JEROME (347-419), all who argued in favor of the pre-existence and survival of souls and believed in the succession of many lives. They pointed out that only in this way there existed a corrective measure to the apparent inequalities of the human condition with compensation in new opportunities, and affirmed that the teaching that came from JESUS OF NAZARETH himself, who imparted them allegorically or directly in his sermons, it can be inferred in his dialog with NICODEMUS where the well-known sentence can be found that says: "It is necessary to be born again." [15]

Wise men of the very first Christians accepted communication with the spirits of the deceased very naturally and wrote down precise instructions on how to evoke and to speak with them, as SAINT AUGUSTINE (354-430) admits in various passages of his *Confessions*, an autobiographical work that is comprised of 13 books. The four centuries of the Patristic period end with the writings of this Bishop of Hippo and give way to the scholastic period, in which philosophy succumbed to the pressures of theology, reflecting an expansion of ideas taking place in the economic, social and political order of the time. This was also when the Christian doctrine began to dis-

---

[15] The Gospel of John 3:1-7

tance itself from its original principles. In addition, starting with the signing of the Edict of Milan by Emperor CONSTANTINE in 313 (which allowed peoples of all faiths the freedom to practice their own religion); the door was opened for it to eventually become the official religion of the Roman Empire in the year 380.

The Scholastic period encompassed all of the theological and philosophical teachings that prevailed during the Middle Ages, where biblical narratives and precepts were reconciled with Aristotelian tradition, framed within two interpretative streams of thought. One of a rationalist character primarily nurtured on the logical writings of Aristotle; which exalted the importance of reason in the attainment of truth and considered that the path to God is through speculation and dialectics. The other was mystical and was supported by the writings of Saint Augustine, who put emphasis on the preeminence of divine revelation and proscribed asceticism and contemplation as the pathway to reach God. Outstanding among the followers of St. Augustine were SAINT ANSELM (1033-1109) and SAINT BONAVENTURE (1221-1274). Among the most prominent rationalists and Aristotelians were PETER ABELARD (1079-1149), ALBERTUS MAGNUS (1193-1280), JOHN DUNS SCOTUS (1266-1308) and SAINT THOMAS AQUINAS (1225-1274).

In order to better understand the origin and development of theological thought, it must be taken into account that Christianity although a philosophy is a religion, founded not on reason but on dogma. Consequently, it is not demonstrated, it is preached; it is not understood, it is believed. Independently from the nuances that can be inferred from each one of its thinkers and the diversity of directions that arise as a result of the many interpretations that are contributed by its internal currents, Christian spiritualism laid its foundations upon the following five cardinal theses:

a)   There exists a personal God, infinite in His essence and in His attributes, transcendent, anterior, superior and independent from the world that is subject to His governance and providence. All beings, especially mankind, are subject to the designs of God.

b)   The human soul is immortal and has eternal life, but lives only one time in a physical body.

c)   God has established rewards and punishments for mankind in accordance to the good or bad works done of their own freewill.

d)   Man will resurrect, his soul will occupy the same body that he animated in life and he will be subjected to a final judgment wherein his ultimate destiny will be determined.

e)   The Christian faith is the indispensable condition for the salvation of the soul.

During the middle Ages, institutional religious pressure suffocated many groups that dissented from official dogmas or those that appeared to be of a mystical, initiatory or esoteric nature by repressing, persecuting and sometimes exterminating them. However, others adopted diverse forms and denominations flourished. They constituted *Guilds* or corporations of artisans and merchants who were united by an oath of mutual assistance and defense, and preserved their knowledge by way of symbols and secret rituals. From them, emerged the guild of the *Maçons* (which means "bricklayer"). It would give rise to one of the most significant philosophical and fraternal movements in the struggle for the moral and social progress of humanity: Universal Freemasonry.

The Italian Cathars (the pure) and the Albigenses (from the Albi region in the south of France) formed religious groups that were austere in their customs and severe in its discipline. They condemned the corruption of the clergy in the Church and rejected certain Catholic dogmas and precepts. They accepted reincarnation, did not believe in the existence of heaven or of a hell, denied the sanction of baptism to children before they reached legal age, considered temples unnecessary, opposed the worship of images, and affirmed that the most essential thing was the practice of virtue in all the circumstances of life.

The Knights Templar or the Knights of the Order of the Temple were a military-religious order that was founded with the purpose of safeguarding the roads that took pilgrims to Jerusalem during the times of the Crusades. However, afterwards they were persecuted and exterminated because of their Gnostic and esoteric beliefs. It was also during the Middle Ages that Kabbalists were at the height of their splendor. *Kabala* is a Hebrew word whose root QBL means oral tradition and refers to knowledge of an esoteric and mystical nature that is transmitted orally among learned Jews in order to keep it from non-Jews. Subsequently, some rabbis and Kabbalists committed it to writing, bringing into existence the *Zohar* and the *Sepher Yetzirah*, works that abound with symbolism and numerological interpretations, and that branch off into two schools of thought: *Effective* (Practical) Kabala that teaches procedures to develop mental powers, and *Speculative* (Theoretical) Kabala which presents a philosophical system with an explanation regarding the creation of the world by God, the connection between macrocosms and microcosms, and the relationship that exists between the body and the immortal soul.

The Medieval period also saw the rise of the alchemists. The word "alchemy" comes from the Arabic and refers to the lime or pith that is formed on the banks of the Nile River. The art of alchemy was first practiced by the Egyptians and was based on the manipulation of metals and their transmutation into gold. The Arabs introduced it into Europe where it evolved into consistent major philosophical and scientific forms until it became the foundation of modern chemistry. In order to understand alchemy in its proper dimension and in its historical and cultural context, it is necessary to delve into the symbolic character of its principles, avoiding the literary and simplistic interpretations. A great many of the spiritualist thinkers of that time were identified as alchemists: RAMON LULL (1235-1315), ROGER BACON (1214-1294), ARNALDUS OF VILLANOVA (1235-1313), NICHOLAS FLAMEL (1330-1418) and the renowned Swiss philosopher THEOPHRASTUS PHILIPPUS AUREOLUS BOMBASTUS VON HOHENHEIM

(1493-1541). This last scholar was better known as PARACELSUS and was the author of over 300 books regarding the most diverse branches of theoretical and practical knowledge. As a doctor of medicine, Paracelsus held reformist ideas regarding the relationship of a human being, composed of a soul and a body, and the universal context that surrounds it, establishing the concept of health as harmony among all the elements. He firmly believed in the medicinal quality of many plants and healed by the laying on of hands.

The decadence of the Scholastic period ends with the work of the English philosopher WILLIAM OF OCKHAM (1300-1349) who categorically rejects the epistemology value attributed to metaphysical speculation, syllogistic reasoning or dogma, and makes a pronouncement in favor of a philosophy that is connected to a philosophy united to science, and preoccupied with the scrutiny of nature and an eagerness to plunge into the everyday world of experience.

Concluding the fourteenth century, after a long and profound medieval parenthesis, there was a resurgence of free-thinking tendencies and criticisms in the intellectual and artistic world which gave rise to Humanism and the Renaissance. Philosophers, scientists and artists converged with great enthusiasm for life and for nature, putting all of their trust in the capacity of the man to forge his material and spiritual progress by using his capacity to reason and in his creative freedom.

The Renaissance represented an era of transition from the Scholastic period to the age of modern philosophy, for which it recovered the cultural legacy of the ancient world. It also signaled a renewal of spiritualism, within a varied gamut of opinions many times contradictory in and of themselves, whether they were neo-Platonic like those of GEORGE GEMISTOS PLETHON (1389-1464), MARSILIO FICINO (1433-1499), GIROLAMO SAVONAROLA (1452-1498); neo-Pythagorean like those of NICHOLAS OF CUSA (1401-1464); eclectic like those held by GIOVANNI PICO DELLA MIRANDOLA and JUAN LUIS VIVES (1492-1540); stoic like those of JUSTIUS LIPSUS (1547-1606); skeptical like those of MICHEL DE MONTAIGNE (1533-1592); humanistic held by DESIDERIUS ERASMUS (1467-1536); free form and naturalistic like those of LEONARDO DA VINCI (1452-1519), BERNARDINO TELESIO (1508-1588), GIORDANO BRUNO (1548-1600); or in his mystical and occultist phase, PARACELSUS, and those of CORNELIUS AGRIPPA (1486-1535), GIROLAMO CARDANO (1501-1576), ROBERT FLUDD (1574-1637), JAKOB BOEHME (1575-1624), and JEAN BAPTISTE VAN HELMONT (1577-1644).

Recognized as the founder of modern philosophy, RENÉ DESCARTES (1596-1650) introduced an all-encompassing and revolutionary thought system able to embrace the physical and the metaphysical within a radically dualist vision, in which the spirit, the thinking substance that does not occupy space and is indivisible (*res cogitans*) is found completely separate from the body, and the physical substance that is divisible by nature (*res extensa*).

Among his greatest preoccupations was to provide science and philosophy with the appropriate method to achieve truth in the knowledge of reality, and he let that method rest in universal doubt. Truth does not come from the testimony of the senses or from opinions; the only incontrovertible truth is the simultaneous consciousness of thinking and existing: *Cogito, ergo sum* [*I think, therefore I am*], for in the very act of doubting, consciousness is affirmed. Thought precedes existence; the spirit precedes matter, as the soul does the body. DESCARTES believed that within human knowledge there pre-existed innate ideas that are independent from experience.

The spiritualism-materialism counter position showed itself in full force during the seventeenth century, in the strong debate within the two philosophical movements that dominated in the Modern Era which took leading roles: rationalism, which is represented in the metaphysical dualism that Descartes proposed, in the pantheistic monism of BARUCH (BENEDICT) SPINOZA (1632-1677), and in the spiritual monads doctrine found in pre-established harmony taught by GOTT-FRIED WILHEM VON LEIBNIZ (1646-1716); and, as opposed to the empiricism propounded by the English philosophers: THOMAS HOBBES (1588-1679), JOHN LOCKE (1632-1704) and DAVID

HUME (1711-1776). For the rationalists, philosophy should be conceived as a universal mathematic, that is to say, a deductive system in which, as it happens in any mathematical model, the sum of its theory and its knowledge can be logically inferred, once a few obvious principles have been set forth. Rationalists took great pains in presenting rational proof of the existence of God and the soul and in defining their essence, their attributes and their relationship. For the empiricists, any one of our ideas, no matter how sublime it may appear to us, is merely a combination of sensations, for all know°ledge has its origins in our sensory experiences. In his fundamental work, *Essay Concerning Human Understanding* considered to be the classical blueprint of empiricism, Locke set out to prove that there are no innate thoughts in the human mind, for at the time of birth it is a *tabula rasa* (blank slate), and any thoughts of God or the soul lack meaning. He sums up his assertion in the following aphorism: "there is nothing in the intellect but what comes from the senses," to which philosopher Leibniz cleverly replied, when he added, "except the intellect itself."

Set within a conciliatory position, the teachings presented by EMMANUEL KANT (1724-1804) emerged. Renowned as one of the greatest philosophers in the history of human thought, Kant took it upon himself to harmonize the rationalist vision with the empiricist position. In his theory of knowledge, which is idealist and critical, he recognized that sensibility as well as rational understanding are processes that complement each other, and which allow human understanding to rise from objective material phenomena to the metaphysical categories of God and the soul. He proposed a type of analysis, which he called "transcendental" that describes knowledge that is universally valid as the result of two processes of synthesis: one that is presented by the facts that come from sensorial perception and gives rise to phenomena; the other in which the mind projects on them a determined category that it previously possessed. In this manner the *a priori* functions of the mind, acting upon matter elaborated by sensations provide true knowledge

The subject of Kantian transcendentalism, with its search for principles of knowledge in the mind, made possible that moment of splendor reached by European philosophy in the so-called school of German idealism, represented by brilliant thinkers like JOHANN GOTTLIEB FICHTE (1762-1814), FRIEDRICH WILHELM SCHELLING (1775-1854), KARL CHRISTIAN KRAUSE (1781-1832), FRIEDRICH ERSNT DANIEL SCHLEIERMACHER (1768-1834), and most importantly by GEORG WILHELM FRIEDRICH HEGEL (1770-1831). With his contribution, the Kantian synthesis *a priori* was transformed into absolute and creative synthesis, when the known object fully identifies with the knowing subject, and all reality is resolved in the creative activity of the "I" and of the spirit.

Among these philosophers, the one who more explicitly presented a vision that was related to Pythagorean and Platonist traditions was KRAUSE. He designated *panentheism* as a concept that is different from deism and pantheism, for he neither accepted an anthropomorphic vision of God nor a God in identification with nature. He rather affirmed that the reality of the world as a world-within-God. Krause proclaims that human individuality will always survive and the soul will maintain all of the attributes that appertains to it, accepts its pre-existence, reincarnation and the existences of the soul in infinite worlds in the Universe.

Hegelian idealism, referred to as logical idealism or panlogism, takes the value of the Idea as a fundamental principle to a culminating point and places all reality in subordination to it. In this light, dialectics is the method that guides reason towards the understanding of the development of the Idea, within a three-pronged process that rhythmically occurs in three stages: affirmative position or **thesis**, counter position or **antithesis**, and the surmounting of opposites or **synthesis**.

Hegel's influence in the world of culture was and is enormous. From his teachings, numerous interpretations and movements split into factions that even reached irreconcilable proportions. It is curious that a system of thought that restores and affirms the values of spiritualism in the philosophical tradition would have wrought directions that are so opposing, such as the one that is known as Hegelian left, which is openly materialist and atheist in its definitions and as principal theorists of scientific socialism, KARL MARX (1818-1883) and FRIEDRICH ENGELS (1820-1895) stand out.

In contemporary philosophy, spiritualist guiding thought found its firmest and best elaborated expression in the movement known as the French anti-intellectualist metaphysical school with thinkers who have shown exquisite sensibility and sensitivity to confront the problems of being and of thought, of liberty and of will, conscience and of spirit, recognizing in the latter a cognitive faculty that is superior to the senses and is conscious of itself. This movement, also known as *spiritual positivism* takes an adversarial position to the materialist mechanism that reduces all reality to its physical elements, and at the same time distances itself from absolute idealism, which exclusively recognizes the value of ideas and moves away from concrete reality. First in this school was FRANÇOIS MAINE DE BIRAN (1766-1824), followed by VICTOR COUSIN (1792-1867), FELIX RAVAISSON (1813-1900), JULES LACHELIER (1832-1918) and EMILE BOUTROUX (1845-1921) until it reached the zenith with HENRI BERGSON (1859-1941), in whose master work all of the reasons for philosophical spiritualism converge and find systematic expression. As the author of: *Essay on the Immediate Data of Conscience, Matter and Memory, Spiritual Energy, Creative Evolution, Thought and Movement,* and *The Two Sources of Morality and Religion,* Bergson has had an enormous repercussion on the culture of the twentieth century and has paved a precious road for philosophical investigation by placing intuition as the most legitimate of paths to the understanding of the intimate realities of the soul. The Swedish academy awarded him the Nobel Prize for Literature in 1927, "in recognition of the richness and fertility of his ideas and in the notable art with which he has expressed them."

In the Bergbsonian vision of the world there is one principle: God, and from which hails the vital impulse, which is distinct and unmistakable from Him. That impulse or "vital élan," identified as a spiritual element, animates and steers matter within an evolutionary plan. Reality is not within the being, but in becoming; in an evolution that we discover within ourselves thanks to intuition, which is the immediate expression of life. Spiritual energy transcends the intellect and reason; it emerges from the limits of time and identifies itself with the duration, in other words, with life itself, taking into account its permanent flow and its maturity.

Among the most prominent spiritualist thinkers of the twentieth century, the following must be acknowledged: the Belgian prelate DESIRÉ JOSEPH MERCIER (1851-1926), who took it upon himself to renew Thomism in light of modern scientific research; the French philosopher MAURICE BLONDEL (1861-1949), whose works were censored by the orthodoxy of the Catholic Church; the Italian historian and philosopher BENEDETTO CROCE (1866-1952) who represented a neo-Hegelian trend known as "Philosophy of the Spirit"; the Swiss KARL BARTH (1896-1968) and the French philosopher GABRIEL MARCEL (1889-1973), who, echoing the Christian existentialist philosophy of the Danish philosopher SOREN KIERKEGARD (1813-1855), set out on the task of giving shape to a theology that was independent of ecclesiastic structure and identified more with a humanist perspective. There was also the notable French anthropologist, philosopher, and theologian PIERRE TEILHARD DE CHARDIN (1881-1955), whose evolutionist and Christian thought expressed with singular beauty in his numerous books, constitute a formidable scientific intent, not free of mysticism, to obtain a definitive closeness between reason and faith, and to construct a vision of synthesis regarding the complete evolution of the universe.

The nineteenth century constituted a particularly special moment in the history of human thought, as a result of the accelerated progress made in the natural and social sciences and the boon brought about by the social and political movements that were revolutionary and material in outlook. They were the product of the French Revolution, in which the rights of men to think freely and to dissent from dogmas were sacred, and in which people were encouraged to liberate themselves from religious tutelage. In this social climate, the positivist doctrine of AUGUSTE COMTE (1798-1857) emerged. According to this doctrine, that which is borne out of experience is the only scientific object; and every notion of God or of the soul is unknowable, indemonstrable, and therefore, outside of the realm of philosophy and science. The evolution of humankind is inscribed within three successive stages: theological, metaphysical and positive. The last one was in response to the needs of a new era which made metaphysics unnecessary, philosophy subordinate to science, and that generalized mathematical methods and experimental sciences to every human and social phenomenon. In substitution for the traditional religious sects, Comte proposed a "Religion of Humanity" guided by this motto: "Love as its principle, order as its basis; and progress as its aim."

More than a philosophy, positivism represented a global trend, a state of mind, a certain mentality, an attitude that was largely widespread in every sector of Western life and culture during the second half of the nineteenth century. Besides in France, it found a favorable climate in England and Germany as a natural consequence to the prevailing empiricism, from which it can be considered a prolongation. In these countries, positivist thinking quickly found an affinity among the representatives of economic liberalism, like JOHN STUART MILL (1806-1873) and scientists of the caliber of HERBERT SPENCER (1820-1903) and ERNST HAECKEL (1834-1919) that set out to systemize the positivist concept in connection with the nascent evolutionist doctrine.

Facing the subjugating thrust of positivism, of Marxism and materialist thinking in general, which dominated the philosophical, scientific, cultural and social scene, idealist and religious doctrines found themselves submerged in a profound crisis, due to their inability to provide adequate responses to the needs of the material progress of cities and to the rationalist and scientific demands of the centers of learning. Materialist euphoria declared that every allusion to the soul or to its immortality only served to numb the human conscience, and sentenced "the death of God." There was only room for that which was material, corporal and physical; that which could be objectively measured, registered and proven. And, at the same time, idealist doctrines with their

metaphysical apriorisms, and religions imprisoned in their dogmas and repudiated for their identification within the old autocratic regimes, beat a retreat, taking refuge in the faith of believ-
ers, surrendering their reins of reason and science to materialism.
It seemed like the ultimate defeat of spiritualism.

It was within this complex and difficult atmosphere that SPIR-
ITISM appeared, specifically on April 18, 1857, when *The Spirits' Book*
by ALLAN KARDEC began to make its rounds in the bookstores of
Paris. It is a work that in spite of featuring on its cover Spiritualist Philosophy when it was presented, boldly proposed to face the immense
challenge of regaining the fundamental value of the Spirit in the philosophical tradition, not from the viewpoints of religious dogmatism
or metaphysical abstractions, but explained in the proper language of
reason and demonstrated by the experimental methodology of science.
Consequently, Spiritism constitutes a particular variant within spiritualism, making it unique because of its rationalist and lay character.

Kardec was preceded by some scholars in Europe and North
America whom came close in their conclusions to what would later be
established as the Spiritist doctrine. One was the famous Swedish psychic and medium EMMANUEL SWEDENBORG (1688-1772), well
known as a scientific authority in his own time, for he had excelled as
a mining engineer and was shown to have had extensive knowledge of
mathematics, astronomy, geology, anatomy, zoology, history and literature. From the time he was a child, he had experienced paranormal
and mediumistic manifestations that intensified in his adult life. He saw
and heard spiritual beings that provided him with diverse information
about the afterlife. It was revealed to him that every spirit was located
in heavens, intermediary places, or hells in accordance with their evolutionary stage of development. One of the fundamental points of his
doctrine is what he called the "law of relationships," in which every
element or object that exists in the material world is the representation
of a model that equally exists in the spiritual world. In an extremely
complicated and abstract language charged with strong religiosity, he
articulated his beliefs as a restoration of primitive Christianity, and

because of that, he insisted on adapting all of the revelations transmitted to him by spirits or "angels" to biblical texts. He was immersed in the firm belief that Christ guided him in his mission to guide humanity in this knowledge and help it in its salvation. He wrote numerous books and each contains many volumes. Among his best known are: *The New Jerusalem, Arcane Celestial, Heaven and Hell, The Final Judgment, The True Christian Religion, Apocalypse Revealed,* etc. These works were studied by famous men and renowned intellectuals (as well as notably influenced them) such as GOETHE, SCHILLER, BALZAC, BAUDELAIRE and WILLIAM JAMES.

The Brazilian author HERMINIO CORREIA MIRANDA, in a brief and substantial biographical essay, analyzed the theories proposed by Swedenborg and provides a psychological and religious profile of his life and work, especially as a medium, acknowledging his merits, critically examining his ideas and historically placing him as a precursor of Spiritism:

> *"I understand that Emmanuel Swedenborg must be justly considered a precursor in the divulgation of the **phenomena** that constitutes the object of Spiritism. He was the first to ponder with authority upon the conditions of existence in the afterlife, bringing many persons to the consoling conviction of the survival of the being upon corporeal death. He also demonstrated with sufficient credibility, the feasibility of interchange with incarnate beings, even though he himself might have not attained the desirable benefit from it. His observations concerning limbo (equivalent to the perispirit in Spiritist terminology) are pertinent and pioneering.*
>
> *Insofar as the **doctrinarian** aspects of Spiritism, his speculations are unacceptable and have nothing to do with the enlightening Doctrine of the Spirits, against which he clashes head on, in relevant aspects like the question regarding successive lives.*
>
> *Regarding questions of theology, strictly speaking, nothing is said with respect to Spiritism, but they do address the traditional dogmatic institutions, his observations are presented full of fantasies,*

> *suppositions, dogmas and theories that would not withstand even a very elementary critical analysis. "* [16]

The studies and experiments carried out by the Austrian physician FRANZ ANTON MESMER (1733-1815) concerning animal magnetism caused a stir in Europe during the eighteenth and nineteenth centuries. By placing as the fundamental basis of his teachings the analogy between the universal physical magnetism and the human magnetic fluid and by retaking the ancient ideas concerning healing that could be achieved by the placing of hands and the transmission of fluids, Mesmer caught the attention of the social and scientific circles of his time with his spectacular and unorthodox therapeutic procedures, and contributed to the promotion of interest in the study of psychic phenomena. Diverting from experimentation of the mesmeric techniques, the majority of the researchers of the time advanced to study of other normal and paranormal manifestations such as somnambulism, telepathy, clairvoyance, suggestion, hypnosis and mediumship, thereby establishing a bridge with the Spiritism that was to come, and upon which it would exercise considerable influence in some theoretical and practical aspects.

MODERN SPIRITUALISM

Another precursor of Spiritism was the U.S. born ANDREW JACKSON DAVIS, who sensitive from a very early age started to show powerful mediumistic faculties that enabled him to hear and see spirits and transmit their messages orally and in writing. From 1844, he started to participate as a medium in sessions that were held in Poughkeepsie, a town in New York State where he resided. There Swedenborg's spirit frequently materialized and offered guidance on the tasks he had to accomplish.

---

[16] HERMINIO C.MIRANDA. *Swedenborg. Un análisis crítico* [*Swedenborg. A Critical Analysis*]. Editora Centro Spírita Léon Denis. Rio de Janeiro, 1991, p.61

Davis cleared the way for the transition between Sweden-borgism and Mesmerism to Modern American Spiritualism. He published various books whose contents were received while he was in trance: *The Principles of Nature, Great Harmonia*, the *Penetralia* and *Nature's Divine Revelations* among others. They are a legacy to the power and diversity of his abilities, in so far as reporting veridical cases of clairvoyance, premonition, out-of-body experiences and xenoglossy. It is important to point out that despite being a person of limited education, his works contain elevated philosophical, sociological and scientific concepts, and are written with impeccable correctness. Some contain information that science had not yet attained, such as the reference he makes to the nine planets of our solar system, a fact that would not be confirmed until 1930 with the discovery of Pluto. He also predicted the invention of the automobile, the airplane and the typewriter, describing them long before they were built, and that is why he is known as the "the Seer of Poughkeepsie."

This "prophet of the new revelation," as SIR ARTHUR CONAN DOYLE would refer to him in his very valuable work dedicated to the narration of the history of Spiritualism[17]paved the way for its advent by gaining recognition through his mediumship experiences, verified with the greatest seriousness and noblest of purposes. It is important to record that among the personal notes of Mr. Davis, there is one dated March 31, 1848 where he wrote:

"About daylight this morning a warm breathing passed over my face and I heard a voice, tender and strong, saying: 'Brother, the good work has begun - behold, a living demonstration is born.' I was left wondering what could be meant by such a message."

It is precisely the date of March 31, 1848 that has gone down in history as a day of great meaning, for it clearly established evidence of the phenomena of mediumship and communication between the spiritual

---

[17] ARTHUR CONAN DOYLE. *El Espiritismo. Su historia, su doctrina, sus hechos* [*Spiritism, its History, its Teachings, its Acts*]. Editorial Kier. Buenos Aires. 1952, p.25. The book in English is entitled *The History of Spiritualism* and was published in England in 1926.

and the corporeal worlds. It happened in the small town of Hydesville, Wayne County in the state of New York at the house of the FOX FAMILY.

This communication with the spirit world signals the starting point of the widespread movement known as "Modern Spiritualism" in the United States of America and in other English-**speaking countries** It is precisely the date of March 31, 1848 that has gone down in history as a day of great meaning, for it clearly established evidence of the phenomena of mediumship and communication between the spiritual and the corporeal worlds. It happened in the small town of Hydesville, Wayne County in the state of New York at the house of the FOX FAMILY.

This humble family, that practiced the Methodist religion, had in December of 1874 leased a modest house in Hydesville, where it was rumored that one could hear mysterious sounds produced from within. The last tenant had been Michael Weekman who later remarked that he heard unexplained raps coming from the walls of the house.

Mr. John Fox, his wife, their daughters, the FOX SISTERS MARGARET and KATHERINE, of ages 14 and 11 years of age respectively, had spent more than three months putting up with the strange noises. That March 31st, close to eight in the evening, it occurred to the girls to interrogate the invisible cause: "Are you a man that knocks?" There was no response to that question. They asked, "Are you a spirit?" And there was a thundering noise. The girls, surprised, snapped their fingers three times and they heard three raps. They summoned their parents, the parents summoned the neighbors, and on that night an improvised mediumship session took place. It was agreed to adapt the number of raps or knocks to the letters of the alphabet, and in that manner they learned that they were speaking to the spirit of Charles Bryan Rosna, a traveling peddler, who had lodged in that house for a couple of days five years prior, had been murdered in order to rob him and he had been buried there. [18]

---

[18] EMMA HARDINGE (1823-1899). *Modern American Spiritualism.* University Books. 1970. Chapters II and III. In 1916, the remains of this house were acquired by Benjamin F.

Nearby neighbors confirmed that a peddler had stayed there during that time, that he had suddenly disappeared, and that the tenants whose last name was Bell, had moved away shortly thereafter. The only thing left was to locate the body which would not happen until 1904, when the walls of the house collapsed revealing a skeleton exposed in an inner wall.

The news of the events of Hydesville spread throughout the country and hastened a true explosion regarding spirit communications by people who purported to be mediums. There was a mixture of authentic phenomena with all sorts of fraud and charlatanism. Some mediums practiced their faculties without any economic gain, while others exploited them commercially. As it was to be expected, this generated an aggressive reaction against all medium-type manifestations on the part of skeptics and traditional religious groups. The Fox sisters, who had participated in mediumship sessions in New York City, were pressured, blackmailed and forced to denounce the phenomena as fraudulent, acknowledging that they had been produced by the cracking of their joints. Much later, regretting these manipulations, they publicly retracted themselves and reaffirmed the truth of everything that had happened at Hydesville.

Many well-known public figures of the American scientific and cultural world joined in the rising movement giving it more credibility and contributed towards its organization. Among those of greater relevancy because of their public status were: ROBERT HARE (1781-1858), chemist, inventor and professor at the University of Pennsylvania, who left evidence of his studies and convictions in the work, *Experimental Investigation of the Spirit Manifestations, Demonstrating the Existence of Spirits and their Communion with Mortals*, published in 1855; his colleague, a professor of chemistry and agronomy, JAMES J. MAPLES; the political leader NATHANIEL TALLMADGE (1795-1864), governor of the state of Wisconsin, who

---

Bartlett, who moved them to Lily Dale Spiritualist Camp in 1916. In 1955, it burned to the ground in a fire. A stone marker stands in its place. Lily Dale is a lakeside spiritualist community in the U.S. in upstate New York.

championed a petition presented before the U.S. Congress in April 1854, backed by 15,000 signatures, to have the phenomena of mediumship officially investigated. There was also Dr. JOHN WORTH EDMONDS (1816-1874), presiding judge of the Supreme Court of the State of New York and Chair of the Senate in 1853, who wrote various newspaper articles in which he professed to be in favor of Spiritualism as a result of his experiences with different mediums. Later, he developed mediumistic abilities of his own, as did his daughter LAURA EDMONDS, who showed a special talent for transmitting messages from the spirits in languages she did not know, such as Spanish, French, Greek, Italian, Portuguese, Latin, Hungarian and different dialects native to India, of which her father gave a detailed narration in his works, *Spiritualism and Spirit Manifestations*. The celebrated English medium, DANIEL DUNGLAS HOME (1833-1866) lived in the United States from 1842 to 1855, and contributed in that initial period by arousing bewilderment on account of his amazing abilities. In his presence the following occurred: the movement and moving of objects in the air, tangible apparitions of spirits and levitations, and with the distinction that these unusual phenomena were observed in plain daylight. It also was of great benefit that these were corroborated by the men of culture and of science in that epoch. [19]

Modern Spiritualism continued to organize itself and become widespread in the entire United States of America. Its followers congregated in "circles" or churches that continued to integrate themselves into national associations or federations. In the City of New York alone there were some 300 spiritualist groups in 1853 with more than 40,000 adepts. By 1860, it was estimated that there were approximately two million followers in the entire country. In many cities the first spiritualist publications began to circulate which recounted the growing progress of the movement, described the sessions that were held to receive spirit communications and also explained the

[19] EMMA HARDINGE (1823-1899). *Modern American Spiritualism.* University Books. 1970. Chapters VIII, IX, and X. This book, whose author lived during the period, is a most detailed, complete and reliable account of the era. She wrote the book in England, starting in 1867, completing it in 1868. It was finally published in 1870.

ideological tenets of the movement that had already begun to show a strong influence on Protestant religious culture.

It was in 1852 when reports of the phenomena at Hydesville and spiritualist ideas reached England. Mrs. W. R. HAYDEN was the first American medium to hold spirit sessions in that country, and despite the strong criticism she received from religious and incredulous persons, she managed to quickly make them widespread and acceptable to cultured and socially well-known men and women. That was the case with the mathematician and astronomer AUGUSTUS DE MORGAN (1806-1871), author of an excellent work on experimental mediumship (*From Matter to Spirit, the Result of Ten Years Experience in Spirit Manifestations*), and the very well-known social reformer ROBERT OWEN (1771-1858). He publicly announced that the sessions with Mrs. HAYDEN had totally convinced him of the existence of spirits and that he had renounced his former materialist convictions.

In England, Modern Spiritualism gradually began to grow until it turned into a powerful philosophical religious movement that was formally organized into several national federations that enjoyed legal status and full official recognition. As its basic principles, it declared the existence of God, the survival of the spirit after death, and the communication between disembodied spirits and incarnated beings, thanks to the faculty of mediumship. The theory of reincarnation was not accepted. Its gatherings contained Christian religious aspects and were held in Spiritualist churches; they included biblical readings, sermons and hymns. The ministers had the official title of Reverend and officiated at weddings, baptisms and other church ceremonies. Besides church donations, many individual mediums received payment for the exercise of their faculties.

Continuing into the mid-1800s it had become fashionable in a few European countries to sit around a table and evoke spirits. The fever of the "talking tables" dominated the times, especially in the highest social circles. The tone of those gatherings was one of complete frivolity, for they were intended as mere distractions, far from any serious purpose and without any regard for the nature of the manifestations that resulted in them.

There were a few scholars and researchers who were the exception, like the case of the French-born ALPHONSE CAHAGNET (1809-1885), who performed important experiments in the areas of hypnosis, mesmerism and magnetism, somnambulism, and mediumship, with the participation of the medium ADÉLE MAGNOT. He made that practical work known in various books, considered to be of great theoretical and experimental value. [20]

Likewise, Dr. JUSTINUS KERNER (1786-1862), a German physician and poet with an excellent reputation, had published in Stuttgart, from 1824 and 1852, many works about psychic phenomena and spirit communications. It was he who made known the noteworthy phenomena produced by the medium FRIEDERIKE HAUFFE (1801-1829), who used to see spirit manifestations while she was in a sleepy trance-like state and who could facilitate materializations, levitations, apports, raps and other physical effects, which she documented in her famous work, *The Seer of Prevorst.* [21]

ALLAN KARDEC and SPIRITISM

During the nine years that followed the events of Hydesville there was much confusion concerning all these strange manifestations where tables turned and messages were transmitted. Their origin, their nature, and the conditions under which they were produced were ignored. A French educator, a learned and cautious man, open-minded but prudent, by the name of HYPPOLYTE LÉON

---

[20] *Magnetisme, Arcanees de La vie future dévoilé* [*Magenetism, Arcane knowledge of the future life unveiled*] (1848). *Sanctuaire au Spiritualisme* [*Santuary on Spiritualism*] (1850). *Encyclopédie magnétique spiritualiste* (1861) [*Magnetic Spiritualist Encyclopedia*].*Thérapeutique du magnétisme et du somnambulisme approprié aux maladies les plus communes* [*Therapeutic Magnetism and of somnambulism suitable for most common diseases*] (1883).

[21] Prevorst is a neighborhood of the town of Oberstenfeld in Württemberg, Germany.

DENIZARD RIVAIL would undertake the task of trying to put these things in their place, through a systematic study of the phenomena. And, in an attempt to explain their cause, he would derive from the experience an entire philosophical system, vast in horizons and profound in moral and social consequences, of which he would be its founder and codifier of what he called: SPIRITISM.

DENIZARD RIVAIL was born in Lyons, France on October 3, 1804 (the eleventh day of the first month according to the calendar of the Republic in the year XIII). He was the son of JEAN–BAPTISTE ANTOINE RIVAIL, a judge and his wife JEANNE LOUISE DUHAMEL. He had a proper and disciplined upbringing, steadied by the principles of honesty and justice. At the age of ten, he was sent by his parents to Verdun, a city in Switzerland near Lake Neuchâtel, to study at the Educational Institute which had been established there in 1805 by JOHANN HEINRICH PESTALOZZI (1746-1827), an internationally renowned and prestigious educator. The students that attended his important educational center came from all over the world. Its classrooms graduated youth who would later attain distinction in the teaching, cultural, social, artistic and scientific fields. In addition, numerous educators from other countries came to study his methods of teaching.

Inspired by the ideas presented by the Geneva-born philosopher JEAN JACQUES ROUSSEAU (1712-1778) and foremost by his teaching methods presented in his *Émile ou Traté de l'éducation* [*Emile, A Treatise on Education*]. Pestalozzi developed in his Institute a scientific method of teaching that was supported by research and was geared toward direct contact with nature. Theory was combined with practical exercises and emphasis was placed on learning that was supported by intelligent comprehension above memorization and rote. The essential methodological principle that ruled in that educational model established a gradual progress in the learning of knowledge, starting out with the most simple concepts, and progressing gradually towards those of greater complexity; going back to those things that are known towards those that are unknown. Pestalozzi fervently defended freedom of thought and religious tolerance, and for that reason, in Verdun, students from all over the world lived in harmony, without regard to differences in nationality, language or beliefs.

It was in that educational atmosphere where young RIVAIL consolidated his intellectual and moral development, assimilating the scientific and educational knowledge of the times and establishing in the depths of his soul those elevated sentiments of equality, liberty, tolerance and fraternity. In 1822, he finished his studies in Yverdun obtaining the degree of Bachelor of Arts and Sciences and returned to France, settling in Paris, where he began to work as a teacher and writer. In 1825 he founded an elementary school [*École de premier degré*] and the following year he established the Rivail Institute, a technical school, where he also taught chemistry, physics, biology, astronomy and other subjects. Both centers of learning followed the Yverdun model.

His first book, entitled *Practical and Theoretical Arithmetic Course, in accordance with the Pestalozzi Method,* first appeared in 1824. It consisted of two tomes and 624 pages. It introduced the theoretical principles of arithmetic and its applications; and, it was recommended for teachers and mothers who wanted to offer their children basic notions of arithmetic by way of a simple and clear method.

In 1828, and as always, signed as, "H.D.L. Rivail, disciple of Pestalozzi," his second work: *Proposed Plan for the Improvement of Public Education* appeared. In it he argued in favor of Pestalozzi's thesis that recognizes education as a science and offered the French government a project for the establishment of a "School for Practical and Theoretical Pedagogy," aimed at educating teachers professionally in three-year courses.

Demonstrating his perfect mastery of the German language, Rivail translated the important French work *Telemachus.* It was written by FRANÇOIS DE SALIGNAC DE LA MOTHE, a bishop who was universally known as FÉNELON (1651-1715). The book was published in 1830 and contained translator's notes explaining the roots of words. In addition to German, Rivail knew and could express himself well in English and Dutch, and understood Latin and Greek without difficulty

Towards the end of January 1831, he published *Classic French Grammar under a New Plan*, in which he explained the basic rules that govern the spelling and syntax of the French language. That same year *Essay concerning the question: Which is the system of educational studies more in harmony with the epoch?* appeared. This work received an award from the Royal Academy of Arrás. Another work, *Essay concerning public instruction* also appeared. It was aimed at the commission in charge of reviewing college legislation in preparation for a new project for a law aimed at public education in accordance with the new French Constitution.

Among other educational works published by H.L.D. RIVAIL, are: *Manual of Exams for Competency Certification* (1846), *A complete Treatise for the solutions and problems of arithmetic* (1847), *Reform project concerning exams and educational institutions for girls* (1847), *Grammatical catechism of the French language* (1848), *Course on mental computations* (1849), *Standard dictations of exams* (1849), *Dictations of the first and second age* (1850) and *Program on the standard coursework of physics, chemistry, astronomy and physiology* (1850).

As one can see, based on the great quantity of works published and teaching tasks accomplished, the learned professor and author enjoyed well-earned respect in the French society of his time, having bestowed it with his books, his progressive teachings, and his exemplary civic contributions. In the first stage of his life as an educator and in the following one as the Codifier of Spiritism, his wife, AMÉLIE-GABRIELLE BOUDET (1795-1883), whom he married in 1832, played an important role. She also excelled in the teaching field. She wrote a few short stories and essays, and was a loyal and loving companion to her husband in his ideals and efforts.

It was in 1854 when RIVAIL came in contact with the manifestations of the so-called "turning tables." His friend, FORTIER, who was a practicing magnetizer, told him about these unusual feats and the following dialog took place:

Fortier: *"Do you know the extraordinary property that I have just discovered in magnetism? Apparently, it isn't just people that I am able to magnetize, but tables as well, which I can make move at will."*

Rivail: *"This is very exceptional, indeed. But, strictly speaking, I confess that I do not think it is radically impossible. The magnetic fluid, which is a sort of electricity, can very well work on inert objects and cause them to move."* [22]

Some months later he ran into Fortier again, who told him:

"See if it truly extraordinary: I do not only make a table turn by magnetizing it, but I make it speak. I ask it questions and it responds."

To that RIVAIL responded:

"This is another matter. I will believe what you tell me when I see it; when you have proven to me that a table has a brain to be able to think and nerves to be able to feel, and that it can turn into a somnambulist. Until then, permit me to only see in it no more than a tale." [23]

From what can be deduced from his own words, Master Rivail received information of this type with skepticism. Although, he admitted the possibility that they might be attributed to a phenomenon tied to the practice of magnetism, a subject he was thoroughly familiar with from a theoretical and mental standpoint. He had been involved in studying it since the age of twenty. In that era, the first half of the nineteenth century, studies concerning animal magnetism and its therapeutic applications had been widespread in Europe, especially in France with the support of learned and serious men. The Marquis ARMAND DE PUYSEGUR (1751-1825), the naturalist JOSEPH PHILLIPE DELEUZE

[22] ALLAN KARDEC. *Obras Póstumas* [*Posthumous Works*]. Ediciones CIMA. Caracas, Second part: My first initiation into Spiritism. p.179.
[23] Ibid. p.179.

(1753-1835) and Baron JEAN DU POTET (1796-1881) all decidedly contributed to its popularization. They were all in agreement in the acknowledgement of its diverse properties, even when there were disagreements concerning explanations regarding its nature and the manner in which it worked. And, with respect to the "turning and talking tables" there were strong differences of opinion; some considered them to be a product of magnetic action and others accepted that they could be attributed to the intervention of spiritual forces. There was already established an intense debate between materialistic-oriented magnetizers (fluid theory) and spiritualistic magnetizers (animist theory).

Of cool temperament, gifted with a sharp critical sense and rational mind, Rivail was involved in the Mesmerist school of thinking, purely of the fluidist school of thought and completely without a spiritualist tendency. It was after direct observation and rigorous study of the phenomena, that he was prompted to modify his first opinion that everything could be framed within the limits of one simple action of the magnetic fluid, and to accept the involvement of spirits in the movements of tables and the intelligent signs they transmitted. The proof he was searching for came in 1855 when he ran into his old friend, Mr. CARLOTTI, who spoke to him with great enthusiasm about the sessions in which spirits manifested themselves. In May of that year, Kardec was invited by FORTIER to attend a session in the home of Mrs. ROGER, known for her faculties of trance. Days later, he witnessed for the first time, at the home of Mrs. PLAINEMAISON, the phenomena of the turning tables, that moved and which by way of raps, gave intelligent responses to the questions that were asked.

In the following sessions, with the participation of various other mediums, he also observed the receiving of messages by way of automatic writing. In the home of the BAUDIN family, and with the participation of their children, CAROLINE, age sixteen and JULIE, age fourteen, who had outstanding abilities and who wrote messages from spirits on a chalkboard with the aid of a basket they tied to their hands (*corbeille-toupie*), RIVAIL could finally clear away his doubts. He now understood that he was facing a fundamental fact that lead to understanding life in all its dimensions and from which all transcendental consequences could be deduced. These were events that, independent of its unusual characteristics, do not escape natural laws, and which he decided to study with the scientific rigor to which he was accustomed to:

> *"I applied to this new science, as I had always done with all others, the method of experimentation: I have never trusted preconceived theories. I attentively observed, compared, deduced the consequences; from the effects I wanted to go back to the causes by the deduction and the logical connection of the facts, and I did not acknowledge as factual any explanation that would not resolve all types of difficulties. That is how I had proceeded in my previous works since I was 25 or 26 years of age. I instantly understood the gravity of the exploration I was about to undertake; I surmised in that phenomena the key to the dark and controversial problem of the past and the future of humanity, the solution I had searched in vain for all of my life; I realized, in a word, that I would provoke an entire revolution of ideas and beliefs, and in view of all of that, I promised myself to work with circumspection and not rashly; to be positivistic and not idealistic, so as to not become attached to beautiful illusions."* [24]

Thus, by this it is proven that only by means of rigorous scientific investigation and by examining everything with a critical sense was how he came to acknowledge and admit that behind those manifestations, that appeared to be childlike, a truly transcendent cause was hiding: the spirit.

The mediumship sessions were radically transformed with the participation of RIVAIL. Instead of having simple or frivolous questions asked of the spirits to satisfy the curiosity of the participants, more serious subjects were put forward, through questions that were

---

[24] Ibid. p. 182

previously prepared by him having to do with philosophy, science, and the nature of the physical world.

After having patiently observed those manifestations and carefully studied the information they yielded, he came to a conclusion that would be fundamental to the definition of the new doctrine that was to emerge: communicating spirits are none other than the souls of persons who are already dead, and are, therefore, not infallible beings; their opinions are personal in nature and are in proportion to their intellectual and moral progress.

In 1856, he started to participate in sessions that were held in the home of Mr. ROUSTAN, with Ms. JAPHET acting as writing medium and using a basket tied to her hand to receive communications. [25] The assortment of mediums that he consulted would allow him to prove that the information received was from the spirit world because the messages maintained the same level of purpose and were not subject to the opinions or particular tendencies of each medium.

By compiling the messages received from the spirits by different mediums, by organizing the responses and arranging them by subject, by adding his personal observations, and by writing the introduction and conclusions, was how RIVAIL gathered ample material that would give birth to a work that would revolutionize human thought; accomplished by means of a rational and scientific explanation of life in its physical and extra-physical dimensions, and offering a new image of mankind and a new vision of the universe. I am referring to *The Spirits' Book,* the most important text of the budding Spiritist Doctrine of which the first edition appeared on April 18, 1957.

Here begins the second stage of his existence. The educator HIPPOLYTE LÉON DENIZARD RIVAIL was now transformed into

---

[25] The procedures to communicate with the spirit world evolved quickly. In the beginning, messages were obtained very slowly when the raps of the tables were adapted to an alphabetical code to assemble words and form sentences. Later, a pencil was adapted onto a basket that was held in the hand of the person. It was found afterwards that only those who had mediumship faculties could produce that phenomenon. If others would place the pencil directly in their hand, they could write by means of an involuntary impulse and receive messages quickly and comfortably; even write books through this procedure. Finally, individuals discovered an infinite variety of ways of communicating with the spirit world.

ALLAN KARDEC, researcher, founder and codifier of Spiritism. Two names that signal different moments of the same being that consecrated his life to the education of humanity. This continuity has been well highlighted by ANDRÉ MOREIL, one of his best biographers:

"Between RIVAIL, the educator, and ALLAN KARDEC there is no difference, nor of method or in scientific rigor." [26]

He adopted this pseudonym at the suggestion of his spirit protector ZEPHYR, who had informed him through a medium communication that they had met in a previous lifetime in the regions of Gaul during the time of the Druids when RIVAIL was named ALLAN KARDEC. Besides being a frequent habit of the writers of the time, the use of that pen name allowed RIVAIL to protect his educational works from the intolerance and aggression that would be unleashed against Spiritism on the part of the clergy and academics. This, in effect, came to pass when his works were placed on the *Index* of prohibited books and were even subjected to the inquisitorial flames in a public *Auto da fe*.

The Spirits' Book is one of those works that is essentially of a universal nature, one that should last throughout the passage of time as an inexhaustible treasure of wisdom and beauty, accessible to all persons in need of true scientific, philosophical and moral guidance, which is based on truth and love. Its development constitutes the most complete demonstration of the active participation of the spirit world in the ideals of mankind. Having as a foundation spirit teachings communicated in numerous sessions, involving the assistance of about ten mediums, KARDEC gathered this material, organized it with impeccable intellectual judgment; and, adjusted it to the rigorous application of the scientific method, in order to offer the world this extraordinary book that inaugurates a new era in the history of thought: the Era of the Spirit. The famous Brazilian Spiritist philosopher JOSÉ HERCULANO PIRES

---

[26] ANDRÉ MOREIL. *La vida y obra de Allan Kardec* [The *Life and Work of Allan Kardec*]. Ediciones CIMA, 1998, p.38.

(1914-1979), who had profound knowledge of Spiritist thought, reaffirms this as follows:

> *"Kardec's method passed into being that of the Doctrine itself, and within its own simplicity it implicitly carries the guarantee of its efficiency. We can summarize it like this:*
>
> 1. *The selection of mediums that collaborated that were beyond suspicion, not only with regard to their moral aspect, but the purity of their faculties and the spiritual aid they received;*
>
> 2. *Rigorous analysis of the communications, from a logical point of view, as well as their collation with demonstrated scientific truths, discarding all material that could not be logically justified;*
>
> 3. *Control of the communicating spiritual entities by means of the coherence of their communications and the tone of their language; and,*
>
> 4. *Universal consensus, it must be noted, regarding the agreement of various communications obtained by different mediums, received simultaneously in different places, concerning the same subject.*
>
> *Based on such principles and rigorously defended by these criteria, KARDEC was able to undertake the difficult task of gathering the type of information that enabled him to organize The Spirits' Book."* [27]

The first edition of *The Spirits' Book* consisted of 501 questions posed to the spirits and their respective responses. It was amazingly successful in France and after that, in all of Europe and America, and sold out after a few months. Stories appeared in several French news-

---

[27] JOSÉ HERCULANO PIRES. *El Libro de los Espíritus frente a la cultura de nuestro tiempo* [*The Spirits' Book facing the culture of our time*]. Editora 18 de Abril, Buenos Aires. 1989, p. 27.

papers about its appearance and immediate repercussions. The famous French playwright VICTORIEN SARDOU (1831-1908), a good friend of KARDEC, and one of the first French intellectuals to state his Spiritist beliefs publicly, wrote KARDEC a letter containing these beautiful words:

> *"This is the most interesting and instructive book that I have ever read. It is impossible that it does not create tremendous repercussions. All of the great metaphysical and moral questions are explained there in a most satisfactory manner; all of the greatest problems have been resolved, including those that the most illustrious philosophers could not resolve. It is the book of life; it is the guide of humanity.*
>
> *Accept, sir, my congratulations, for the manner in which you classified and coordinated the material offered by the spirits themselves. Everything is perfectly methodical, it all fits together well and your introduction is a prime work of logic, discussion and exposition."*

The second edition saw the light of day in March of 1860. Revised, and considerably enlarged, it consisted of four parts and contained 1,018 questions and answers, in addition to the introduction and conclusion. It would be the final and definitive edition. On the cover, one can read an excellent summary that anticipates with precision the unfolding of the work:

> *"It contains the principles of the Spiritist doctrine, concerning the immortality of the soul, the nature of spirits and their relationship with mankind, moral laws, the present life, the future life and the future of humanity, according to the teachings imparted by superior spirits, with the help of different mediums."*

On the uppermost part of the frontispiece it reads: *"Spiritualist Philosophy,"* perfectly explained by KARDEC in the first considerations that he made in the Introduction:

> *"The Spirits' Book contains, specifically the Spiritist doctrine, and as a generality, its connection with the spiritualist doctrine, presenting one of its aspects. For this reason one can see in the heading of its title the phrase Spiritualist Philosophy."* [28]

The rapid spreading of Spiritism driven by the publishing of *The Spirits' Book* prompted KARDEC to take measures to organize the movement around one key point. On January 1, 1858, he started the publication of a Spiritist journal called the *Revue Spirite*, and with singular wisdom introduced it with the subtitle, "Journal of Psychological Studies," thus giving Spiritism academic status, since it involved the integral study of the human soul in all its dimensions as an incarnate and disincarnate being. Combined within its pages, were doctrinal articles, as well as debates and polemics from detractors of Spiritism. It also contained: reports on the progress of the new doctrine in the world; commentaries on books, pamphlets or daily news articles that spoke about Spiritist subjects; communications received by the spirits; and, accounts relating to the phenomena of mediumship of physical or mental effects from all around the world. Showing an impressive capacity for work, KARDEC edited the *Revue Spirite* monthly and uninterruptedly until the moment of his own disincarnation, which occurred the 31st of March, 1869. Eleven years and four months of intense labor were translated into a beautiful collection of 136 magazines that illustrate, step by step, the initial moments and progressive development of Spiritism. [29]

---

[28] ALLAN KARDEC. *El Libro de los Espíritus* [*The Spirits' Book*]. Caracas, 1992, Introduction to the study of the Spiritist doctrine, p. 11.

[29] The entire collection of the *Revue Spirite* constitutes an essential complement for the study of Spiritist teachings. Happily, it has been preserved for posterity and is available to new generations, having been published in twelve tomes by Editora Cultural Espirita (EDICEL)

In that same year, 1858, on the 1st of April, KARDEC founded the first regularly established Spiritist society: *The Parisian Society of Spiritist Studies*, [30]with the purpose of systematically studying the new doctrine, holding mediumship sessions in a methodic manner, and guiding the expansion process of the Spiritist movement within the rational and ethical standards that come with it. Article 1 of the by-laws of the *Spiritist Society of Paris*, as it was also known, established that its purpose is, "the study of all phenomena relative to spirit manifestations and its application to the moral, physical, historical and psychological sciences," underscoring that, "any political, as well as religious and socio-economical controversies are prohibited." There were two different types of meetings: general and special, and both were private in nature. Any new participant had to be invited or recommended by one of the members. In this manner the institution was preserved from the curious and its seriousness could be guaranteed. Different speaking and writing mediums participated in the experimental sessions. Some of whom were famous personalities of French society such as the astronomer CAMILLE FLAMMARION, the bookseller and editor of KARDEC's works PIERRE PAUL DIDIER, and the young ERMANCE DUFAUX, who despite being only fourteen years of age, had received through mediumship works of great historical wealth dictated by the spirits of JOAN OF ARC, LOUIS XI, CHARLES VIII and LOUIS IX. These works received much praise from KARDEC and other scholars of the time.

Two months later, *Practical instructions regarding spirit manifestations* appeared, set on explaining the experimental foundations of Spiritism. It was introduced as a "complete exposition of the necessary conditions to communicate with spirits and the ways to develop the mediating faculty in mediums." It included an extensive chapter entitled, "Spirit Terminology" with the intention the Codifier had to later write a Spiritist Dictionary. In August 1860, KARDEC informed the readers of the *Revue* that, "the work is completely sold out and

of Sao Paulo (1976), with the magnificent translation into Portuguese by the distinguished writer JULIO ABREU FILHO.

[30] The by-laws of *The Spiritist Society of Paris* were placed in the *Mediums' Book* as Chapter XXX of the second part.

will not be reprinted. It will be substituted by a new work, already in progress, that will be more comprehensive and will follow a different outline." Obviously, he was referring to *The Mediums' Book.*

KARDEC next published *What is Spiritism?* in June of 1859. In its preface it states: "Introduction to knowledge of the invisible world and of the spirits, the fundamental principles of the Spiritist Doctrine and answers to some unfavorable objections." Due to its instructive quality and the ease of use for consultation, this work is a most excellent guide for all who want an adequate initiation into knowledge of Spiritism, where one can appreciate its grandeur and positive influence on the future of humanity. By combining simplicity and profoundness, it engages in dialog with three characters that are representations of society: the materialist, the skeptic and a priest. These respectively personify the critical, skeptical and dogmatic viewpoints that boldly confront Spiritism in the book, and which KARDEC refutes with admirable logic.

In January 1861, the first edition of *The Mediums' Book* appeared. The second edition, revised and enlarged, in November of that same year, would be the final edition. As was his habit, KARDEC succinctly summarized the book on the cover: "Experimental Spiritism. A guide to mediums and evokers. Contains the special spirit teachings about the theory of all types of manifestations, the means of communicating with the invisible world, the development of mediumship, and the difficulties and obstacles that can be found in the practice of Spiritism." And, he added: "A continuation of *The Spirits' Book.*"

In this masterpiece of experimental Spiritism, the scientific rigor that KARDEC placed on the study of psychic phenomena and the different theories, positive and negative, that have emerged to explain them, is expounded upon and explained in logical detail. The most complete theory of all being the Spiritist one, for it came about from the application of strict scientific methodology as well as from the invaluable contributions from the spirit world, where superior intelligences always assisted him in his work and his mission. It is a tremendous treatise on mediumship, indispensable for all who are interested in properly and seriously executing experimental mediumship work, and in understanding the principles that govern them; that is why it is the principal book of Spiritist Science.

KARDEC teaches that mediumship phenomena are far from marvelous or supernatural, and if they have been considered as such, it is because what caused them was not known. That is why it has been up to Spiritism to explain and place them within the realm of natural events. Parting from those of whose ignorance, gullibility, superstition and charlatanism have predominated in environments where there has been supposed establishment of communications with spirits.

The Mediums' Book is a work of absolute relevance to modern day interests, and to date, contains all research concerning the paranormal, starting with metaphysics and ending with parapsychology. It is the most extensive technical and ethical guide to the theoretical and practical study of spirit manifestations that exists, and no other book has been able to replace it as such.

The progress made by Spiritism in such a short time, which awakened in thousands of people a tremendous enthusiasm for its ideals of renewal and transformation, would not be inconspicuous to those representatives of old and dogmatic systems. Many books and articles were published attacking its principles.

In particular, quite a few in the Catholic faith waged an aggressive campaign against Spiritist ideas from the pulpit, accusing them of being "harmful to morality" or "satanically inspired." The *Bibliographie Catholique*, a widespread publication, launched a violent article against Spiritism. The fury of the clergy reached its culminating point on October 9, 1861, when in the city of Barcelona, Spain, the bishop publicly executed an *Auto da fe* and three hundred Spiritists books and magazines were burned. KARDEC had sent them to that city at the request of JOSÉ MARIA FERNANDEZ COLAVIDA, the distinguished pioneer of Spanish Spiritism.

Having consulted his spirit guides concerning the unusual event that revived the bygone practices of the Inquisition, KARDEC decided not to pursue the matter legally. He considered, with precise intuition, that this would help the propagation of Spiritism because it would draw the attention of many enlightened and progressive people who were open to its ideals. He stated:

> *"We examined the case from the point of view of its conse-*
> *quences, and we will say to begin with, that there is no doubt*
> *nothing could have been more useful for Spiritism. Persecu-*
> *tion has always been beneficial for an idea that people want*
> *to outlaw. Thanks to that imprudent zeal, everyone in Spain is*
> *going to hear talk about Spiritism and will want to know what*
> *it is. This is all we wish. They can burn books but ideas they*
> *can't: the flames of the fires have stimulated instead of smoth-*
> *ered them. Moreover, these ideas are in the air, and there are*
> *no Pyrenees [mountains] high enough to detain them.*
>
> *Spiritists of all countries: do not forget that date of*
> *October 9, 1861. It shall be etched in the annals of Spiritism.*
> *Let it be a day of celebration for us, and not of mourning, for*
> *it constitutes a token of our next triumph."* [31]

Towards the beginning of 1862, *Spiritism in its simplest expression* appeared. It is a short work that is intended to facilitate the spreading of the Spiritist doctrine by providing a brief vision of its fundamental principles in a text of few pages that was reasonably priced. Once the spirits were asked how far reaching this short work would be, they announced that, "it would have an unexpected effect and its adversaries will be furious to find that a publication, because of its low price, would be able to spread among the masses and in that way penetrate in all parts."

Entitled *Spiritist Journey in 1862*, KARDEC published in December of that year a small book that encompasses matters of high importance to the progress of the Spiritist movement. It consists of four parts: general impressions of the six-week journey covering more than 20 cities where he presided over some 50 meetings; the speeches he gave to the Spiritists of Lyons and Bordeaux; the special instructions he gave to Spiritist groups

---

[31] *Revue Spirite*, November 1861. Editora Cultural Espírita EDICEL, Sao Paulo, 1976, p. 339.

in response to certain matters of doctrine and institution; and, proposed by-laws to serve as a model for the Spiritist societies to come. [32]

On April 1864, *Imitation de l'Evangile* or *In Imitation of the Gospel* was published. It is a work of profound moral content and whose title would be finally modified in the second edition the following year to, *l'Evangile selon le Spiritisme* or *The Gospel according to Spiritism*. In its presentation, KARDEC wrote:

> *"It contains the explanation of the moral principles of CHRIST, their agreement with Spiritism and their application to the many situations of life."*

And he added the following sentence:

> *"Unshakable faith is that which can stand face to face with reason in all epochs of humanity."*

In the introduction, explaining the goal of the work, KARDEC specifies the following, which is necessary for its understanding:

> *"We can divide into five parts the subjects contained in the Gospels: 1) the ordinary acts of the life of CHRIST; 2) the miracles; 3) the prophecies; 4) the words that have served to establish the dogmas of the Church; and, 5) the moral teachings. Therefore, if on*

---

[32] It is important to point out that in addition to this one, KARDEC made another five trips to propagate and defend Spiritist ideas: In 1860, he traveled to Sens, Mácon, Lyons, and Saint-Étiènne; in 1861, he visited Lyons and Bordeaux; in 1864, he went to Belgium and met with the Spiritist societies of Brussels and Amberes; in 1867, he attended a banquet offered by the *Spiritist Society of Bordeaux*, and he also visited the cities of Tours and Orlèans, which were en route. It was in Tours where he met a young LÉON DENIS who would become his most loyal follower and disseminator of the Doctrine. In response to shameful attacks of some adversaries of Spiritism who accused KARDEC of becoming wealthy through Spiritism, he distinctly clarified by stating the following:
"Various persons, especially outside the capital, had thought that the expenses for those trips were covered by the *Society of Paris*. We find it necessary to rebut that error, whenever the occasion presents itself... Travel expenses, as well as those that are necessary for our involvement with Spiritism come out of my own pocket and personal finances, product of our labors, without which it would have been impossible to afford all of the debts incurred by the task we have undertaken. I say this without pride, only to showcase the truth and for the enlightenment of those who think that we are becoming rich." (*Revue Spirite*, November 1862).

one hand, the first four parts have been the object of controversy, the last part, on the other hand, continues to be irrefutable...And that part is the sole object of this work." [33]

As one can see, it was not KARDEC's intention to write a text that was religious in nature, as it is sadly often proclaimed, nor did he proceed to engage in a meticulous examination of all of the verses of the four synoptic gospels. That would not have been useful and it would be far from the interests of the Spiritist Doctrine. He also did not discuss the aspects of the life and work of JESUS that could have been historical or myths. If anything, he made his position clear concerning the human condition of the extraordinary man from Nazareth and took great pains in placing, within the context of natural acts, any miracles and prophecies, and that they can be explained scientifically.

KARDEC's exclusive objective was, as he insisted, to project the enormous moral force of the transforming message of love disseminated by the great Master, often times obscured by dogmas and buried in literal, opportunistic and decontextualized interpretations of the Christian religions.

This book, a treasure of consolations and hope, is so vastly widespread throughout the world, that KARDEC confirms this basic statement: **The moral teachings of JESUS are the same moral teachings of Spiritism.**

In the face of the publication of this work, that tore down all sorts of mythologies, and at the same time presented the ethical vision of Spiritism as a beautiful song of praise to truth and love, the wrath of the Catholic clergy was made evident. A few days after the circulation of its first edition, it was anathematized. In effect, on May 1, 1864, the Church of Rome included this and the rest of the books of ALLAN KARDEC in the *Index librorum prohibitorum* (An Index of books their church members were forbidden to read). [34]

---

[33]   ALLAN KARDEC. *El Evangelio según el Espiritismo* [*The Gospel According to Spiritism*]. Ediciones CIMA, Caracas, 1995, p. 11.

[34]   Based on a decision of the Council of Trent, Pope PIUS IV ordered the publication of the first *Index* in 1546. During four centuries, this was a powerful instrument used by the Church to condemn any expression of thinking that was not in agreement with its dogmas. Almost the entirety of the basic works of universal culture is included there. It is sufficient to recall

Also in April 1864, a brief essay by KARDEC was published; it was titled *Summary of the law of Spiritist phenomena*, with the following subtitle: *An introductory initiation for those unfamiliar with knowledge of Spiritism.* Once again he continues to confirm his academic training as an outstanding disciple of PESTALOZZI, when he insists on making the learning of the doctrine easier by way of introductory works that synthesize the basic principles of the teachings, and at affordable prices.

The following year, on August 1, 1865, *Heaven and Hell or Divine Justice according to Spiritism* is presented to the public. On its cover, it reads: "Contains a comparative examination of the teachings concerning the passage from material life to spiritual life, the penalties and recompense of future rewards, angels and demons, eternal suffering, etc.; followed by numerous examples regarding the actual state of the soul during and after death."

Historically speaking, it was the first scientific study with respect to the status of spirits after death, supported by their own accounts through mediumship communications. Heaven, hell, purgatory, angels and demons, rewards and punishments, eternal suffering and other notions typical of major religious teachings are discussed with incontestable arguments. They are examined and explained under a new prism in the light of an evolutionist philosophy which included reincarnation and that is in harmony with a more logical, rational and just vision of life, which allows one to understand the infinite presence of the Creator in the fulfillment of universal laws.

---

some of the names of the literary figures, artists, philosophers and scientists whose books were censored to have an awareness of the opposition carried out by the Catholic Church to all manner of expressions of progress and innovation: FRANCIS BACON, GIOVANNI BOCCACCIO, GIORDANO BRUNO, DANTE ALIGHIERI, RENÉ DESCARTES, DENIS DIDEROT, DESIDERIUS ERASMUS, GALILEO GALILEI, THOMAS HOBBES, VICTOR HUGO, DAVID HUME, IMMANUEL KANT, ALPHONSE DE LAMARTINE, JOHN LOCKE, MARTIN LUTHER, MICHEL DE MONTAIGNE, CHARLES DE MONTESQUIEU, BLAISE PASCAL, JEAN JACQUES ROUSSEAU, BENEDICTUS SPINOZA, VOLTAIRE, etc.

ALLAN KARDEC would not be deprived of having the honor of appearing on that list alongside such distinguished names. The conquest of freedom of thought and conscience, secular education, and the independence of nations, forced the Church, in 1966, to suspend the publication of the Index and render it legally powerless.

During 1865, KARDEC published two short works, for which he chose a few extracts and chapters from *The Gospel according to Spiritism*. They were titled *Collection of Compositions* and *Compilation of Spiritist prayers*. While others accept prayer as a ritualistic action or one that is charged with religious mysticism, KARDEC makes it very clear that it is a demonstration of psychic power, a loving expression of the spirit:

> *"Prayer is an invocation; through it we put ourselves in mental contact with the being we are directing [our thoughts to]. It can be for the purpose of requesting a favor, giving thanks or praise...Spiritism makes it possible to understand the action of prayer in explaining the manner in which thought is transmitted, be it so that the being we pray to responds to our call or so our thought reaches him."* [35]

> *"The spirits have always said: the form is nothing, the thought is everything. Pray in accordance with your convictions and in the manner that moves you the most, for a good thought has more value than many words wherein the heart is absent."* [36]

The *Revue Spirite* of February 1867 reports that the book *Poetic echoes from beyond the grave* is available to the public. It is an extensive collection of poems received by LOUIS VAVASSEUR, a writing medium of the *Spiritist Society of Paris*, and dictated to him by the disincarnated spirits of famous poets. As a means of introduction, KARDEC wrote a *Study of medianimic poetry*, a beautiful work that is a pioneer on the subject matter. [37]

The last of the great books that ALLAN KARDEC published during his lifetime appeared on January 6, 1868. It was entitled *Genesis, Miracles and Prophecies according to Spiritism*. The impact of

---

[35] ALLAN KARDEC. *El Evangelio según el Espiritismo* [*The Gospel according to Spiritism*]. Ediciones CIMA. Caracas, 1995, Acción de la plegaria y transmisión del pensamiento [Action of prayer and the transmission of thought]. p. 310.

[36] Ibid. *Compilación de oraciones espíritas* [*Compilation of Spiritist prayers*], p. 321.

[37] In his book *El Espiritismo y la creación* poética [*Spiritism and the creation of poetry*], (Ediciones CIMA, Caracas, 1995) we already have noted that Kardec was already aware of the clear relationship between art and mediumship, as well as the immense creative possibilities that are possible with a Spiritist interpretation of art.

this work was so tremendous it had to be reprinted three times during the first year of its publication. The first chapter entitled *Character of the Spiritist revelation* was also edited as a separate pamphlet. The following maxims were placed at the beginning the book:

> *"The Spiritist doctrine is the result of the concordant and collective teachings of the spirits."*

> "Science is in charge of explaining genesis in accordance with the laws of nature."

> *"God proves His grandeur and His might through the immutability of His laws and not by the suspension of them."*

> *"For God, the past and the future are the present."*

The book is divided into three parts. The first part introduces interesting studies concerning God and the creation of the Universe, the formation of the Earth and the origins of life within it, as well as organic evolution and spiritual evolution. KARDEC demonstrates the vastness of his knowledge here when he undertakes subjects concerning astronomy, physics, geology, biology and the other sciences of his time. In the second part, he explains rationally and scientifically many events in the life of JESUS that are considered to be supernatural by Christian religions. There is an examination of the "miracles" as interpreted by Spiritist principles, explaining they involve psychic or mediumship phenomena whose laws were unknown at the time. Refuted with solid arguments are the false theories that accept the physiological condition of Jesus' body solely as a fluidic body. [38]

---

[38] KARDEC makes clear that some Christian sects like the Apollinarists and the Docetists maintained JESUS only appeared to have been born and never had a body that was physical or organic in nature. This theory was inserted into Spiritism by the French lawyer of the Court of Bordeaux, JEAN BAPTISTE ROUSTAING (1806-1879), who published in 1866 a three-volume work entitled *The Four Gospels, Christian Spiritism or Revelation of the Revelation*. The work contained the spirit communications received by the medium EMILIE COLLIGNON that were attributed to the evangelists and other biblical persons. Besides supporting the theory of a fluidic body of JESUS, it also contains other incredible affirmations that mix Spiritist concepts with Catholic dogma. These were quickly challenged by KARDEC and subsequently by almost all of the Spiritist philosophers. Yet, *Roustaingism* still prevails today,

KARDEC's essential purpose of this book was to stimulate the alliance that should exist between Spiritism and science, as they both reciprocally complete each other:

> "Science, properly stated, aims to study the laws of the material principle, in the same manner that the aim of Spiritism is the learning of the spiritual principle; but, because the latter is one of the forces of Nature and works continuously upon the material principle, as this acts upon the other, the results are that knowledge of the one cannot be complete without the knowledge of the other. Consequently, Spiritism and science mutually complete each other. Science without Spiritism is powerless to explain certain phenomena, considering only the laws that govern matter, as Spiritism without science would lack support and control. The study of the laws of matter should precede the study of spiritual laws, since it is matter that first affects the senses. Had Spiritism arrived before scientific discoveries, it would have been a useless work, as is all that happens before its time. "[39]

The term revelation, frequently used in this book, must be understood in the scientific and not in a theological sense, as a research process of investigation that allows mankind to expand the limits of its knowledge concerning material and spiritual reality. It is a revelation that is defined, as divine and scientific, inasmuch as it comes from the spirit world and has been elaborated upon by human beings. It is a revelation that possesses a progressive nature. Therefore, it has not been definitively established and should continuously follow, regarding its ideas, the march of progress:

> "One has to bear in mind the ultimate distinguishing characteristic of the Spiritist revelation, and that is, it stems from the same conditions in which it was actualized, that is, being supported

supported by the Brazilian Spiritist Federation, which is the only institution that defends and spreads it, in opposition to the opinion and wishes of many within the Brazilian Spiritist movement, which happens to be, by the way, the largest in the world.
39 ALLAN KARDEC. La Génesis. [Genesis] Ediciones CIMA. Caracas, 1995, Ch. I, No. 16. P. 19.

*by facts, its nature is essentially progressive, as is all the observa-
tional sciences...Spiritism marches to the rhythm of progress and will
never lag behind, for if new discoveries prove that it is mistaken on
something or if a new truth is revealed, it will have to rectify itself.*" [40]

The last work published by KARDEC during his lifetime was
a *Reasonable catalogue of works that serves as the foundation of a
Spiritist library*. It appeared towards the end of March 1869 and was
distributed to the subscribers of the *Revue Spirite* as an independent
supplement. It relates all the basic texts of the Spiritist doctrine, afterwards with a list of authors in alphabetical order, followed by a complementary list of Spiritist works. It also lists a series of works that
are in opposition to Spiritism, some of them with a brief commentary.

On January 1890, *Posthumous Works* was published. This
work contains a great quantity of manuscripts on a variety of subjects
that had not yet been published, and which KARDEC had previously
announced would be included in a new book that he was preparing,
whose title was to be, *Book of considerations concerning Spiritism*.
It was PIERRE GAETAN LEYMARIE (1827-1901), a close friend
and collaborator of KARDEC and Director of the *Revue Spirite*, who
compiled and collated those documents and published them as a book.

Following logical and chronological sense, part one of the
work includes essays on transcendental subjects such as: the many
physical and intellectual forms that are assumed by spirit manifestations; explanations of psychic phenomena, like telepathy, clairvoyance, premonition and somnambulism, highlighting the role that the
perispirit functions in these; historical studies surrounding the life of
JESUS and his message of redemption; music and art examined from
the Spiritist viewpoint; and, a discussion on the philosophical and
religious alternatives that mankind is faced with.

The second part includes writings that are of an autobiographical nature that KARDEC, with characteristic modesty and humility,
had kept private. And, that is how it has been possible to learn about

---

[40] Ibid. Ch. I, No. 55, p. 36.

his initiation into Spiritism; his relationship with the superior spirits that advised him and that revealed to him his mission on Earth; the details about the publication of his works and his great concern for doctrinal pureness; the progress of the Spiritist movement in the world and its future; and finally, about his concerns and his state of mind in facing and overcoming all manner of adversity.

ALLAN KARDEC disincarnated in his home (at rue Saint-Anne, 59), between eleven and twelve in the morning of March 31, 1869, after having suffered a ruptured aneurism. He returned with a peaceful conscience to the world of spirits, to those with whom he had established such a noble relationship with, granted by having fulfilled his duty by delivering a complete philosophical, scientific and moral doctrine that may illuminate for humanity the path it needs to travel toward the conquest of its superior destiny.

The burial of his remains in the Cemetery of Montmatre took place in a strictly civil ceremony before approximately a thousand persons, the majority of whom were members of Spiritist groups from all over France. Among the funerary speeches that were offered, the oration expressed by the famous astronomer CAMILLE FLAMMARION stands out. He highlighted the intellectual and moral qualities that graced the great Master of Spiritism and exalted the immense value of his work:

> *"He was what I will simply call: good sense incarnate. Of just and critical reasoning, he always applied to his work the indications of common sense, and that was not of a minor quality. It was, it can be affirmed, the finest of all and the most precious; without it the work could not have become as popular nor sow in the world its immense roots...*

> *Because, gentlemen, "Spiritism is not a religion, but a science, of which we only know its abc. The time of dogmas is over."* [41]

The following year his physical remains were transferred to the Cemetery of Père-Lachaise and on March 31st, the well-known

---

[41] *Revue Spirite*. May 1869

monument raised in his memory was inaugurated. It consists of a bronze bust placed within an imposing dolmen that perfectly symbolizes his remote Druid origins. It continues to be the most visited and flower-covered site of this historical place in the City of Lights.

The following inscription is found on the front portion of the dolmen:

FOUNDER OF THE SPIRITIST PHILOSOPHY

ALL EFFECT HAS A CAUSE
ALL INTELLIGENT EFFECT HAS AN INTELLIGENT CAUSE

THE MAGNITUDE OF THE CAUSE IS IN PROPORTION
TO THE GREATNESS OF THE EFFECT

TO BE BORN, TO DIE, TO BE REBORN ALWAYS AND PROG-
RESS WITHOUT END
THAT IS THE LAW

Fifteen years had passed since the moment that he became interested in the phenomena of the "turning tables." In such a short time, this laborious and methodical man, full of integrity and honesty, wisdom and prudence, derived from those acts the foundations that would open a new stage in the evolution of humanity. One in which the values of sentiment and of the intellect, and of faith with reason are joined together, and it was possible to answer that most ancient question of knowledge: scientific proof of the spirit.

In order to appropriately understand Spiritism, one must consider the precise relationship of the doctrine with its founder, the epoch in which he lived, the cultural influences that prevailed during that time, and, of course, the cooperation offered by the spirits during all of the process of its development.

The affirmation that Spiritism is as old as mankind or as old as the Creator is not accurate. These statements are usually repeated very casually in Spiritist circles and causes serious confusion, for it is the same as identifying Spiritism, which is a doctrine, with the phenomena that it studies. It is obvious that spirit manifestations are as old as the appearance of mankind on Earth. However, it is also evident that Spiritism, the doctrine that studies and explains them, emerges with the work of KARDEC upon which superior spirits actively participated in. When one insists on that concept, one incurs, from an epistemological point of view, an error of inversion, since the object being studied is being confused with the subject that is studying it. It is the same as saying that astronomy is as old as the Universe, given that the stars that serve as the object of the investigation have been there almost an eternity. Likewise, spirits have existed since the dawn of life, since by definition, the spirit is life itself, inasmuch as Spiritism, the science that studies it, makes its appearance in a given moment of the development of human thought, specifically with the works of KARDEC.

The confusion of equating mediumship phenomena and Spiritism has prompted certain writers to note the episode with the FOX SISTERS at Hydesville as the starting point of the Spiritist movement, while the historical truth being completely different. When writing about the history of Spiritism, it is imperative to refer to April 18, 1857 as the starting date, for it was the day in which the first edition of *The Spirits' Book* entered into circulation.

In that first work of the codification [42]KARDEC featured on the cover the phrase **Spiritualist Philosophy**, thereby establishing with complete semantic and conceptual precision the characteristic of the new doctrine. However, he suggested the term "Spiritism" as a new word to differentiate it from the word "Spiritualism," avoiding the ambiguity that could result, and by employing each term according to its exact dictionary acceptation or meaning.

Spiritism has to be situated and differentiated as a specific variant within spiritualism. As it has already been mentioned, every

---

[42] In some Spiritist groups, the expression "Kardecian Pentateuch" has been widely spread, which is inappropriate, for as it can be seen, KARDEC wrote more than five books. Moreover, they have no historical or ideological connection with the first five books of the Old Testament, which exactly constitutes the Pentateuch.

person who accepts within his or her belief system the existence of a spiritual principle as a separate identity from the physical body, which it outlives after death, is a Spiritualist, no matter how he or she conceives that spiritual component. Therefore, there are those who accept the immortality of the soul or even believes in spirit communications, but who do not share Spiritist explanations. A Christian is as much a Spiritualist as a Buddhist or a Moslem, the same as a Theosophist, a Rosicrucian or a Spiritist. This allows us to establish that all Spiritists are Spiritualists, even though not all Spiritualists might be Spiritists.

Bearing in mind its doctrinal structure, Spiritism ought to be catalogued as a philosophical spiritualism, clearly differentiated from other alternatives of Spiritualist thinking, be they philosophical, theological or esoteric. The Spiritist practice does not include the following: dogmas, sacred books, liturgies, ceremonies, ecclesiastic hierarchies. It does not use symbolism or have initiation rituals. In addition, Spiritism is distinguished from other types of spiritualism because it has its own specific terminology which allows it to accurately and clearly express its entire doctrinal context.

The logical and progressive thinking that makes Spiritism so unique comes from the consolidation of many historical, cultural, social and spiritual elements. KARDEC, its founder and codifier was a man who was brought up in the culture of the nineteenth century. This was a century of profound scientific changes, of revolutions and stirring political and philosophical controversies, which had a marked influence on his vision of the world. Fifteen years before his birth, in 1789, the Bastille was taken, and later the Declaration of the Rights of Man was proclaimed, in an effort to build a new society upon the foundation of the power of the citizen before autocratic regimes. The universal principles of liberty, equality and fraternity were declared and reason was consecrated as a discernment of the truth instead of faith or dogma, thereby diminishing the power of the Church.

KARDEC's century witnessed the birth and rise of positivism, a doctrine founded by AUGUSTE COMTE that was perfectly in tune with the rationalist and intellectualist movements that prevailed at the time. For the positivists, heirs of rationalist Illuminism that inspired the French Encyclopedists, all references relative to the spirit or the notion of God did not go beyond futile speculation, due to the impossibility of their being demonstrated objectively.

It was an age where many revolutionary political movements sprang up, like Marxism and Anarchism, bent on the transformation of the socio-economic structures of capitalist society into a socialist model. Their ideology was rooted in materialism and advocated class struggle as an instrument for the conquest of power.

It was a time of great inventions and discoveries in all of the fields of science: DARWIN and evolution; MENDEL and genetics: PASTEUR, KOCH and vaccines; GALVANI, VOLTA, FARADAY and electricity; FULTON, WATT, STEPHENSON and steam power; MORSE and the telegraph, to cite a few relevant examples.

A learned man with great curiosity for different branches of learning, KARDEC carefully studied what was happening; he absorbed everything that his sound reason and good judgment advised, and the influence of that renewing atmosphere is perceived in all of his works, before and after Spiritism. Being a disciple of PESTALOZZI, he never strayed from the teaching criteria of his teacher with regard to critical observation and investigation. He adopted as his own, the teachings that he received in Verdun regarding respect and tolerance. He adopted from rationalism its general guidelines without arriving at extremes, because he recognized that besides reason, there are other sources to obtain knowledge, like intuition or through mediumship. For him, reason and faith did not constitute an insurmountable dichotomy. He tried to reconcile them through a proposition of "rational faith" that can be summarized in the following categorical sentence:

"Unshakeable faith is that which can stand face to face with reason in all epochs of humanity." [43]

---

[43] ALLAN KARDEC. *El Evangelio según el Espiritismo* [*The Gospel according to Spiritism*]. Ediciones CIMA, Caracas, 1995. Ch. XIX, No. 7, p. 24

To a certain degree, KARDEC identified with the positivist movement, which required any discipline that aspired to be recognized as scientific to be firmly supported by solid experimental support and to offer an irrefutable demonstration of its basic principles. That is why he always insisted on a definition of Spiritism as a science and on the application of the scientific method to all of the phenomena it studied. He never accepted the concept of the supernatural, for everything in the Universe is in accord with natural laws, and spirit manifestations also obey the natural laws that Spiritism has come to discover and explain. Notwithstanding, while he obtained some theoretical and methodological suppositions from positivism, he rejected the materialist, atheist or agnostic inclinations of the majority of its supporters. It can be said, then, that the Spiritist doctrine can be placed within a positivistic spiritualist perspective, recognizing its rationalist and research-oriented inclinations.

Social issues also gravitated within the concerns of the wise man from Lyons. The harsh quality of life suffered by the working class and the conditions of the poor aggrieved his sensibilities. Many times he spoke and wrote on the subject, demanding a life of dignity for them and making it clear that according to the principles revealed by Spiritism, we are all equal; we are called to fulfill our duty so that we can reclaim our rights; and, that social injustices does not occur by the design of God, they are a product of mankind and we are bound to struggle to overcome them. Nevertheless, at the same time, he explained that it is impossible to think about social revolution without a moral transformation achieved by each individual; one that would lead to the eradication of selfishness, pride, hatred and the lower passions, and this would succeed in getting mankind's thoughts and feelings to vibrate with the sublime notes of fraternity, solidarity and love.

KARDEC had the intelligence to examine that world of new ideas and the wisdom to discern its merits, the good, its limitations or errors, and to take advantage of as much of the positive that he could identify in each one. This eclectic outlook that he adopted gave Spiritism a humanistic and universal aspect, as well as a secular and progressive dimension which cannot be found in any other expression of spiritualist thought.

The strength of Spiritism and the guarantee of its continuity stem from its doctrinal unity, the consistency of its basic principles, the coherence with which they have been combined, and of course, from the noble consequences that are derived from its great moral significance. The protection of that doctrinal unity is essential to the accomplishment of its mission on Earth. This is only possible if Spiritism is preserved within the basic parameters established by KARDEC. However, at the same time, one can understand the evolving and progressive worth of a doctrine that was not wrought in a complete or definitive form, that does not pretend to have a monopoly on all truth, and that accepts new discoveries as they are revealed and is prepared to accompany the evolution of ideas in the world.

Unity and progressiveness are terms of the same equation demonstrated by the nature of the Spiritist doctrine and its unremitting commitment to the truth. Unity that is centered on its basic principles (Creator, spirit, immortality, evolution, reincarnation, and plurality of inhabited worlds), these of which have gained more strength each day. And, its progressiveness allows it to incorporate new scientific advances maintaining it current in order to incorporate concepts that belong to another era and have already been surpassed or to correct errors, if necessary.

With his proverbial good judgment, KARDEC left open possibilities so that Spiritism would always be brought up-to-date by way of the incorporation of the advances taking place in the cultural and scientific fields, for we are not dealing with a sect or a religion with dogmas or definitive truths, but with a scientific philosophy of moral consequences:

> *"The third point, in short, is inherent in the essentially progressive nature of the doctrine. By the fact that it does not surround itself with unattainable dreams, it does not follow that it*

ought to immobilize itself in the present. Solely based on the laws of nature, it cannot vary as long as those laws do not; but if a new law is discovered, it has to place itself in agreement with that law. Under penalty of suicide, it cannot close its doors to any progress. Having assimilated all ideas considered just, no matter of what order they are, physical or metaphysical, it will never be over-come, this constituting one of the guarantees of its perpetuity." [44]

"Spiritism solely stands on absolute principle that which is demonstrated by evidence or that which results from logical observation. It is joined to all branches of social econ-omy, to which it provides the support of its own discoveries; it integrates itself with all progressive doctrines, without regard to the order they pertain to, leaving behind the dominion of utopias and having converted into practical truths; if it leaves by the wayside what it is, it would deny its origins and its providential finality and end up annihilating itself. Spiritism marches to the beat of progress and will never fall behind, because if new discoveries prove it wrong on something or if a new truth should be revealed, it would have to rectify itself." [45]

Statements such as these, reiterated throughout his works, give a complete portrait of a cultivated and humble man, a progressive thinker who never pretended to possess the absolute truth or the last word; and, who always acted with amazing prudence by not pronounc-ing definitively on subjects that required greater proof. Additionally, he only wrote down his own opinions as hypotheses, thereby prepar-ing the way for his followers and the progress of ideas, in general.

ALLAN KARDEC was and always will be, on the moral con-science of humanity with his immense prestige as the wise researcher of cosmic realities, with his profound sense of humanity, and with

---

[44] ALLAN KARDEC. *Obras Póstumas [Posthumous Works]*. Ediciones CIMA. Caracas, 1995, Constitución del Espiritismo. De los cismas [Constitution of Spiritism. Regarding schisms]. p. 240

[45] ALLAN KARDEC. *La Génesis* [Genesis]. Ediciones CIMA. Caracas, 1995, Caracteres de la revelación espírita [Character of the Spiritist revelation]. No. 55, p. 37

his moral pureness. His untiring generosity prompted him to offer his knowledge to people and nations, as well as to beings of all races and social stations, in order to help and steer them towards the ideals of intellectual and moral progress. Now Spiritism, his life's work, is ful-filling its historical and spiritual commitment by successfully rising to the challenges that have been placed on it by the philosophical and scientific culture of these modern times. It allows humans to under-stand their spiritual nature through the full and conscious exercise of their reason and the sum of their intellectual capabilities. The Spiritist doctrine, codified by KARDEC, has sufficient strength and stability to transform the world by victoriously facing the religious dogmatism and materialism that still prevail in current society and by bringing together human beings in an embrace of peace and fraternity.

Chapter Three

PHYSICAL AND SPIRITUAL CONSTITUTION OF A HUMAN BEING

"Gnothi Seauton" ***"Know Thyself"** - **Inscribed on the portico at the Temple of Delphi attributed to Socrates***

The human being is composed of three essential parts, three elements that correlate with each other, forming a totality that identifies and individualizes it as a person: the organic or **physical body**; the **soul**, in the nomenclature of the Spiritist doctrine, and considered a spirit when it is incarnated; and, the **perispirit**, the essential intermediary which envelopes the spirit and connects it to the physical body. Each one of them possesses its own particular characteristics, but integrated within a process towards the accomplishment of a common objective. Understood as a system, an incarnated being functions in this way: the spirit thinks and desires; the perispirit transmits this information; and, the physical body acts.

As long as an incarnated human being finds itself on the physical plane of life these three components remain united, but when death occurs there is disengagement and the soul recovers its liberty within the spirit world, retaining its perispirit.

Man is not only a physical, biological, psychological, and social being it is much more, it is a spiritual being. With its conception of a human being in this unified aspect, the Spiritist doctrine develops a systematic and holistic approach in perfect harmony with modern philosophical and scientific thought. In addition, the spiritual world and the material world constitute two faces of the same reality – LIFE. They are dimensions that eternally intermingle within the dynamic process of evolution.

Given that the physical body is the agent through and wherein the spirit manifests itself, Spiritism highly values its extremely important role. Therefore, it acknowledges the old aphorism *mens sana in corpore sano* or "a healthy mind in a healthy body." Consequently, since it is in the best interest of the spirit and its incarnated body to fulfill its purpose in each material existence, it is necessary that it have a healthy organism, one full of energy and in the best possible condition.

Therefore, Spiritism recommends as essential the education of children, young people, and adults aimed to the formation of strong bodies; one that takes into consideration the primary factors such as healthy food, proper hygiene, recreation and sports, education, appropriate work, etc., necessary for integration in the proper development of a personality and a social life in order that the noble faculties of the soul may find an adequate and coinciding complement for its manifestation and expression within each incarnation.

Endeavoring to seek an exaltation of the soul through neglect of the physical body considering it to be "the fountain of all sin and evil" is the product of dangerous theological opinions and of ancient mysticism; ideas held in past ages that have been mostly overcome. Contempt of physical life or tormenting the body through voluntary suffering or self-flagellation or by any other means is rejected by the doctrine of Spiritism. Therefore, one should not renounce the just and natural enjoyments brought to us by living a healthy, honorable, and intelligent material life. Self-mortification or imposed hardship of the body and soul can be the result of psychological disturbances or a false mystical, religiously devout idea for a defense of self-inflicted pain and suffering. It is not a means beneficial for the purification of the soul.

Moral elevation of the soul is not achieved by running way from the realities of everyday life, but through the procuring of living in harmony with natural laws, educating ones intellect, cultivating good sentiments, practicing virtues, and fortifying our will in our daily engagement with humanity, and, to earn our living in an honest and dignified way.

The spirit, responsible for all intelligent phenomena, is that which thinks, desires, loves, and is the central force of all our potentialities; a substance of a subtle and delicate nature, the soul constitutes within man his true individuality, its indestructible "I," its consciousness which manifests its intelligence, sentiments, emotions, memory and will. These qualities arise from acquisitions obtained from previous material incarnations, combined with the ones obtained in the current lifetime. The spirit never dies or ages.

The physical body, the tangible expression of material life, is that which ceases to exist at death. It inherits physiological aspects, but not spiritual elements. The reproductive cells, by the action of hereditary mechanisms, cause individuals to have resemblance to their parents, although they present themselves in many diverse variations. Spiritism, with its central thesis related to the preexistence and survival of the spirit, accepts similarities in physical characteristics, but not in the spiritual elements. Attitudes, tendencies, and other intellectual and moral characteristics, and all other exclusivities of the personality have their explanation within the spirit itself and its past reincarnations. These are exclusively part of the soul's inheritance and have been formed by a vast number of successive incarnations. Physical hereditary aspects are the byproduct of gene peculiarities, biochemical structures organized in the chromosomes of the cells. Spiritual heredity is a product of the spirit's prior learning and experiences that have accumulated and that it has been synthesizing through innumerable incarnations down through the epochs.

The customary use of the word "death" is truly not an accurate description for the dying process, for it should not be understood as annihilation rather as a metamorphosis; a period of transformation which involves the liberation of the soul from a material body whose deterioration has caused disharmony for a variety of reasons. In the terminology of Spiritism, this process is called disincarnation which is considered much more appropriate. The soul abandons the material body taking with it all meaningful characteristics such as: acquired intelligence, sentiments, emotions, moral qualities, conscience and freewill. It survives and continues to be active with its personality in the spiritual domain. This change of circumstances modifies essentially nothing; it does not convert an ignorant person into a wise one, nor change a morally elevated person into an evildoer. Each entity retains its individual characteristics; it still carries the same beliefs, tendencies, good and bad habits, and intentions. Each human being occupies a specific place on the ladder of progress in accordance to their level of intellectual and moral progress. On material death, the spirit does not instantly acquire the Light of Universal Truths nor arrive more elevated than what they were in the material world, although it can advance upon comprehending its new situation, recognizing its past errors and is willingness to undertake conquest of higher goals.

Upon the physical death of the body, the spirit falls into a stage of disorientation that clouds and confuses it; that will last, accordingly, depending on its level of evolution, and particularly on how much it understands what is happening to it. Awakening in the spirit world and adapting to a different form of existence will be, more or less easy, or difficult, depending on the cause that brought on the disincarnation, the mental and moral disposition that dominated the spirit in accordance with its beliefs and expectations and the quality of the outcome of its last material existence.

When it is a natural death, one that occurs by age or infirmity with the departure of natural life forces, the ties that unite the perispirit to the physical body progressively loosen. For the person that is knowledgeable about spiritual realities and as to what is occurring, and has relinquished attachment to terrestrial things, the detachment is not traumatic; it is smooth, gradual and almost automatic. The individual's philosophical and ethical conviction instills hope in the future and allows him or her to bear death with tranquility, resignation and peace of mind.

For one that is self-centered, materialistic and has lived for the accumulation of wealth or as a slave of vices or irresponsible pleasures, with total neglect of moral principles, the separation of the body from the spirit can cause suffering because there is a clinging in desperation to material life, for it sees nothing else, and wants to retain the feelings that escape it, but the only thing this does is prolong the agony.

The conditions are different in those deaths that occur due to accidents or violence. While organic life has instantly ceased and there has been a sudden rupture of the fluidic link, the separation of the spirit and its enveloping perispirit may be gradual, especially if there has not been complete destruction of the organic body. The spirit, taken by surprise and bewildered, believes it is still incarnated, and this illusion persists until it realizes its true condition. This period of confusion is of short duration for those on a more spiritually evolved level, and they succeed in recuperating rapidly, very naturally becoming members within their new environment. For others, the confusion could last for days, weeks and even more.

In the case of suicides, the spirit's condition can be even more difficult. Suicide is the worst cruelty a person can inflict upon him or herself. If it would be possible for that person to understand at that very moment the consequences derived from that one act, he or she would probably prefer to suffer all the miseries and disappointments that life is full of before choosing a course of action so detrimental, extreme and contrary to the laws of self-preservation and evolution.

Many and varied, are the motives that can carry a person to the point of committing suicide. Some believe that they will find eternal rest or nothing at all. Others act out of desperation due to hurt pride, or because they suffer from an incurable disease, or when facing an economic or family crisis, thinking that death is the end of everything and seeing it as a door to escape. Nevertheless, suicide does not erase or extinguish anything; the act is an unproductive one. On the contrary, instead of liberating themselves from suffering, they have added to it. Since life does not disappear with physical death, since the spirit continues to exist when passing into the spiritual plane, it may be confronted with painful sensations, for in addition to the frustrating discovery that he or she still exists, the consequent feelings of repentance can produce bitter moral distress. However, situations do vary depending on the particular individual circumstances. Spiritism provides comprehension of the process of death; and the conditions of the spirit after it takes place by the knowledge it offers and the sentiments it inspires. Its teachings help us overcome the unhealthy fears our society generates with respect to death, and at the same time educates us regarding the law of self-preservation that we should all respect. Our own self-confidence assured by a hopeful optimism, and sustained with the certainty of our immortality, is the best guaranty for us to reach an adequate physical, psychological, and moral equilibrium.

With knowledge of Spiritism, we can exclaim, there are no dead. Those that have left before us, continue living a spiritual life and return in new existences; and where they are in space, can take an interest in and influence us according to the principles of affinity. Our dear loved ones live; and, can always be by our side, concerned over our progress, helping us mentally and inspiring us with good thoughts.

Our society dedicates one day on the calendar for those souls who have parted, and consecrate it with a formal memorial service, some held at cemeteries where all that is there are the mortal remains. In accordance with Spiritist teachings, we should not spend just that one day remembering our loved ones, placing flowers on a tomb. We should, as much as possible, send them our loving vibrations, and in their memory perform acts of fraternity and solidarity to help those who need us most here on earth. These good thoughts and noble actions fortify our loved ones in the spirit world and allow them to be closer to us.

By assimilating Spiritist teachings, contemporary man learns not to view death with perplexity, anguish, or the fear of that of his ancestors based on false religious or materialistic notions inculcated in them.

It is now understood, that in the harmoniously united natural laws that govern the world and life, it is not chance, but causality that is the foremost guiding principle. In the spirit world, the immanent laws of justice rule, functioning to balance and compensate, providing that each one receives exactly what they deserve. When we reach the spiritual dimension all superficial masks, exterior disguises and all pretentiousness that surround so many upon the earth disappear, revealing for all to discover, one's true thoughts and sentiments. Cause and effect, action and reaction; each person, or rather each spirit's situation is the result of its own conduct.

Loving beings of progress that have overcome much in the way of their own moral imperfections view things with excellent judgment. They understand the benefit of each earthly existence and continue in their fervent desire to continue advancing in their progression. Those that have lived their life on earth attached to things of a material nature, those that have lived solely for the satisfaction of their selfishness, and have not tried in any way whatsoever to enhance their capabilities, yet have developed somewhat intellectually to serve their own personal interests, will find that when they arrive in the afterlife they will have dragged along their passions, vices and their attachment to materiality. Instead of elevating themselves like those eager for light and progress, they remain stagnate, self-deceived by ignorance, holding on to earthly things, and in consequence, suffering longer periods of confusion.

It is as if a principle of attraction and repulsion operates, as if a law of spiritual density regarding those individuals exclusively of a materialistic mentality and conduct stay psychically full of dense particles that make it difficult for them to elevate themselves to superior planes. Meanwhile, those persons that are characterized by their unselfishness acquire the ability to detach themselves from the physical world and to project themselves to superior spiritual planes. Clearly, between these two extremes, there is a broad spectrum of intermediate levels corresponding to the different scales of human values which reflect the moral and intellectual diversity of humanity.

are the anti-physical ones dragged down
also because of their (anti?)-physical obsessions(yes?)

Since spirits are the souls of the deceased and preserve their psychological characteristics, their virtues and imperfections, it is quite obvious that in this spiritual landscape the populace is a clear representation of all those in the physical world. In this spiritual domain, advanced spirits that have maintained their inclinations towards study and their devotion towards serving mankind coexist as well with those spirits that are extremely ignorant with perverse tendencies, although separated and placed in homogenous groups, for spirits are united by ties of affinity. *Similia similibus*, like attracts like.

There are no divine rewards or punishments, but only the fulfillment of universal laws. One should not infer from this principle of compensation a mechanical view that divides spirits in an absolute manner into definitive groups of the good or the bad because in reality, the evolutionary ladder of life represents a *dynamic continuum* wherein every spirit occupies a relative and transitory position, and possesses the intrinsic tendency to progress and strive to new evolutionary levels. This explanation is not an apology for suffering, but to reveal the reality implicit within the mechanisms of life, in the processes of reincarnation, to contribute in the formation of a higher level of social conscience within our humanity, and that each day there is learning more from love, and not by pain. And, in this educational undertaking, highly advanced spirit benefactors work in the afterlife to offer their support to those that are incarnated. Later, they help from the beginning and throughout the disincarnation process, calming our worries, explaining to us regarding our new situation, as well as assisting us in our evolutionary journey in future existences.

By these facts, Spiritism has confirmed that the soul, or rather the incarnated spirit, while consisting of the constant agent of the human personality that integrates psychic factors within a coherent totality, is not the derivation of vital brain functions and is not destroyed by the death process. On the contrary, thought is a function of the spirit, and the brain acts as the organic instrument that permits it to manifest its faculties in the physical dimension.

Spiritism's spiritualism differs from traditional religious and philosophical speculations which tend to stray into abstractions attached to an absolute idealism of the metaphysical school. Therefore, it has been very hard for them to find the *substratum* that can serve as a solid base regarding how the soul could transmit thought. Since remote times, philosophers, theologians and other intellectuals have encountered insurmountable difficulties trying to find a connecting link between the imponderable soul, on one side, and the organic physical body, on the other; both with such dissimilar natures. The gap between both was so immense that it held up the comprehension of the nature and functioning of the human psyche for centuries. Spiritism came to fill this space when it proposed the existence of the **perispirit**, a fluidic body that envelopes the spirit and fulfills the function of intermediary between the spirit and the physical body, actively participating in a wide range of biological, psychological, paranormal phenomena, as well as in the use of the faculty of mediumship. The perispirit is the fluidic envelope of the spirit; as such, it never separates from it, even before or after death, forming a sole structure. It was ALLAN KARDEC who gave it the name perispirit, alluding to the perisperm or the membrane which surrounds the seed of a fruit.

Before Spiritism, numerous cultural and religious traditions had knowledge of this "spiritual body" although they knew little regarding its true nature and properties. It was called *ka* by the Egyptians, *linga shira* by the Hindus, *nephesh* by Jewish esoterics, *subtle cart of the soul* by PYTHAGORAS, *spiritual body* by PAUL of TARSUS, *sidereal body* or *evestrum* by PARACELSUS. After Spiritism, other names appeared, such as: *astral body* or *etheric double* within distinctive esoteric schools, *psicosoma* in the books by the spirit of Andre Luis through the Brazilian medium FRANCISCO CANDIDO XAVIER, *biological organization model* in the works by Brazilian scientist Dr. HERNANI GUIMARES ANDRADE, and *bioplasmic body* proposed by scientific researchers investigating paranormal phenomenon in what was previously the Soviet Union.

Based on his investigations, experiences and on information received from spirit communications, KARDEC came to the conclusion that the perispirit holds a very important function in spirit activities, in both those that are incarnated and disincarnated. He refers to this extensively in his writings:

> "The link, or perispirit, which unites the body with the spirit, is a type of semi-material envelope. Death is the destruction of the material body, which is the grosser of man's two envelopes; but the spirit preserves the second one, the perispirit, which constitutes for him an ethereal body, invisible to us in its normal state and which can be made visible, and even tangible, as has been seen in the phenomena of apparitions." [46]

> "Therefore, a spirit is not an abstract, undefined being, only to be conceived of by our thought, but a real circumscribed being which is appreciable, in certain cases, by the sense of sight, hearing, and touch."

> "The perispirit is an integral part of the spirit, as the physical body is an integral part of man. However, the perispirit itself is not the spirit, in the same manner that the body itself is not a man. Because the perispirit does not possess the faculty of thought and is in relation to the spirit, as the physical body is to man: the agent or instrument of its action." [47]

In accordance with the Spiritist doctrine, the perispirit is a product of the **Universal Cosmic Fluid**, the primary substance of the universe, of which in numerous modifications and transformations, is the origin of a myriad of diverse bodies in nature. The perispirit is the fluidic condensation that surrounds an intelligent focal point, or the spirit. Formed from the cosmic fluids surrounding each particu-

---

[46] ALLAN KARDEC. *El Libro de los Espíritus* [*The Spirits'Book*]. Ediciones CIMA. Caracas, 1992, Introduction to the Study of the Spiritist Doctrine, p. 21

[47] ALLAN KARDEC. *Libro de los Médiums* [*The Mediums'Book*]. Ediciones CIMA. Caracas, 1994, No. 54 & No. 55, pp. 63 & 64.

lar planet, its characteristics depend on the evolutionary level of its inhabitants, and it is more or less dense or subtle in conformance with the grade of purification of each particular spirit. [48]

Therefore, the spirit gives orders and instructions that are received by the perispirit (the bond that joins the spirit with the material body during incarnated life), and it transmits them to the material organism, exercising its action on the central nervous system. The brain transforms these energy impulses into instructions that can be attended to and differentiated by all the systems of the material organism for execution of their corresponding tasks. At the same time, any external impressions that are captured by the physical body are sent to the spirit, after being modified and adapted by the perispirit, executing in this way its function as a mediator that relates and sustains a constant equilibrium; the intelligent powers of the spirit with the mechanical functions of the material organism.

During the incarnated state, every one of the physical senses has a specific organ through which is perceived a determined order of sensations. Therefore, the impressions of physical life are being diverted into various physical faculties. Meanwhile, when the spirit is disincarnated and in the spiritual plane, where no physical organs are present, sensibility is concentrated in only one place and is dispersed throughout the structure of the perispirit. In the spiritual plane, there is a centralized faculty operating as one general consciousness with the potentialities of the spirit. A process of analysis occurs in the incarnated being; the intellectual, emotional, and sensitivities of the soul are distributed in an extensive range of activities. Meanwhile, in the disincarnated spirit a synthesis is produced that condenses and unifies all the attributes that identify that particular spirit. In light of theoretical studies and from a great variety

---

[48] We continue to use the term "fluid" although it does not comply with the language of modern physics, but in order to continue within Spiritist terminology. In the middle of the 19th century, this term was the scientific expression for designating whatever natural substance was not related to solid or material bodies. It was applied to invisible and imponderable forces emanating from solid bodies, like magnetic or vital fluids. Actually, an appropriate equivalent for the word fluid would be "energy"; therefore, in this case, it is basically a question of semantics. The state of the fundamental concepts that support the basis of Spiritist doctrine enhances with further scientific advancements, for it is necessary to maintain an open attitude in providing for adjustments that may be imposed by proofs that are duly confirmed.

of experiences, we can assert certain basic characteristics that identify the nature of the perispirit. We can say that: it is **semi-material** (a term employed due to a lack of a more precise one to express its subtle constitution); it is **invisible** to humans in the material world (even though it is visible under special circumstances); it is **expandable** (it is able to project itself outside corporeal limits as in astral projections or out- of-body experiences); it is **highly sensitive** (it is intensely impressionable by the mental energy of the spirit that controls it, as well as through the action of magnetism and hypnosis); it has **plasticity** (it constantly is modifying its appearance in response to the biological changes of the incarnated being, and when it is participating in psychic, paranormal, and/or mediumship experiences); and, it possesses the property of **luminescence** (it forms a luminous atmosphere or aura around the physical body, that contracts or expands, according to the thoughts of the spirit).

One should not confuse the functions of the spirit with that of the perispirit. The spirit is the thinking and intelligent principle that commands all vital processes. The perispirit is the fluidic envelope of the spirit, and serves at its discretion. The perispirit does not possess intellectual attributes, it does not think, it is not the seat of memory, it does not direct the biological or psychic processes during reincarnation. It is the structure that the spirit avails itself to fulfill its objectives. And, all this was expressed very clearly by KARDEC:

> "The perispirit of itself is not intelligent, although material, but is the vehicle of thought, of the sensations and the perceptions of the spirit." [49]

The perispirit is not a mere reflection of the physical or material body, but on the contrary, it's as if the material body serves as a sort of mold in preserving the semblance of the human form and a variety of peculiarities that is identified with it, as a manifestation of the person that it was in its last existence. In the spiritual dimension, wherein every human being becomes a member after disincarnation, the spirit discovers it is endowed with a body similar to that which it had in its

---

[49] ALLAN KARDEC. *La Génesis* [*Genesis*]. CIMA, Caracas, 1995, Cap. II. No. 23 p. 51

most recent earthly experience: its *perispiritual body*; that preserves its identifiable appearance and provides for a concrete and definite being.

There exists a direct relation between the appearance of the spirit and its level of moral evolution. This occurs due to the sensibility and plasticity of the perispirit which is highly susceptible to the influence of a spirit's thoughts and will. An aggressive spirit, that lies, is cruel, envious, and perverse, will cause distortions of its fluidic body; the result of negative mental vibrations. Meanwhile, the opposite effect occurs with those beings that distinguish themselves by the ethical quality of their ideas and by their conduct of love for their fellow beings.

At each incarnation, in the process that gives rise to a new material organism, the spirit with its individual perispirit is present at the very moment of fertilization and conception. It progresses along in its attachment throughout all the stages of the embryonic process until finally, acquiring its full autonomy at the birth of the organism. The spirit directs the cellular division that occurs in the embryo by means of the perispirit, imparting to the embryo certain characteristics within a complex mechanism, uniting to it cell by cell, and organ by organ. This union persists throughout the physical life of a given individual, and is solely broken when death, or rather disincarnation, occurs. Understood from this perspective, one can realize that the perispirit functions as an organizing matrix in the formation and development of the physical body.

All the phases of embryonic and organ development are highly specialized processes, and numerous observations and experiences suggest the intervention of a superior force that directs and guides these transformations. No other functional cellular mechanism, or anything within any of its internal structures, can explain the perfect orientation that follows the process of mitosis, completing the stages of prophase, anaphase and telophase, to obtain the duplicity of all the elements and distributing them equally between the two daughter cells. In addition, it is not possible to explain the embryonic development and the perfect differentiation that occurs in the endoderm, ectoderm and the mesoderm, to give origin to specialized tissues and organs of the human body, solely from an anatomic and physiological perspective. It is necessary to recognize the presence of the spirit as a biodynamic force that prefigures beforehand the function that each organ should carry out and its harmonic relationship with the rest of the organs within the general structure of the system that configures the incarnated spirit.

In the last decades of the twentieth century, scientists from different countries have come to the conclusion that all living beings are surrounded by an energy field, and this is where instructions specifying the construction of organic forms are transmitted. A curious fact well known by embryologists, is that when a cell is extracted while it is engaged in the first stages of the formation of an embryo and in the beginning process of differentiating into a particular structure, and then grafted into another tissue related to a different organ, that cell will retrocede to its previous stage of differentiation and reprogram itself to give way to develop into the new structure. Different names have been suggested to define this force that can configure biological forms or structures: *Idée directrice* was suggested by the celebrated French physiologist CLAUDE BERNARD (1813-1878). *Entelequia or Entelechy*, was the denomination suggested by the well-know German biologist and philosopher HANS DRIESCH (1867-1941), well known for his contributions to parapsychology. Professors HAROLD SAXTON BURR and F.C.S. NORTHRUP of Yale University, proposed what they called *fields of life* to certain electrodynamics fields that molded and controlled living beings, and representing to biological beings the equivalent to fields known in physics.

A Brazilian engineer, notable for his research in the fields of Spiritism and parapsychology and one of the founders of the Brazilian Institute of Psychobiophysical Research (IBPP), HERNANI GUIMA-RAES ANDRADE presented the work of his investigations in various books fundamental to these two disciplines on such topics as: survival of the soul after death, reincarnation, paranormal phenomena and mediumship, presenting theoretical models representing one of the major contributions for the establishment of a scientific theory of the spirit. [50]

---

[50]   Some accounts of ANDRADE'S research can be found in English, in the book *The Unknown Power* (also published under the title *The Flying Cow*) by parapsychology writer

In his books, he wrote extensively about the perispirit, explaining its participation in the reincarnation process by following the spirit's instructions; the perispirit acting as *biological organizational model*, providing form for organisms and determining its characteristics. With acceptance of this model, many mysteries that are due to materialistic, chemical, or genetic conceptual thinking as well those in various fields of biology, are resolved. The following interesting case is offered for consideration:

"Another inexplicable fact by the theories of the reductionists and is the result of certain genetic experiments conducted with the fruit fly Drosophila melanogaster. The cross-breeding of flies possessing a recessive mutant gene corresponding to the characteristic of obtaining "flies without eyes" which could result in a pure stock of flies with no eyes. According to the strict laws of genetics, if one proceeds ahead from this in cross-breeding of these "flies without eyes," of a pure line, their descendents should exactly be all of the type of "flies with no eyes." But that is not what occurs. Within a certain number of generations within these cross breeds of the "flies with no eyes" there will newly emerge normal flies with eyes." [51]

The mechanisms of inheritance receives its determinant influence from the instructions that emanate from the spirit, which are processed by the perispirit to penetrate within the vital energy of the cellular nucleus, reaching the genes situated in the chromosomes. By this process, the experiences acquired by the spirit down through the ages in the reincarnation process, and which is found synthesized in numerous programs of information, proceed to orient the genotype (united with hereditary factors)

and translator Guy Lyon Playfair. Among ANDRADE'S most well-known books are: *Teoría Corpuscular del Espíritu* [*Corpuscular Theory of the Spirit*];*Nuevos Rumbos en la experimentación espiritica* [*New Directions in Spiritistic Experimentation*];*Parapsicología Experimental:La materia* PSI [Experimental *Parapsychology:the matter of PSI*] ; *PSI quántico* [*Quantic PSI*]; *Reencarnación en Brasil* [*Reincarnation in Brazil*]; *El Poltergeist de Guarilhos, El Poltergeist de Suzano* [*The Poltergiest of Guarilhos, the Poltergeist of Suzano*]; *La transcomunicación a través del tiempo* [*Transcommunication across time*]; etc.

[51] HERNANI GUIMARAES ANDRADE. *Muerte, renacimiento, evolución* [*Death, rebirth, evolution*]. CIMA, Caracas, 1993, p. 58.

and the phenotype (characteristics that visibly manifest in the individual and express the interaction of its genotype within its environment), producing the guidelines specific for each individual. This approach permits the comprehension, in a concrete and objective way, the relationship that can exist between certain body injuries or functional disturbances affecting a newborn starting at birth, and/or even from the fetal stage, with psychic or physical traumas that derive from past life existences. This information opens an immense field of study in medicine that can completely modify traditional concepts of illness, its etiology and treatment.

Continuing with Andrade's ideas relating to organized biological fields, he presents the following reflection, that perfectly signifies his acceptance with the concepts developed so far:

> "Let's return to the simple experience of [the action of] magnets on a paper cartoon and covered with iron filings. What does this phenomenon suggest to us? Could it be that in biological processes there is also present an orderly action of fields of organizing forces? Furthermore, could it be that these fields were produced by a principle that was formed concomitantly at the beginning of primordial life itself? In this case, the principle can, thanks to a space-time structural constitution, save all previous experiences, converting itself into an informational historical domain. This being the case, in its interaction with organic molecules, it could conduct the embryo to reproduce, to sum up, during the ontogenesis, the decisive phase with its phylogenesis. We could in that way justify the phenomena of recapitulation.
>
> The principle we have brought about then functions as a model biological organizer. Perhaps it could possibly identify itself as part of what religious doctrines call the spirit." [52]

---

[52] Ibid. p. 59.

The Spiritist vision of mankind, of life, and of the universe is clearly in harmony with the new scientific paradigms of the beginning of the twenty-first century by revisiting the traditional materialistic, mechanistic, and reductionist teachings in light of the advanced discoveries in quantum physics and relativity, astrophysics, biology, psychosomatic medicine, transpersonal psychology and parapsychology, all of which are advancing to a point where they can demonstrate that the world we perceive through our physical senses only represents a small fraction of reality. [53]

The new paradigms that are emerging can be classified as holistic, systemic, ecological and spiritualistic, in as much as they present man as a system, with its respective physical, chemical, biological, social, cultural, and spiritual aspects integrated into other systems of a plural-dimensional universe, sustained by numerous experiences that have required a modification of traditional concepts of physical reality and of human nature.

In 1982, at the University of Paris, scientific experiments were conducted based on the Einstein-Rosen-Podolsky paradox (ERP) which demonstrated that the thesis is well founded that everything is interrelated, and that interdependency exists between all particles of the universe and they previously have interacted. It is the same idea proposed by the German biologist LUDWIG VON BERTALANFFY (1901-1972) in his work on the *General Theory of Systems*, regarding the interconnection that exists in nature, including human behavior. This also relates to the work by Belgium educated, Russian born scientist ILYA PRIGOGINE (1917-2003), who was awarded the 1977 Nobel Prize in Chemistry, while a professor at the University of Texas, for his studies on the irreversible processes of thermodynamics, in

---

[53] Plato's use of the term paradigm was to refer to the world of ideas as a prototype for the world of the senses. However, the word "paradigm" was given a new meaning by a North American physicist and philosopher Thomas Kuhn in his book, *The Structure of the Scientific Revolutions*, to indicate a model of reality, that is, a system of facts, theories and philosophical concepts that are widely accepted and are converted in appropriate conceptual agreement for carefully thinking about a scientific problem. When new discoveries put to doubt an existing paradigm, a substitute paradigm is produced.

relation to certain systems which gave a name to dissipative structures, demonstrating the existence of an ordering principle that could
counteract entropy, that is to say the degradation of a system's energy.

From the quantum perspective, physics presents concepts
completely removed from the old mechanistic model. It is now known
that information between subatomic particles cannot be interpreted
using the classic principle of causality, and that the change of position
of a particle simultaneously provokes modifications in another one
without registering physical signals between them, and, that the presence of an observer affects the phenomena studied, interacting with it
at a level that is not of a physical nature.

In conclusion, these are times of change for physics. That discipline known as the "dictator of science" which fervently embraced
itself with a materialistic vision, has moved in such a way that it
opens the possibility to give credit to a spiritualistic interpretation of
the cosmos. In the works of the French physicist JEAN CHARON,
like *The Spirit, this unknown;* or in *The Tao of Physics* by FRITJOF
CAPRA; or in the revolutionary works published by known physicists known as the "Gnostics" from Princeton University, they found
a relationship, sustained in a scientific way, that exists in the universe
between those two essential elements: the spirit and matter.

Another notable scientist, DAVID BOHM, proposed an holo-
graphic model of the universe, wherein our sensory and conscious
perceptions can solely grasp only the partial reality of things, the
"explicit order," energetic, that manifests itself in the physical and
three dimensional field, can only be accessed by an expanded state
of consciousness that can be reached by way of relaxation, meditation, or by mediumistic or paranormal trance. Similar ideas has been
put forth by psychiatrist STANISLOV GROF, one of the foremost
exponents of transpersonal psychology and creator of the technique
of "holotropic respiration" to facilitate access to modified states of
consciousness and facilitating the acquisition of extra-physical levels
with extra-sensory means.

Also in medicine, some very significant changes have been occurring. In as much as the bio-medical model is still in use, that considers an organism as a machine, that sickness is looked at as damage of one of its parts, and the act of therapy is the repairing of damage, each day appear new alternatives. These different approaches take into consideration the involvement of mental, psychic, or spiritual factors in the chemical and organic dynamics of the human body, and, that they may be responsible for the formation of pathological symptoms or in their cure of them. Namely, psychosomatic medicine has been gaining ground in today's medical vision, deepening the relationships between the biological and psychological components of health, and reclaiming a practice of medicine oriented towards psychotherapy and natural healing, towards strategies that diminish or eliminate treatment with pharmaceuticals.

Heading in this same direction, a new medical specialty emerged at the end of the twentieth century called psychoneuroimmunology (PNI) to study the reciprocal interaction that occurs of a permanent nature between human behavior and the structure of the central nervous system, that is, of the endocrine and immunological systems. This science explains what has always been known concerning the powerful influences the mind has over the physical body and that what happens to one has repercussions in the other, demonstrating an anatomical-physiological basis in that interaction. Positive thoughts of optimism, happiness, wellbeing and peace, are beneficially reflected in the personality of an individual, returning them to health and facilitating congenial relations around them by the good impressions they make. On the opposite side of the spectrum, negative thoughts of sadness, doubt, anguish, or selfishness, deteriorates the immunological defenses rendering it vulnerable to illnesses that are already present and exposing it to the risk of encountering new diseases. Furthermore, a psychic atmosphere is created able to generate unbalanced vibratory energies that hurt the sensibility of those that are found encircled within its field of action. A pioneer in PNI and an American from the United States, O. CARL SIMONTON, a physician has obtained remarkable successes in cancer patients, combining psychotherapeutic strategies to confront stress and in modifying the thoughts and attitudes that can upset the patient, by using relaxation and visualization techniques with the intention of eliminating sick cells.

The more understanding we have regarding human nature as well as the physical and spiritual laws that rule their evolution, the more confident and liberated we will be, and be more able to head toward the advent of a more superior moral state. From the world of science, and thought in general, everything is culminating into the configuration of a new paradigm that aims to establish a new vision of reality, backed by proof of the existence of the manifestations about a double aspect of the universe, of life, and of man: the material and the spiritual.

Spiritism, uniting science with philosophy and moral principles, offers a decisive contribution for the emergence of this new paradigm, that leaves behind superstitions, dogmatic creeds, materialistic guidelines that used to characterize previous stages, and opens a new horizon regarding the evolutionary process of humanity.

Chapter Four

COMMUNICATION WITH SPIRITS THROUGHOUT HISTORY

> *"The phenomena of mediumship is as old as man. In the East it has been known since remote times. The Greek Pythia, the Roman Sibyl, the Oriental Fakir and the magician of the ancient legends are similar to the medium as psychic transmitter and receiver, human telescope for whom therefore science sees the invisible and penetrates the impenetrable."*
>
> ***Manuel S. Porteiro***
> **Spiritist Author and Activist from Argentina (1881-1936)**

There are no people or religion that does not contain a belief in the soul and its immortality or in the manifestations of spirits, whether expressed in a primitive or sophisticated manner according to the time, place or the established customs. In fact, a bibliographic run through the multiple studies made by anthropologists and sociologists about the types of life characterized by primitive peoples or the diverse civilizations prior to ours demonstrate that at the base of all their beliefs were always found the same fundamental principles, and also reveal that in those communities there had already appeared profound and enlightening concepts in their essence, even though they may have been obscured by crude forms and confused with any manner of superstitions.

All the fundamental beliefs of humanity had at their beginning a common acceptance of the survival of the soul after death and the communication between the dead and the living, or rather, between disincarnated spirits and incarnated spirits. These beliefs are lost in distant antiquity but are based on concrete acts related to visions, apparitions, transmission of thought, trances, communication with spirits, prophesies, healings, and great quantities of other unusual phenomena, all of which have continued being produced throughout human evolution and among people and cultures all over the entire world. This admirable fact of universality and concordance prompted the eminent Italian paranormal researcher ERNESTO BOZZANO (1862-1943) to write an authoritative and scholarly book entitled *Pueblos Primitivos y manifestaciones supranormales* [*Primitive peoples and supernormal manifestations*] with the purpose of compiling numerous occurrences of psychic and spiritual manifestations, in primitive cultures already extinct as well as in others that still existed, and to demonstrate that those phenomena were similar in essence to the ones that could be verified currently in the modern societies of our planet.

> *"It is truly interesting how prominent the supernormal manifestations among the savages are not only related to the kind of manifestations with the ones that are made among civilized people, but also that among the savages and the civilized, a perfect relationship is also found in the procedures that they use to select the subjects indicative of becoming 'witches' on one hand and 'mediums' on the other; moreover in the empiric systems of 'training' adopted to favor the emergence of the supernormal subconscious faculties in the new adepts."* [54]

In this work, Bozzano reviews the opinions discovered by outstanding historians and social scientists that did research on these topics during the first decades of the twenty century to demonstrate

---

[54] ERNEST BOZZANO. *Popoli primitive e manifestazioni supernormali.* [*Primitive peoples and supernormal manifestations*]. Luce e Ombra, Genova. 1926. p. 9.

that they had made identical conclusions: the belief in the survival of the soul after the death and the influence of the dead over the living is the universal idea that gave origin to worship and religions; that there have existed primitive peoples that did not develop a concept of God in an exact meaning of the word but that in no case was there one found without belief in spirits; that the psychic supernormal manifestations among the people called savage or primitive should be considered as real and indisputable as the analogies that are verified in current societies; that the ceremonies and rites that were practiced by those ancient peoples have been perpetuated from generation to generation and are manifested in the ancient cultures that still exist on our planet, the customs and beliefs of their ancestors having continued in these populations for millenniums.

It suffices to summarize and reaffirm these concepts, by the following quote by illustrious positivist British researcher and philosopher HERBERT SPENCER (1829-1903), to whom BOZZANO admired with enthusiasm:

> *"We find, everywhere, the idea of the survival of the spirit after death of the body, with all the numerous and complicated derived conceptions. We find them identical, even in the Arctic regions and in the tropics; even in the woods of North America as in the deserts of Arabia; as well as in the valleys of the Himalayas and on the Islands of Polynesia. That idea is expressed with great clarity by races so different, that specialists consider that its transformation occurred before the present distribution of the lands and of water; it is as much among straight haired people as much as among those of curly hair; among white and yellow races, red or black; among the savages, the semi-civilized and those that are found at the vanguard of civilization."* [55]

In the ancient sanctuaries, from the crypts of the Himalayans to the Egyptian hypogeums, from the Greek oracles to the Roman catacombs, the communication with the so-called dead was always the basis

---

[55] HERBERT SPENCER. *Sociology Principles*. Volume II.

of beliefs, myths, and liturgies. In all religions, the literary works that were adopted as sacred books show characteristics that allowed considering them as mediumship works. Formed on the basis of communication with spirits, given orally mostly, and that were transmitted down through generations until writing allowed them to be set down. These messages resulted in being seriously adulterated by a very long oral tradition, since there is a lot of time between the epoch when they were received and when they were written, as well as by the participation of numerous interpreters and intermediaries who distorted and adapted them to their convenience.

The same prophets that are venerated in diverse religions, declared that the spirits had revealed the messages, but it was the priests of all sects that attributed them to God, to give them an absolute character to the doctrines that they propagated and to cover them with an unquestionable authority. [56]

So therefore, the Brahmans consider the *Vedas* [57] as revealed by the Supreme Intelligence to be spirits that were the intermediaries for men. The *Manava-Dhrama-Sastra* or *The Laws of Manu*, a code in which Brahman morality is based, is taken as revealed to the first Manu by its proper Brahma. It teaches that "the spirits of the ancestors, in invisible state accompany the Brahmans invited to the ceremonies in commemoration of the dead" and that of the *pitrs*, or spirits could manifest by means of the rishis or wise ascetics with special psychic faculties.

The Chinese people consider their *Kings* [58] as books revealed from Up High and were received by FOHI in a state of trance when

---

[56] Therefore, each religion proclaimed itself the authentic representative of God on the earth, as a unique depositary of the divine truth, and considered the others as false or heretical. When it is understood that these messages come from spirits, with their accordingly high or low level of progress, and not directly from the Creator, an era of tolerance will be established of respectful and happy coexistence among the peoples of the world, because it will be calmly accepted that each one has received learning adapted to its own distinctiveness and for which it was prepared to receive, each according to their particular epoch and level of evolution.

[57] These are sacred books written in Sanskrit. The Vedic literature is composed of four *Samhita* or collections: the *Rig-Veda*, the *Yajur-Veda*, the *Sama-Veda* and the *Atharva-Veda*. Also, the origin of the Brahmanas, the Aranyakas and Upanishads goes back to very ancient epochs. The *Mahabharata* is attributed to the sage Vyasa, about the 14th century B.C.E., and finally edited when writing was introduced to India, between the 18th and 19th centuries B.C.E..

[58] The *Kings*, that oral tradition transmitted for many generations, it is supposed that it had

he entered in a cavern that he chose for his acetic refuge. In China, the mediums, those that they knew had the faculty to establish contact with spirits, were called *Wu*. Among the Japanese evocations to receive spiritual messages was very well established. There were two categories of mediums: the *kan-nagi*, those that served the imperial authorities, and, the *kuchiyose*, of the general populace. In addition, as in other peoples, they accepted sacred books like the *Nihon Shoki*, the most important of these, as revelations of a superior spirituality.

In Egypt, books attributed to HERMES TRISMEGISTUS were dictated by a mysterious voice priests felt came from the divine. The *Zend-Avesta* (the live word) [59]sacred book of Mazdayasna (or Zoroastrianism) the religion of the Persians was revealed to ZOROASTER or ZARATHUSTRA, prophet of the old Iran (VI century B.C.), by *a*mshaspandan a spirit of an elevated degree that appeared to him by the margins of River Daitia, where he had withdrew to prepare for his spiritual mission. The Chaldean Magi lived a life of purity and meditation that permitted them to enter into contact with spirits of an elevated hierarchy. In Babylonia and Assyria, evocations to spirits of the dead were allowed and they were consulted for particular issues or to make decisions of state. The Druids evoked the spirits in the forests of Gaul, and in the life of the Celtic people, spirit manifestations were always welcome. The bards were poet mediums that composed during trance the anthems that glorified their nations. The historians say that VERCINGETORIX, hero of the fight for the independence of the Welsh, interned himself in the woods to communicate with the souls of those who had died for the homeland, and that before the uprising against the Roman occupation led by JULIUS CEASAR, a spirit appeared to him and predicted his defeat and martyrdom, to which he submitted.

---

its beginning nearly twenty centuries before the Christian era, and was later revised and organized by CONFUCIOUS (551-479 B.C.), eminent philosopher and moralist, whose teachings are based on the cult of reverence to one's ancestors and have in their country the power of law. The principal ones are *Shu-King*, canon of history; *Shi-King*, canon of poetry; *I-King*, canon of changes; *Li-Ki* and *Hsiao-King*, books of moral character.

[59] The *Zend-Avesta* as it exists today constitutes fragments of the primitive *Avesta* originally on twelve parchments of which only a part are preserved.

In communication with spirits, its geographical and cultural universality is a key factor to get an objective and authentic interpretation of human history. The most well-known researchers of these processes took them to each of the peoples of the world and they have elaborated on their belief systems and values which offer ample testimonies about the constant relationship they had with spirits and practiced in all times, among all peoples. LUCIAN of SAMOSATA in his *Dialogues of the Dead*, FLAVIUS PHILOSTRATUS in *Life of APOLLONIUS of TYANA*; FLAVIUS JOSEPHUS in *Antiquities of the Jews*, PLUTARCH with his *Parallel Lives*, STRABO's *History* provide much evidence of this. The same Fathers of the Church [60]also make reference to mediumship activities that were made with much frequency in the beginning epochs of Christianity and contributed powerfully to its final victory and consolidation as a religion.

The Spiritualist thought that marked the Greco-Roman civilization was held on the most varied of mediumship experiences which was beautifully expressed in its mythology, literature and philosophy. ORPHEUS evocates his lover EURYDICE and he attempts to fruitlessly bring her back to the world of the living. In the Odyssey, Ulysses interrogates several spirits by means of CIRCE. [61]In the Iliad, we find the dead prophesying many events and ACHILLES[62], the most important hero of Troy, is visited in his tent by the soul of PATROCLOS that had just died in battle. AENEAS descends into hell to consult with his father ANCHISES [63]and PERIANDER, one of the seven wise men of Greece, talks to the spirit of his dead wife Melissa. SOCRATES receives by his auditory mediumship advice and warnings by his *daimon* or spirit guide and are decisively important in his thought and in the most relevant acts of his life. PLATO rests his theory of knowledge on the reminiscences of prior lives and inspiration that comes from the spiritual world. The soul

[60] TERTULLIAN, *Apologetics*, XIII, XXII; LACTANTIUS, *Divine Institutions*, Book IV, 27; EUSEBIUS, *Ecclesiastical Histories*, VIII, 10, etc.

[61] HOMER. *Odyssey*, Rhapsody XI, *Evocation of the Dead*.

[62] VIRGIL. *Aeneid*, Book VI.

[63] HERODOTUS. *The Nine Books of History*, Book V, No. 92.

of SCIPIO AFRICANAS, who had been Consul of Rome, presents himself to his adoptive grandson SCIPIO AEMILIANUS, who had also been Roman Consul, and predicts to him that he would triumph in Cartage and Numantia, and he also relates an interesting description regarding the soul's immortality and its continued existence in the spirit world. [64]

The followers of Plato, the Pythagoreans, the Stoics, as well as the Romans and Neo-Platonists, esteemed the practice of communication with spirits and continuously visited the places where the oracles were. At the zenith of Greek culture, the oracle was recognized as the official way of communication between the inhabitants of the two worlds. It was especially consulted by government officials and philosophers, and it was respected as an institution created by the gods or spirits, for the instruction and orientation of humanity, and therefore was of prime importance in the lives of the Eurasian peoples. The oracles were actually centers of mediumship, and they only differed from others by their particular method of practicing it. The Greek pythoness and the Roman sibyls were mediums that predisposed themselves to trance by fasting and inhaling thick vapors, sulfurous or aromatic, coming up among the rocks, and then afterwards they were raised on a tripod or table to transmit the message. The spirits counseled and prophesized using a language of great beauty, using simple sentences or given in hexameter verse. When MNESARCHUS and PARTHENIA, future parents of PYTHAGORAS, consulted the fortune teller at Delphi about their child about to be born, and the response was that he would become a man full of wisdom and beauty, and be of great benefit to the human race. The accuracy of the response would honor who would come later. About SOCRATES, the oracle predicted with amazing accuracy, "He will be the wisest in Greece." The oracles maintained their influence during the first centuries of the current historic chronology, until their members started to be persecuted by the Christian Church authorities. The oracle of Delphi, the one with the most superior reputation among all the rest, was closed by emperor Theodosius I at the end of the fourth century.

---

[64] CICERO. *The Republic*. Book VI.

The Hebrew sacred books also present themselves with support of an authority that comes from revelation. They were dictated to the prophets by Jehovah, their God. In this way, MOSES, liberator and legislator of Israel, received the *Decalogue* when he was in a spiritual retreat among the brambles of Sinai.

The Bible is full of the phenomena of mediumship like all of the other religious books in the world, and to pretend that only devils (according to the distorted meaning given to evil spirits by the Christian Church) could manifest to men, is the equivalent of destroying the fundamental principles of the creation of religion by denying the value of revelation and ignoring the evidence of the historical testimony. The prohibitions given by MOSES regarding mediumship were perfectly justified at that time, since the practice demands certain proper conditions that some of the Hebrew people at that time, dominated by ignorance, superstition and idolatry, were not able to respect. On the other hand, there was no comprehension of the importance that the prophets reached among the Hebrews, "Before time in Israel, when a man went to inquire of God, thus he said, *"Come and let us go to the seer, for he that is now called a Prophet was before time called a seer."* [65]

In the *Old Testament*, is described an impressive scene that shows in a forceful way the knowledge that Hebrews had about the possibility of consulting the spirits of those who had died. In this story of mediumship, it was instigated by KING SAUL (XI B.C.), who decided to consult a fortuneteller or medium, on the eve of the battle of Gilboa during which there would be a confrontation between the Israelites and the Philistines. The spirit of SAMUEL, last of the judges of Israel that had disincarnated years before, rebukes the king and predicts his imminent death:

> *"Then Saul ordered his officials," Find me a woman who is a medium, and I will go and consult her."*
>
> *"There is one in Endor," they answered. So Saul disguised himself, he put on different clothes, and after dark he went with two of his men to see the woman. "Consult spirits for me and tell me what is going to happen, "He said to her. "Call up the spirit of the man I name."*

---

[65] 1. Samuel, 9-9

The woman answered, "Surely you know what King Saul has done, how he has forced the fortunetellers and mediums from Israel. Why then are you trying to trap me and get me killed?"

Then Saul made a sacred vow, "By the living Lord, I promise that you will not be punished for doing this." He told her.

She then asked, "Whom shall I bring up for you?"

He replied, "Samuel."

When the woman saw Samuel, she cried out at the top of her voice, and said to Saul, "Why have you tricked me? You are King Saul!"

The king said to her, "Don't be afraid. What do you see?"

The woman said, "I see a spirit coming up out from the earth."

"What does he look like?" He asked.

"An old man wearing a robe is coming up," she said. Then Saul knew it was Samuel, and he bowed down to the ground in respect.

And Samuel asked Saul, "Why have your disturbed me? Why did you make me come back?"

And Saul responded, "I am in great trouble! The Philistines are at war with me, and God has abandoned me. He does not answer me anymore, either by prophets or by dreams. And so, I have called you, for you to tell me what to do."

Then Samuel said, "Why do you call me, when the Lord has abandoned you and become your enemy? The Lord has done to you what he told you through me, he has taken the kingdom away from you and given it thy neighbor, even to David instead. You disobeyed the Lord's command and did not completely destroy the Amalekites and all they had. That is why the Lord is doing this to you now. Tomorrow you and your sons will join me. The Lord also will hand over the army to the Philistines." Immediately, Saul fell down and lay stretched out on the ground, terrified by what Samuel had said." [66]

The next day the Israelites were completely defeated by the Philistines and SAUL lost his life with his three sons, and most of his army.

---

[66] 1, Samuel 28, 7-20

Those who consider that the Bible is a sacred book and that it contains the Word of God, do not have another alternative but to accept as an unquestionable truth that disincarnated spirits can manifest through the faculty of mediums when the conditions are favorable. To deny it, is equal to denying the authenticity of the Bible.

To understand religious books in their truest meaning, one should keep in mind not only their historic and cultural context, but that there teachings contain an exoteric element, written in a simple way for the masses and adapted to the mentality of the people of the times, and another part esoteric, reserved for the people of a higher intellectual and moral level, in which the most profound truths are revealed. In the *Gospels* [67], for example, there are found numerous ambiguous texts, whose true reading could only solely be done by those knowledgeable and privileged disciples, of which JESUS made reference to when he told his disciples after they asked him, why he spoke in parables:

"The knowledge about the secrets of the Kingdom of heaven has been given to you and not to them." [68]

The *Koran* or *Kitab-Allah* (Book of Allah) also presents notable characteristics of mediumship revelation. MOHAMMED, who presents himself as an "illiterate prophet" affirms that the Koran is not his work but that it was dictated to him by an angel through dreams, voices and visions: "The Koran is a revelation that was done." (Koran, LIII-4). MOHAM-

---

[67] The Gospels were only written years after the death of JESUS. The word Gospel, of profound roots in Greek literature, signified the payments given to the messenger that carried *good news*, and very gradually changed to designate the new meaning. The narration of MARK, which is the most ancient, appeared near the year 60, MATTHEW's AND LUKE's at the end of the first century, and JOHN's, at the beginning of the second century. At the same time of these Gospels that the church knows as synoptic or canonical, many others existed that were apocryphal. In the year 284 Pope DAMASUS I commissioned the ecclesiastic writer JEROME to write a Latin translation of the Old and New Testaments which is known as the Vulgate Bible, which would be considered since then, the only one with official character inside the Church. With the purpose of agreement, the texts that show strong differences and contradictions, Jerome chose the ones that harmonized best with the interests of the Church and introduced alterations that matched. That translation supposedly definitive was modified in 1588 by the order of SIXTUS V, as well in 1598 by CLEMENT VIII.

[68] Matthew, 11, 10-13

MED makes reference in the Koran to the permanent action of spirits over men (XIII-12) and those spirits could be good or bad (LXXII-11). And he, himself, offers his testimony to recognize the previous prophets, "We have given you the revelation that we gave to NOAH and the prophets that came after him. We gave it to ABRAHAM, ISHMAEL, ISACC, to JACOB, to the twelve tribes, to JESUS, JOB, JONAH, AARON, to SOLOMON and we gave the psalms to DAVID (IV-16).

It is not reasonable to suppose that the original messages in the revelations of all religions were given by direct intervention of the Creator, because it would also be attributing to the Supreme Intelligence the responsibility of the absurd concepts and trivialities that are also found in these sacred books on par with its sublime teachings and transcendental truths. It is necessary to have a general knowledge of these books to understand and recognize that the source of such revelations is found in the transmitted communications of spirits. Therefore, it undoubtedly appears that, MOSES, BUDDHA, ZORO-ASTER, JESUS and all the prophets and moral reformers of humanity, in all times, have offered their lives in order that TRUTH and LOVE shine within the human conscience.

The first Christians were absolutely convinced that the spirits were the ones who talked through their prophets' mouths, following the Greek tradition that designated every intermediary with the name of *pneumaton*, which literally means "he who is directed by the spirits." And, precisely due to that conviction that the messages came from spirits, and not from God, is that they were also alert to whatever deceptions could occur and recommended that their origin be examined carefully, as is deduced from this advice that JOHN the evangelist provides, emphasizing the use of discernment when receiving information from the other world:

> *"Dear friends, do not believe every spirit, but test the spirits to see whether they are from God."* [69]

---

[69] I John 4:1

In a book that stands out for its historical rigor and its ample documentation, the talented Brazilian writer, PEDRO GRANJA (1909-1969), shows a meticulous relationship about mediumship phenomena that one can find in the Bible, citing cases of apparitions, materializations, levitations, luminous effects, transfigurations, clairvoyance, spirit messages transmitted orally or written, and many others. [70]

The adoption of Christianity as the official religion of the Holy Roman Empire marks the starting point of a degenerative process in which dogmas progressively obscure the truths of the loving and tolerant message of JESUS. Religious liturgies fused with the pomp of paganism, flames consume the libraries containing the treasures of ancient knowledge, anathemas and excommunications censured consciences, and, fanaticism and superstition was skillfully driven to eliminate dissenters, resolve rivalries and satisfy ambitions. Sadly, the Church considered torture and bonfires legal in order to impose its dogmas and eradicate spiritual truths that seemed to contradict them. It was precisely because of this that communication with spirits was fiercely persecuted, and those who practiced mediumship were accused of witchcraft and thrown into bonfires as heretics or possessed by devils. This is what happened to millions of people endowed with psychic faculties; it was solely because in their presence phenomenon were produced, of which its study brought moral and philosophic light, meanwhile the Church decided to maintain in darkness with its dogmas and fanaticism.

Nevertheless, the atrocities did not succeed in detaining the spontaneous torrent of progress or destroy the yearning for liberty, and, amidst all the persecutions, mediumship phenomena never stopped being produced. Those thought possessed by devils were nothing more than mediums, although they may not have known it, and the same priests that rejected as wicked and sinful these manifestations from the spirit world, secretly practiced evocation

---

[70] PEDRO GRANJA. *Afinal, quem somos?* [*In the end, who are we?*] Editora Cultural EDI-CEL. Sao Paulo, 1981. p.102.

and contact with spirits. Doctors and saints of the Church were endowed with powerful psychic and mediumship faculties which were manifested in diverse phenomenon. A German Benedictine nun named SAINT HILDEGARD OF *BINGEN* (1098-1179), became widely known for her visions of spirits and for having received prophetic messages, some in other languages. The life of ST. BERNARD of CLAIRVAUX (1090-1153), French theologian and mystic, founder of the Cistercian order, was continuously associated with spirit apparitions, healings and paranormal phenomena.

The Middle Ages is a time full of spirits that made themselves visible. Numerous cases of spiritual obsession or mental disturbances were declared as demonic possession and were confronted with violent techniques like exorcisms. ROGER BACON (1220-1292), Franciscan monk, philosopher and English scholar bestowed with the title Doctor Mirabilis because he was so knowledgeable was accused of evoking spirits through the magic arts and was imprisoned. The celebrated DANTE ALIGHIERI (1265-1321), presented his *Divine Comedy*, a classic work of universal literature that provides an allegorical description of life after death, revealing how the disincarnated spirits respond to the evocations of the living. JOAN OF ARC (1412-1431) was condemned to burn for hearing spiritual voices that incited her to struggle for the liberty of France. Paradoxically, the same Church, whose tribunal of Inquisition ordered her execution, canonized her five centuries later.

From the fourteenth century on, after the somber processions of the medieval night came forth the dawn of the Renaissance and the refreshing breeze of the greatness of Greece, due to the resurgence of its Art, Science, and Philosophy. Standing out with grace and liberty were spiritual manifestations, promoting the transition of theology to science, and from the monasteries to the universities, and from dogmas towards reason. PARACELSUS and BRUNO taught the infinity of inhabited worlds, the revolving journey of the spirit through reincarnation and communication between the living and the dead.

TORQUATO TASSO (1544-1595), the celebrated Italian author of the 1851 epic poem *Gerusalemme liberata* [*Jerusalem Delivered*] confessed to have had a good or familiar spirit that accompanied him. The greatest among English writers, WILLIAM SHAKESPEARE (1564-1616), displays a procession of occasions throughout his literary masterpieces where spirits provide advice, ghosts manifest by diverse psychic means, revealing the constant communication between the material and invisible worlds. *Hamlet*, his most famous play, is based on the appearance the main protagonist's father, as an apparition who reveals his own assassin to obtain vengeance. The central figure of the Protestant Reformation, MARTIN LUTHER (1483-1546), heard spirit voices that guided him and he perceived tangible apparitions. Many times, within Protestant churches, spirits manifested which brought about new religious movements. One of these were the Quakers (from the English, to shake or tremble) founded in 1652 by the preacher GEORGE FOX (1624-1691) who received spiritual instructions to establish a religious society characterized by fraternity and tolerance. A group called the Shakers split from them and their meetings were characterized by people in trances where there was much agitation. [71]

SWENDENBORG starts to have visions and hear voices from the Beyond; having a dramatic and impressive mediumship and obtaining minute details regarding the conditions of spirits in the afterlife.

The first songs of Romanticism at the end of the eighteenth century, combined diverse intellectual and artistic movements wherein thrived the free expression of internal sensibilities, breaking

---

[71] It is well known that many religious groups throughout the world have originated due to manifestations of mediumship that were adopted in many diverse forms. It is about disincarnated spirits that present themselves as angels or messengers of God or even as the Creator. In this category can be included the Convulsionaries of the Cevennes in France; the Church founded by EDWARD IRVING in Scotland (1830); the communications of the Shakers in the United States (1835) that facilitated mediumship communication with disincarnated Native American Indians' the Mormon Church founded in 1830 by JOSEPH SMITH who received instructions from the spirit Moroni; the Shintoist sect Tenri Kyo organized around the spirit communications received by the medium MIKI NAKAYAMA (1998-1887); the Oomot spiritualist movement (in Japan, great cause) initiated by the writing medium NAO DEGUCHI (1835-1918); and in addition the Caodaist religion created in ancient Indochina (now Viet Nam) taking as its basis the communications of the spirit Cao-Dai, etc.

away from the rigidness of the normal classics. In this way, one may consider Romanticism, by its dominant characteristics the esthetic precursor of Spiritism.

GOETHE'S poem *Faust*, is profoundly esoteric, inspired by the exceptionally renowned working miracles of the nineteenth century. The poetry and paintings of WILLIAM BLAKE (1757-1827), are a plethora of exuberant mysticism, representing a phantasmagorical demonstration of what is possible with art through the communion of living souls with those that are disincarnated, when circumstances present themselves that facilitate their interaction. Artists, such as poets, musicians or writers, transform the subtle perceptions they receive from the spirit world into a creation of abstract form. PERCY BYSSHE SHELLEY (1792-1822), celebrated English lyricist and poet said, "Man is an instrument over which a series of external and internal impressions are driven, like the alternations of an ever-changing wind over an Æolian lyre, which move it by their motion to ever-changing melody."

The American and European Transcendentalists experimented with various currents of spiritualism, from both Eastern and Western sources, and they include themes of the occult in verse and in essays with beauty and mastery: EMERSON, TENNYSON, MILTON, SCHILLER, THOREAU, WORDSWORTH, COLERIDGE, LONG-FELLOW, WHITMAN, and POE, proclaimed openly the reality of the invisible world and its constant action on the material plane.

The British novelist ROBERT LOUIS STEVENSON (1850-1894) was persuaded that he was assisted in his work by an invisible collaborator, and that the plot of his most famous novel, *The Strange case of Dr. Jekyll and Mr. Hyde*, was presented to him in a dream. The Frenchman GUY DE MAUPASSANT (1850-1893) evoked in his short stories and brief narratives, the influence of the spirits in everyday life and admitted that his writings were written in special psychic states, that he called "somnambulism."

In the writings of VICTOR HUGO (1802-1885), the same as HONORE DE BALZAC (1799-1850), JAMES FENIMORE

COOPER (1789-1851), CHARLES DICKENS (1812-1870), JACK
LONDON (1876-1916), RAINIER MARIA RILKE (1875-1926) and
GABRIELE D'ANNUNZIO (1863-1938), spirits intervene in the life
of humans with messages that have profound ethical and social implications. During his exile in Jersey, VICTOR HUGO, the national poet
of France, argues passionately in verse with the invisible inhabitants
of space and from there emerging, is a vibrant combination of his own
genius with psychic writings, impressive books like *Contemplations,
Sunbeams and Shadows, The Legend of the Centuries, Toilers of the
Sea, At Infinity's Edge.* This is his conviction, "The dead are living
beings mixed within our struggles, that at times have for the mark
good, others the bad. On occasion, we hear the whistle of their invisible arrows." DICKENS has confessed that each phrase expressed by
his characters in *The Adventures of Oliver Twist* or in *David Copper-
field*, he heard audibly pronounced, with him doing nothing else but
to write them down. The same was hinted at by GUSTAVO ADOLFO
BECQUER (1836-1870) the most genuine example of Spanish
Romanticism, when he wrote at the end of the Rhyme V:

> *"I am the invisible*   *I, in short, am that spirit*
> *ring that's attached,*   *unknown essence,*
> *to the world of form*   *mysterious perfume*
> *the world of the idea.*   *that is the poet's vessel."*

In 1929, the talented German writer THOMAS MANN (1875-
1955) received the Nobel Prize for literature. Within his vast work *The
Magic Mountain* stands out as his most well known novel and one of the
most important within the European literary panorama of the twentieth
century. Within it, he dedicates the next to the penultimate chapter named
"Supreme Doubts" to describe a mediumship session that culminates with
the materialization of a spirit. MANN accepted Spiritualism and his conviction was born of his numerous participations in experimental reunions
with the well-known medium RUDI SCHNEIDER (1908-1957) whose
specialty was the phenomena of the production of ectoplasm.

Under the powerful influence of the invisibles, HARRIET BEECHER-STOWE (1811-1896) wrote *Uncle Tom's Cabin*, of such influential force in the struggle for the abolition of slavery within the United States of America. In various interviews, she recognized that she heard a voice that was dictating the book absolutely independent of her own literary ideas and will. She called it in her own words, an "inner ear by a spirit voice." It is well known that ABRAHAM LINCOLN (1809-1865) participated in séances with the young NET-TIE COLBURN MAYNARD who acted as a speaking and writing medium. Also, through her intercession the spirits solicited earnestly of Lincoln to hasten issuing the Emancipation Proclamation of which he signed January 1, 1863. [72]

This is not an isolated case, because being that these spirits are humans who have already been on this physical plane, those who were preoccupied and struggled for the moral and social redemption of humanity, can and do continue with the same ideas and inspire those who are in concordance with them. Spirits have always influenced in the process of obtaining liberty for peoples, as can be verified in the lives of all the heroes and their deeds and examining all the facts. [73]

And, if we continue to also examine the other major names of the universal literature received, overtly or subtly, the influence of the spirits in the creation of their works, inserted within them as an undeniable truth the possibility of communications between

---

[72] In 1967 the publishing company of O Clarim of Matao, Sao Paulo, Brazil, published a volume entitled *Spirit Sessions in the White House* in which it is mentioned that LINCOLN participated in numerous mediumship experiences. Diligently translated into Portuguese by the Spiritist writer WALLACE LEAL V. RODRIGUES, it includes the book of NETTIE COLBURN MAYNARD entitled *Was Abraham Lincoln a Spiritualist?* and within its pages are found related firsthand accounts of the instructions that were given from the spirit world to the great American president.

[73] Books on this theme regarding the presence and influence of the spirit world in the creation of works of literature, art and science are available, unfortunately they are not in English, however, they are: *Literatura del mas alla* [*Literature from the Beyond*] by ERNESTO BOZZANO, *Investigaciones sobre la mediumnidad* [*Investigations regarding mediumship*) by GABRIEL DELANNE, *Escritores y fantasmas* [*Writers and apparitions*] by JOGE RIZZINI, *Muertos-vivos/vivos-muertos* [*Dead-living/ living-dead*] by WALTER JOSE FAE, *Victor Hugo el poeta del mas alla* [*Victor Hugo the poet from Beyond*] by HUMBERTO MARIOTTI, and my own book *El Espiritismo y la creacion poetica* [*Spiritism and the creation of poetry*].

this world and the other, that are definitively, two faces of the same reality.

One cannot adequately comprehend the historical evolution of humanity without the aspect of mediumship influence. It is well that we occupy ourselves with the primitive beliefs of the aboriginal peoples, of the rise and consolidation of religions, or of the observed and chaotic phenomena of the order of the paranormal that presents itself with all its most diverse nuances in all parts of the globe and in all times, or that of the controlled, positive and useful mediumship manifestations, these all put into evidence the determinate influence of the spirits. They, the so-called "dead," how alive they are! Like all of us, we are in various phases of the immense evolutionary process that pushes us forward without stop in conquest of new and superior horizons.

It was the phenomena of mediumship that called itself to our attention in modern society so that it could fortify the base of spiritualistic thought that had been distracted by dogmas and abstractions and had become impotent before uncontrolled advance of materialism. Since the mid-nineteenth century, there has been a powerful spiritual rebirth that started with the manifestations at Hydesville with the Fox sisters and expanded rapidly and dynamically through America and Europe. Then it found an adequate direction with the Spiritist codification by ALLAN KARDEC, who had the lucidity and intelligence to organize and compile acts of mediumship, adequately study and interpret them, strip them of any aspects of superstition and put them together in harmony with the natural laws that govern the Universe.

Mediumship helps us to comprehend history, and it is Spiritism that helps us to understand mediumship!

Chapter Five

MEDIUMSHIP

> *"The phenomena of mediumship is encompassed in all ages, and speaks brilliantly with vivid light, it speaks somberly veiled depending on the level of the people, it has not stopped one solitary instant to guide humanity in its terrestrial peregrination. All great works are the children of the great beyond. All that has revolutionized thought in the world, all that has determined intellectual progress, was born by an inspired breath."*

> ***Léon Denis***
> **French Spiritist Author and Lecturer (1846-1927)**

DEFINITIONS

According to its Latin etymology the word "medium" means intermediary. A medium is a person that has been provided with a particular psychic and physical constitution and can act as an intermediary between the spiritual world and the material world. Mediumship is a faculty that distinguishes that person, and it serves as a bridge to establish relations between the both sides of life (the visible and the invisible).

Mediumship is the capability of incarnate persons to serve as intermediaries so that the spirits can manifest themselves. Therefore, it is for that reason that we cannot properly discuss mediumship without also discussing the intervention of these disincarnated spirits.

In addition, it is necessary to differentiate between the term mediumship and other types of spirit phenomena. It is known that the inhabitants of the spirit world have spontaneously manifested in all parts of the world and in all epochs, and it is among these mixed primitive spiritual interchanges that we can acknowledge what can be called spirit phenomena. **However, for Spiritists, the word mediumship is designated as the faculty that permits communication with the spirit world when exercised within certain rational and ethical parameters**. In this sense, we find it appropriate to identify the vast repertoire of practices as simply spirit phenomena, frequently occurring among those with a mixture of different philosophical or religious beliefs and cults, and reserve the term mediumship for the spiritual exchange practiced under the guidelines of the Spiritist Doctrine. Therefore, there is the empiric practice of mediumship; while in the latter is the Spiritist practice of this faculty.

Mediumship is a natural human faculty, and is not to be considered magical, miraculous or abnormal. Communication between the two dimensions is a perfectly natural process that has its own conditions and distinctiveness. There is nothing supernatural about mediumship, even though there is still much unknown about its mechanisms, and it has not received official recognition from the academic and scientific community.

In its widest scope, every human being has mediumship abilities, and this was clearly recognized by Kardec when he stated:

> *"Any person, who feels in any degree the influence of spirits, is by this very fact a medium. This faculty is inherent in man, and consequently not an exclusive privilege; and, there are few persons in whom some rudiments of it are not found. We may therefore say that practically everyone is a medium."* [74]

---

[74] *El Libro de los Médium* [*The Mediums' Book*] Second part, Ch. XIV. No. 159.

If we adopt stricter criteria, the condition of mediumship would be reserved for all those who exhibit the faculty in a more ostensible manner, well characterized, and with frequent manifestations and of a certain intensity or force. We could speak of it as a dynamic mediumship, meanwhile calling one that is latent and dormant within every human being a static mediumship, occasionally expressing itself in slight and undifferentiated ways.

This faculty is independent of sex, age, race, nationality, or the social, economic, educational level or cultural condition of the medium, or regardless of the person's particular philosophical or religious beliefs that they may or may not have. Therefore, mediums can be found in all countries of the world, in all social classes and in the adherents of all religions. In addition, the faculty of mediumship is not dependent on the level of morality of a particular person. There are mediums that are conscious of the value of the faculty they possess and the responsibility that it implies in satisfactory service towards a good cause, while there are others that become involved in disorganized, superstitious and erratic practices. Therefore, mediumship being a neutral faculty by nature, its level of morality is determined by its correct application.

THEORIES REGARDING MEDIUMSHIP

It is well known that the phenomenon of mediumship has accompanied the historical evolution of humanity, integrating itself into all of its cultural, religious, social and moral manifestations. Yet, this universality does not imply that there has existed uniformity in the identification or explanation of the acts of mediumship, and the reason for this is that there have appeared numerous interpretations that differ regarding its authenticity, its causes, its consequences and its significance. Among the possible explanations, theories and hypotheses, we present the following:

Fraud:

Supporters of this theory affirm that mediums fake trance states, dramatizing so-called spirit communications and utilize tricks to provoke physical effects. In this category, the majority of skeptics and materialists do not even consider paranormal or mediumship phenomena worthy of study. To them, "to think" is a function of the brain and therefore the existence of intelligence cannot exist without it, nor that objects can be modified without the action of a physical force, therefore attributing this to misrepresentation and fraud.

Many commit the error of unjustly accusing all mediums of being fraudulent because some have been found to be so. One has to keep in mind that the subject of spirit communications is delicate and complex, and one who has been the object of charlatanism and exploitation, may also be subject to human ignorance about its reality. Nevertheless, mediumship experiences have been and are, so widespread and plentiful throughout the ages with numerous testimonials so solid, that objectively speaking, one cannot deny the reality of psychic and mediumship phenomena in spite of the existence of people that do fall into fraud, willfully or involuntarily.

Today, as always, there exist backward beings that turn into a farce something that should be a sublime experience taking advantage of the incredulity of some or the fanaticism of others. There are then, false mediums, but it is easy to recognize and unmask them when one undergoes a Spiritist education that promotes a critical and rational approach and advises one to suppress a superficial enthusiasm and to adopt every precaution required in the practice of mediumship.

Even in his own time KARDEC denounced impostors and egotistical mediums that were not only those that wanted material gains, but even those that were motivated by pride and ambition, faking the phenomena with special effects, illusion and prestidigitation, misleading those who then remain under their control and dominance.

Regarding physical manifestations, numerous frauds have been detected that have been attributed to various motives: monetary interests, the temptations that pride and vanity provoke, and the promise to produce phenomena at any cost to meet the demands of attendees and/or investigators. These circumstances are due to a lack of moral values in the supposed medium and their accomplices.

It is necessary to clarify, taking into account certain well-known cases like those of EUSAPIA PALADINO (1854-1918), that some mediums were surprised because of being caught in the act of trying to trick investigators because at that particular moment no real manifestations were occurring. However, these particular instances cannot invalidate the entirety of all notable experiences in many other sessions properly controlled, monitored, and photographed where psychokinesis, manifestations of ectoplasm, and other types of psychic and mediumship phenomena did take place.

It is appropriate to emphasize the need for a medium's ethical behavior as he or she continues orientation studies, attends to the advice of good spirit entities, and leads his or her life, and to use mediumship faculties according to the highest moral principles. Here we have examples like the Scotsman DANIEL DUNGLAS HOME (1833-1886), one of the most prestigious mediums in the world, who was never found using suspicious behavior or tricks, while accepting all the trials of undergoing rigorous testing and controls to verify his faculties. Mediums, ELIZABETH D'ESPERANCE (1855-1919) from England and ELEANORE PIPER (1859-1919) from the United States of America, were both possessed of remarkable mediumship abilities and were exhaustively investigated in both countries. When they realized these abilities where decreasing as a consequence of age and many years of intense work, they stopped attending séances, fearing that their well respected and accomplished amount of work might be put at risk. They both retired to private lives without anyone having the right to reproach them.

In the Spiritist library, many books may be found where proper advice is given about the possibilities of people being misled and deceived by unscrupulous persons at spirit sessions, and recommendations as well as precautions are provided that should always be established. One of these books, written by a first class expert on mediumship phenomena and a meticulous researcher, ANTONIO J. FREIRE (1877-1958) a physician from Portugal, below he wrote clearly about the Spiritist approach:

> *"Due to the decisive importance that experimental studies of Spiritism are evaluated, it is easy to acknowledge as concerns all Spiritists, individually or collectively, that they are interested in combating fraud, and unmasking tricksters and mystics that present themselves as mediums pretending to exploit this new science for their own monetary interest and for vanity.*
>
> *There is evidence, including, of which some religious sects had been trying to bribe mediums and their accomplices, to provoke scandals of fraud in order to discredit Spiritism and obstruct its expansion.*
>
> *Fortunately, many false mediums have been denounced in international Spiritist magazines, having been unmasked and discovered while in acts of fraud."* [75]

It remains clear, that if any theory that should try to reduce mediumship to the simple production of fraud, is inconsistent, does not explain absolutely anything, and errs when generalizing and mingling particular situations in conjunction with all other manifestations. Also, one thing has to remain very clear, that Spiritism, far from being responsible for deceptions, it has made itself worthy by the most rigorous investigations achieved by its scientific approach in exercising mechanisms of control in experimental spirit sessions,

---

[75] ANTONIO J. FREIRE. *Del Fraude en el Espiritismo experimental* [*Fraud in experimental Spiritism*]. Ediciones Fiat Lux. El Palomar, Argentina. 1952. p. 33.

with its essential ethical position in favor of the practice of principled and honest mediumship, and with the utmost and sincere intent to not produce any type of fraud whatsoever.

Suggestion:

There are those who intend to explain mediumship phenomena as a process of unconscious auto-suggestion that involves the mediums as well as the participants of the session and, that they are all the victims of their own deception.

The supporters of this theory concentrate their arguments based on the simplicity and mediocrity of the messages transmitted by the "presumed' spirits, pointing out that the content of these communications do not contain information that surpasses the knowledge of the mediums or the attendees, and that they simply reflect the opinions or reflections of the members of the group, and that the group itself keeps reinforcing this by an ambience of suggestion, individually and collectively.

This theory can be rebutted with convincing arguments based on an objective and thorough review of the information. In the first place, we are speaking of manifestations of mental mediumship, since physical phenomena are not subject to explanation by illusions of thought. Also, it can be said that the moral or intellectual quality of a message does not exclude the possibility of it coming from a spiritual entity outside of the group. It is true that on many occasions spirit communications can be unsophisticated, trivial and mediocre which can reflect the moral condition of the medium and of those spirits about them. However, it is also true that the low level of a communication does not negate that its origin is spiritual. Actually, spirits are not powerful supernatural beings, but the souls of human beings without their material bodies that are found in another dimension, and have retained their own particular cultural and moral qualities.

The theory of suggestion is insufficient to explain the multiple manifestations when sentiments as well as the contents expressed in the messages are entirely new, unexpected, and with ideas contrary to the ideas of the mediums and of all those in attendance at the session. It should be enough to demonstrate this with the following, citing some cases selected from the extensive spiritualist, Spiritist and parapsychological literature:

There is CAMILLE FLAMMARION, the celebrated astronomer and author of *Lo Desconocido y los Problemas Psiquicos* [*The Unknown and Psychic Problems*], that at one of the customary mediumship sessions that were regularly held at the Observatory of Juvisy, at which only notable European personalities of science and culture were invited, he was surprised by the reply that no one expected before the question formulated by the spirit:

> *"Erdnepmoc ed simrep erocne sap tse suov en li'uq snoitseuq sed ridnoforppa ruop tirpse'l sap zetnemrot suov en"*

He asked what that enigmatic message meant and received this reply:

> *"Read it backwards."* And, this was the answer the spirit gave so unusually:

> *"Ne vous tormentez pas l'esprit pour approfondir des questions qu'il ne vous est pas encore permis de comprendre."* [See translation below][76]

The mediumship faculties of EILEEN GARRETT (1893-1970) born in Ireland, were thoroughly investigated by the foremost researchers around Europe and in the United States during various parts of the decades of the twentieth century. Along with her exceptional psychic and mediumship abilities, came her love for scientific investigation. She therefore created in New York *The Parapsychology Foundation* in 1951, one of the most prestigious institutions dedicated to the study of the paranormal.

---

[76] "Do not torment the spirit anymore by going too deep into questions that he is not yet permitted to comprehend."

In 1930, while she was living in England, a famous story occurred about the British air ship the dirigible R101 that afterwards would be known as one of the most spectacular occurrences in mediumship history. On October 4, 1930, the dirigible departed from England en route to India on its maiden flight, it contained 54 passengers on board. Right after having crossed the canal of the Mancha, in the early morning of the 5th they were caught in a storm that damaged its motors causing its descent and explosion close to the French city of Beauvais killing 48 passengers.

On October 7, Mrs. GARRETT was participating at a séance directed by HARRY PRICE (1881-1948), at the National Laboratory of Psychical Research, an institution he founded. In the middle of the séance, UVANI, Garrett's spirit guide announced the presence of an unexpected visitor, H. CARMICHAEL IRWIN, the spirit of the deceased captain of the dirigible who through the medium in trance, described the details of the cause of the accident using such specialized language that only an expert in aeronautical engineering could understand it. IRWIN was very disturbed while communicating, and among other things he spoke of secret information of which it was later found out were plans the Germans were developing. He also described other specific details regarding the accident. It is necessary to explain that at the time of the séance there was no knowledge of any specific details available about the tragedy. Afterwards, transcripts of the séance were acquired by the British Air Ministry. An official inquiry was conducted into the accident and its investigation revealed that every detail received through mediumship was later confirmed by an official.

The case of dirigible R101 has become known as one of the most convincing cases of evidence of the afterlife and communication with spirits of the deceased. Evidently, one cannot explain these types of incidents by "suggestion" or maintain that the information received through the medium was telepathic because all those who knew the details revealed, had died in the accident.

Satanic Intervention:

One of the oldest beliefs regarding the source of mediumship phenomena is attributed to the perverse action of Satan and/or his demons. This theory was proposed by the various Christian denominations, Catholics as well as Protestants, in order to censure and combat the practice of mediumship, even though not all of their adherents believe this is true.

In the truest sense of the word, and in accordance with its Greek etymology, the word *demon* refers to "a protector spirit or guide" that assists each person providing them with advice; the way it was with Socrates and his familiar *daimon*. The Christian religions distorted this concept by designating it to that of an evil spirit. It was eternally devoted to the fatal mission of separating human beings from taking a good path in life and therefore also away from God. Human souls would then be tormented by the devil after death in a horrific inferno where he was the absolute ruler. Truthfully, we believe it unnecessary to give reasons that such a horrifying personage does not exist since cultural progress has generally disposed of such a concept. In addition, many progressive theologians have requested it not be mentioned in catechism, since it is an anachronistic idea incompatible with the justice and love of the Creator.

The dignitaries of the Catholic Church know that spirit communications via mediumship is an incontestable reality and that it is confirmed in the Bible and in the millions of experiences lived through by priests and nuns, by theologians and pontiffs as well as their own saints. There are some Catholic books that were granted their respective *imprimatur* and were dictated by disincarnated spirits. There was *Le Manuscript de Purgatoire* of 1922, with authorization by PALICA, Archbishop of Philippi and Vice General of Rome, and within its pages are the narrative conversations that a nun encountered from 1874 to 1890, with another nun that had died in 1871. The same thing occurred with the book *Lettera dal mondo di la* published in Rome in 1952, with the express approval of Monsignor TRAGLIA that contains messages by a young Italian woman who had died.

DR. JOSE LAPPONI, first physician to popes LEON XIII and PIO X, felt obligated to acknowledge the authenticity of mediumship manifestations in his book *Hipnotismo y Espiritismo* [*Hypnotism and Spiritism*] and confirming they have accompanied humanity throughout its historical progression.

The *Museum of the Souls of Purgatory*, that is adjacent to the Church of the Sacred Heart of Sufferance in Rome, keeps hundreds of objects that are the tokens made by disincarnated souls for those left behind on earth and are a representation of the "souls in purgatory." The museum was created by VICTOR JOUET a French priest who realized his religious task in the Italian capital where he died in 1912. There are Bibles, crucifixes, tunics and others ritualistic objects with burnt traces of hands on them that belong to those of the deceased and attached to each one documentation guaranteeing its authenticity. Obviously, the Church recognizes that these are not left by demons but by the souls of disincarnated humans.

Before the evidence of its actions, we can affirm that notwithstanding the denials of the theologians and bypassing the prohibitions and persecutions, mediumship will continue triumphantly on its course, eventually establishing itself as the most efficient means to proving the immortality of the soul.

Pathological:

Those who support this theory affirm that mediums display, in various degrees, states of mental disturbance which may extend from neurosis to acute cases of hysteria or schizophrenia.

On certain occasions some have endeavored to identify mediumship phenomena with alterations of a hallucinatory character pointing out that what occurs at sessions, or what the mediums are seeing, hearing or feeling is a false perception of reality that does not have an objective existence. It is simple to demonstrate the well-defined differences that separate acts of mediumship from the pathological view within the nosologies of psychiatry by the characteristics that accompany it as well as by its results. Those who attribute the conditions of paranoia or of hallucinations to mediums cannot manage to explain why, once the trances conclude, the mediums return to their normal psychological state and behave as absolutely sane individuals.

There is no lack of supporters of the theory that proclaim that Spiritism, because it promotes the practice of mediumship, "drives people crazy." This constitutes not only ignorance, but a terrible injustice because it has been precisely Spiritist institutions that have promoted the scientific study of the phenomena of mediumship and have insisted that it be practiced with prudence and within the parameters of the highest moral and rational principles. Thanks to this orientation, millions of persons with mediumship tendencies that were psychically and emotionally affected because they did not know how to properly manage their own natural faculties have been assisted. Many of them felt alienated and were declared as having psychological problems. Some had been in and out of public and private psychiatric institutions and subjected to unnecessary medications and shock treatments without an appropriate solution to their problem. They then were finally assisted in a place where they could be properly guided and educated about their mediumship, and receive the chance to practice and develop it, in the safe environment within the ambience of a Spiritist center duly trained for this task.

On the other hand, it is the same Spiritist Doctrine that continually advises against the carelessness of some directors of spirit sessions that tend to identify as mediums those persons that may be behaving in an unusual or atypical manner.

Authentic mediumship has no relationship whatsoever with mental disturbances, and this has been made evident each time there have been psychiatric and psychological studies done of mediums. Furthermore, when authentic mediums have presented with some type of mental disturbance, it was a consequence of an inappropriate use or due to carelessness of their faculty, which can sometimes develop into a spiritual obsession.

Esoteric:

There are many diverse theories that have surfaced about mediumship within the wide world of esoteric spiritualism. Some affirm that mediumship practices are not useful solely because one may make contact with spirits of a low evolutionary degree. These promote only meditation exercises in order to try and create a telepathic relationship with superior entities. Others consider mediumship practices dangerous to the medium's health and to any others participants, therefore it is completely rejected.

Certain authors state that contact through mediumship is not in fact accomplished with disincarnated spirits, but with fragments or a residue of the perispirit the remains of which each person's spirit will gradually dispose of when they die and which gradually disintegrates. This residual, called larva, astral shells, psychic remnants or fragments would partially conserve some of the specific contents of the disincarnated being's psyche and that would be the information the mediums would receive. This is the explanation most favored by theosophists.

Experimental demonstrations that had been done regarding mediumship tend to confirm that a spirit and its perispirit remain united after disincarnation. Consequently, it is not possible to attribute the information received by mediums to some supposed personality fragments like the so-called astral larvae, when we find ourselves confronted with literary works, either scientific or philosophical, and magnificent poetry by entities that identify themselves as spiritual authors and confirm their permanence in another dimension as complete beings enjoying in plenitude their abilities and knowledge with a complete personality.

While examining the wide range of literature about the afterlife, wherein millions of spirits of different intellectual and moral levels have participated, it is not reasonable to imagine that this is all due to mediums establishing contact with astral shells in the process of disintegration or with "elementals" or inferior entities. For example, one can read the amazing works received through writing mediumship by

VERA KRIJANOWSKY, FERNANDO DE LACERDA (1865-1918), PEARL CURRAN (1883-1938), GERALDINE CUMMINS (1890-1969), YVONNE PEREIRA (1906-1984), and FRANCISCO CANDIDO XAVIER (1910-2002) among so many others, instruments of spirituality, to clearly understand the great possibilities that mediumship interaction can bring about when it is done with elevated intentions.

Animism:

According to this theory, mediumship originates within the consciousness of a person believed to be a sensitive or medium. These types of trances are altered states of consciousness that precipitate the unfolding or expansion of the personality of the medium, the maximization of his or her senses and the exteriorization of dynamic forces or energies, so that it would not be a true communication with different spirits but in essence the manifestation of the sensitive's or medium's own spirit in a special emancipated state. Therefore, mediumship phenomena such as these known as paranormal, in this scenario, would be expressions of an immense and powerful psychic force that emerges from a human's consciousness.

Within this explanation, one will find various theories proposed by researchers in metaphysics and parapsychology. Although they differ in details, they all agree on a central idea, that the phenomena comes from the human subconscious and they negate any possibility of the participation of communication with deceased beings. Some picturesque names have been given to this phenomenon. RENE SUDRE (1880-1968), called it "prosopopesis" which is "all sudden modification, spontaneous or provoked, of the psychological personality, produced by suggestion, by either pathological conditions or by the supposed spirit manifestations." British physicist MICHAEL FARADAY (1791-1867) and French chemist EUGENE CHEVREUL (1786-1889) attributed physical mediumship manifestations to the "unconscious muscular movements" provoked involuntarily by mediums and their assistants. Charles Richet (1850-1935) created the term "cryptesthesia" for mental mediumship to explain an extensive unconscious faculty that allows the acquisition of knowledge without the use of the ordinary senses. This corresponds with "extra-sensory perception" (ESP) used in modern parapsychology. EMILE BOIRAC (1851-1917), a well known French metaphysician, proposed the name "psychodynamism" to mediumship, which included:

> "the group of phenomena where an animated being seemed to act over other animate beings (psychodynamia vital) or over physical material (psychodynamia material), through a sui generis force, different from all known forces, although analogous to radiant and circulatory forces, like heat, light, electricity and magnetism." [77]

There is no doubt that the hypothesis of animism (or extra-sensory perception) is useful to explain many incidents that have occurred within the vast amount of paranormal phenomena occurrences, but it is not sufficient to eliminate the authenticity of the many acts of mediumship, and that is how Spiritism has always acknowledged it. In *The Spirits' Book*[78] published by ALLAN KARDEC, there is a chapter entitled "Emancipation of the Soul" in which he examines the wide psychic possibilities of the spirit in its incarnated condition when it momentarily frees itself from its corporeal bonds. Therein, he provides explanations about dreams, visits that a person can spiritually make while its physical body is asleep, about thought transmission experiences, lethargy, catalepsy, apparent death, somnambulism, ecstasy and second sight. For him, it was quite clear that an incarnated spirit, when it finds itself emancipated from the physical body, can produce the same manifestations that a disincarnated spirit can do, including its spirit communicating through a medium.

[77] MILE BOIRAC. *La Psychologie inconnue*. [*The Unknown Psychology*]. Félix Alcan, Editeur. Paris, 1908, p. 86.
[78] Second Book, Ch. VIII

In classic Spiritist works by authors like GABRIEL DELANNE (1857-1926), ERNESTO BOZZANO (1862-1943), ALEXANDER AKSAKOF (1832-1903) and KARL DE PREL (1839-1899), there are numerous studies about the relationship between animistic and mediumship acts and instead of being contradictory, they complement each other. Therefore, if the human soul has the capacity to produce paranormal phenomena, it is with a much greater reason that it should be able to do it when it is disincarnated.

Among the proofs that offer much solid evidence in favor of an explanation of mediumship and demonstrates the insufficiency of solely the animist hypothesis are the cases called the "cross correspondences." These are certain experiments in which one spirit sends different fragments of the same message through two or more mediums that do not know or have any relationship with each other. Each medium receives a piece of the message, which by itself lacks any meaning, and only when putting all the partially received messages together is when they represent one coherent and complete idea. To make this demonstration more convincing, it can happen that either the method or characteristics of the test are not decided by the researcher, but by the spirit that desires in this way to give unequivocal proof of its existence. Illustrious British researchers like FREDERICK MYERS (1843-1901) and OLIVER LODGE (1851-1940) experimented with this system, and they also used it themselves to provide evidence that they continued to exist after their own physical death.

Spiritism: The Spiritist concept of mediumship explains with clarity, simplicity, logic and scientific rigor the combination of acts and all the situations that can arise within the vast world of relationships between disincarnated beings and the inhabitants of the physical plane.

One must not confuse mediumship with Spiritism. Mediumship is the faculty that permits the establishment of relations between the spiritual and the material world. It is a communication process wherein the psychic and organic composition of the medium functions as an intermediary, receiving energy waves of information emitted by an external agent, and retransmitting them in diverse ways. Spiritism teaches that mediumship is not abnormal or super-natural; therefore, it does not have a pathological character and it is not a violation of natural laws. It simply constitutes a natural and normal path so that disincarnate spirits may manifest to incarnated spirits creating a relationship between the both sides of life.

Mediumship is the phenomena and Spiritism is the doctrine that studies and explains it. Mediumship has always existed, but Spiritism originated with the doctrine codified by ALLAN KAR-DEC. Mediumship can exist, and in fact does, without Spiritism, although Spiritism would not make much sense without medium-ship. Confusion, as well as not acknowledging this fact has caused damage to Spiritism. Many times mediumship practices, supposed or real, conducted in an ambient that are superstitious or ritualistic are being presented under its name, even though they are completely distinct from the proper orientation, the technical and moral norms that distinguish the Spiritist Doctrine and its proper practices.

ANIMISM AND MEDIUMSHIP

The term *animism* has multiple meanings and has acquired diverse sentiments of opinion depending on the field of study in which it is employed. In the social sciences, it is applied to the belief that all objects in the Universe are living beings and it endows every natural phenomenon with a spirit or a soul, and within this viewpoint it should be revered, be placated or dominated. In this context, it is related to the fetishism and totemism of primitive peoples. In some philosophi-cal schools, it is used to designate any type of spiritualist nature. In parapsychology, animism was originally adopted as the fundamental hypothesis that explains paranormal phenomena since it is produced by psychic forces, consciously or unconsciously, by living beings.

In Spiritism, animism is designated to that particular state of trance in which the incarnate being (the particular sensitive, psychic or medium) is producing, or is the origin of, the mental or physical effects of **psychic phenomena.** If it was being produced by a disincarnate spirit this would be called **mediumship phenomena**.

It was ALEXANDER AKSAKOF, the Russian investigator who introduced the word *animism* when he reached the conclusion that the same phenomena can be produced either by the disincarnate spirit (mediumship) as well as the incarnate spirit (animism):

> *"The light, for me, did not break until the day that I was forced to introduce the title of animism, that is to say, after attentive study that the acts obliged me to admit that all mediumship phenomena, regarding its type, can be produced by the unconscious mind of a living being, a conclusion that cannot rest on a simple hypothesis or on an unfounded affirmation, but on the irrecusable testimony of the facts themselves, wherein that consequence is derived: that the unconscious psychic activity of our being is not limited to the periphery of our body and that it does not only present exclusively a psychic character, but that it can go beyond the limits of the body and produce effects not only psychical as well as [with] plasticity, and that this activity can be intracorporeal or extracorporeal."* [79]

AKSAKOF also produced another neologism with the term "personism" to facilitate the study and comprehension of the wide variety of phenomena that presented itself in this field, classifying them in accord with their characteristics and peculiarities. The concept of animism includes within it those unconscious psychic phenomena that are produced "outside the limits" of the corporeal action of the sensitive, like the transmission of thought or the movement of objects without contact. Meanwhile, personism covers the unconscious psychic phenomena produced "within the limits" of

[79] ALEXANDER AKSAKOF. *Animismo y Espiritismo* [*Animism and Spiritism*]. Casa Editorial Maucci. Barcelona, 1906, Tomo I, p. 28.

the subject's corporeal sphere with its distinct trait of personifica-
tion, or in other words, the adoption of a different personality, as it
can occur with certain supposed spiritual communications.

In experimental research, KARDEC had already observed
that during certain trances what was manifesting was the medium's
own spirit. He dedicated to the study of those facts, innovative at that
time, an entire chapter in *The Mediums' Book.*

When Kardec asked if the communications could be coming
from the medium's spirit, he obtained this significant response:

> *"The soul of the medium can communicate like any other;*
> *if it enjoys a certain degree of liberty, it recovers its qualities of the*
> *spirit. You have proof of this in the souls of living persons that come*
> *and visit you and often through writing, even without being called*
> *upon by you. Because it is necessary that you understand, among the*
> *spirits that you evoke, there are those that are incarnated upon the*
> *earth: then they speak as spirits and not as men. Why would it not*
> *proceed in the same manner with the spirit of the medium?"* [80]

In light of the Spiritist Doctrine, there exists no contradiction
about the natures regarding those of animism and of mediumship. The
error of the followers of animism is in denying the possibility that in
certain cases there is a manifestation of a spiritual entity unconnected to
the medium. And, for those who solely allow for a mediumship explanation attributing all phenomena to the action of spirits, the mistake is
not in acknowledging that sometimes what is occurring is the spiritual
expansion of the unconscious faculties of the particular medium.

Within the wide spectrum of psychic phenomena, animism
and mediumship, far from excluding each other, they represent
diverse degrees of the same scale that extends from the most elemental forms to the most complex expressions of the paranormal and of
mediumship. A comparative analysis of the phenomena that form the

---

[80] Segundo Parte, Capítulo XIX: Rol del médium en las comunicaciones [Second Part,
Ch.XIX: Role of the Medium in Spirit Communications]

vast repertoire of psychic manifestations suggests that some of them may have its origin upon involuntary acts of an unconscious character in an expression of the personal and individual psychic resources of the subject, while in others it is an authentic intervention between two planes of existence. The same phenomena, whether physical or mental, may be animism or mediumship, and that is why guidelines are recommended to determine the phenomena's origins; generalizations should not be made, and there should be no dogmatic or preconceived positions as each situation should be thoroughly analyzed.

Although it is clear that on some occasions it is falsely attributed to spirits what is nothing but unconscious fantasies, one should not suppose that this always occurs in the same form. Animism does not invalidate mediumship, because, as a last resort, in producing a trancelike state considered as animistic, the subject is actually acting as an intermediary for its own spirit, thereby acting as its own medium. This concept which harmonizes both alternatives was adopted by researchers and Spiritist writers as the most convincing explanation of the causes and nature of psychic phenomena. This is how Italian psychic researcher BOZZANO, in his important book *Animism or Spiritism? Which of the two explains the entirety of the acts?*, where in the preface he states:

> "Neither animism nor Spiritism will explain, separately, the entirety of supernormal phenomena. Both are indispensible for this purpose and cannot be separated, since they are both effects of the same cause and this cause is the human spirit, that, when it manifests, in fleeting moments, during incarnation, determines animic phenomena, and, when manifesting through mediumship, while it is in a disincarnated existence, determines spiritist phenomena."

Therefore, continuing further with these ideas it convenient to point out that paranormal phenomena are due to *animism* [81] and not

---

[81] In this context, English speakers customarily use the terms "extrasensory perception (ESP)

mediumship, for the former are produced by the unconscious forces of an incarnated spirit - a human being. Among these phenomena, one must give emphasis to the following capabilities: telepathy (thought transference), clairvoyance (ability to perceive things beyond the usual range of human senses), precognition (ability to foresee what is going to happen in the future), and psychokinesis (ability to use the mind to affect physical objects). A person who manifests paranormal aptitudes may be called a sensitive or **psychic**. One should reserve the term **medium** for those that possess the faculty to serve as a vehicle for communication of disincarnated spirits.

A sufficient knowledge of the theory and practice of mediumship is required to differentiate it from animism, and animism from actual fraud. *Animism should not be categorized as fraud; it is an unconscious psychic action.* Meanwhile, fraud is the deliberate act of a false medium and any accomplices with the purpose to deceive, and commonly for material gain at the expense of the unwary. It should also be taken into account as well, that in many cases excellent mediums begin with psychic manifestations (expressions of animism or psychic abilities) which serve as an adaptive and transitional phase before producing their full authentic mediumship faculties. However, even among highly educated and experienced mediums, spirit messages may become unintentionally and unconsciously infiltrated and mixed in their content with some elements from the medium's own mental structures.

Similarly, it is convenient to clarify what mystification really means. It is the deception caused by a spirit that provides false information, even regarding its true identity pretending to be someone else.[82] It should be noted that this can occur with an authentic medium, and in this case the communicating spirit is responsible for the deception.

Overcoming unsystematic practices and deception in mediumship activities, placing its direction in knowledgeable and competent hands, educating the participants so that all can contribute to the creation of an

---

and psychokinesis (PK)" depending on the type of paranormal phenomena.

[82] ALLAN KARDEC. *The Mediums' Book*, Ch. XXVII. Contradictions and Hoaxings. Lake – Livraria Allan Kardec Editora. Ltda. Sao Paulo. 1975. Translated into English by Anna Blackwell. The same chapter, in the translation by Emma Wood of the same book is entitled "Contradictions and Mystifications." These two were the first to translate this book into English.

adequate spiritual atmosphere can overcome obstacles and prevent fraud. This will allow for a productive progression of psychic manifestations, and as a result authentic mediumship can emerge in all its splendor and glory.

MEDIUMSHIP CLASSIFICATION

Even though mediumship is essentially unique, it is extraordinary because it exists in many forms and manifests in various categories and circumstances. Different classifications can be established depending on the criteria used. Taking into consideration the psychic and physiological reactions of the medium, as well as the profound degrees of the *levels of trance*, the faculty may be:

Conscious: The medium is in a light trance, knows what is occurring and once the manifestation is over remembers all the details. In conscious mediumship, the basic ideas come from the spirit but the verbal form is wrought and molded by the medium based on his or her cultural, educational and personal concepts. Therefore, there will always be a certain degree of influence or interference by the medium. Intuition and inspiration are typical variations of conscious mediumship.

Many times a medium can suffer inner turmoil due to confusion and doubt about the origins of the spirit messages received. The medium wonders whether it is from a spirit or from his or her mental world. This doubt also empowers those spirits that accompany them.

Having a reasonable concern regarding the possibility of whether only animism (their own psychic resources) are being manifested instead of mediumship is a prudent attitude of vigilance and control that should be taken by the medium. However, this should not develop into an obsessive behavior driven by fear, since this will create a state of psychological inhibition within the medium that can block spirit reception.

The education of the medium, the experience as it is acquired and the person's moral elevation constitute the best guaranty of success when the mediumship faculty is of this type.

Semi-conscious: The medium is only partially conscious of his or her mental and physical reactions as well as what is happening during the spirit manifestation. After the trance, there is generally some retention of fragments of what has occurred. The medium's mind interferes little in the spirit communications, causing only minor distortions in language and emotion. This is the most common variety of mediumship.

Unconscious: The mediumship trance is complete and has reached its deepest intensity. The spirit manifests control over the medium's nervous system. The medium is asleep and his or her consciousness is dazed. When the experience is concluded, the medium will not remember anything that has happened and may even be surprised when told.

In some groups, an unconscious mediumship is called a "medium of incorporation" (or a medium that joins with a spirit body) which is quite inappropriate, for this suggests that the medium's spirit has "left" its body and is being "occupied" by part of the spirit that is communicating. In reality, the magnetic control that the spirit exerts upon the medium's nervous system causes its consciousness and critical reasoning to become temporarily lethargic in a process where the spirit superimposes its perispirit upon the medium's perispirit.

Since the medium's interference is minimal, unconscious mediumship is of the type that preserves the most fidelity and reliability of the feeling and original form of the communication permitting a better identification of the spirit.

This especially occurs in cases of xenoglossy (a term coined by Dr. CHARLES RICHET founder of metaphysics) wherein spirit messages are transmitted in languages unknown to the medium, verbally or through writing.

Depending on the particularities that the different mediumship phenomenon displays, mediumship is classified into two main categories: mediumship of mental (or intelligent) effects and mediumship of physical effects.

However, it must be clear that there are no absolute boundaries wherein they can be placed as if in separate compartments, since many times they may intermingle. Again, GELEY expressed it well in that mediumship, in spite of its multiple and distinctive manifestations, is essentially unique.

MEDIUMSHIP OF MENTAL EFFECTS includes those phenomena in which psychological and intellectual aspects predominant, and that is why many researchers call it subjective mediumship. These are its principal categories:

Speaking Mediumship: Here, a spirit projects psychic magnetic energies over specific sensitive as well as motor areas of the cerebral cortex of a medium, and then utilizes the vocal organs in order to communicate.

Generally, the message is transmitted in the medium's language, but in some cases of deep trance, it can be expressed in the language of the spirit unknown to the medium, providing an action called xenoglossy. Spiritist literature provides impressive cases in this category. Suffice it to mention an excellent example of trance mediumship of LAURA EDMONDS, daughter of Judge JOHN EDMUNDS (1816–1874), Justice of the Supreme Court of New York in the United States of America and an early psychic researcher. His daughter only spoke English and a little French, yet spirits manifested speaking diverse languages such as Italian, Spanish, Latin, Greek and others. [83] On one occasion, when LAURA was in trance, a communicating spirit gave news to a Greek visitor who spoke very little English that his son had died and this was later confirmed. [84] It is appropriate to differentiate *"xenoglossy,"* which is a form of mediumship and when a spirit that is well identified expresses itself in a coherent and clearly articulated way from what is called *"glossolalia,"* in which some

[83] EMMA HARDINGE. *Modern American Spiritualism*. University Books. New Hyde Park, New York. 1970. Ch. IX p.86 & Ch. XI p. 101.

[84] ROBERT F. ALMEDER, Ph.D. *Death and Personal Survival: the evidence for life after death*. Rowman & Littlefield Publishers. 1992. Ch. 5, pp. 205-206.

psychic contents emerge from the subject's unconscious and presents in "unknown, archaic or extraterrestrial languages" and are mere false or fantastic languages. A psychical researcher and professor of psychology at the University of Geneva, THEODOR FLOURNOY (1854-1920), studied this type of phenomena with the medium Helen Smith of which he wrote a book in 1900 entitled *Des Indes á la Planéte Mars* [*From India to the Planet Mars*]. In these cases, the medium during trances may adopt various involuntary postures, move arms and hands about or produce voice inflections when speaking.

Writing Mediumship: (Kardec called it "psychography") In this type, the communicating spirit projects control over the medium's arm and moving the hand in order to write a message. Mechanical writing mediumship is when the medium is totally unaware of what is being written or may be unconscious since the spirit moves the medium's hand as if it was a tool, in an action independent from the will or control of its intermediary. A semi-mechanical medium feels an impulsion given its hand and may know what is being written. There are many very interesting cases in which the medium simultaneously writes with two hands, providing information in two messages, received from two different spirits.

Sometimes a medium writes a message in an unknown language. Originally from Canada, the medium MINA STINSON CRANDON (1889-1941), best known as "MARGERY," wrote spirit messages during various séances mainly in the city of Boston in the late 1920s, many signed by the spirit CONFUCIUS in Chinese characters. These messages of a philosophical nature where later translated by experts in the language. In another case, VICTOR HUGO (1802-1885), while in exile on the isle of Jersey and during one of the many séances he participated in with his son CARLOS HUGO as medium, received the following verse signed by Lord BYRON (1788-1824):

> *"Vex not the bard;*
> *his lyre is broken,*
> *His last song sung*
> *his last work spoken."*

Victor Hugo clarified that a friend was visiting from England and had participated in the séance and had wanted to evoke the famous English poet. However, his son did not speak or write English.

In the book *Investigaciones sobre la mediumnidad* [*Investigations regarding mediumship*] one of the most complete works on mediumship due to its diversity of documentation and scientific rigor in the analysis of the phenomena, GABRIEL DELANNE dedicates one chapter to the examination of numerous cases of writing mediumship.[85] In this same work, the distinguished French Spiritist, researcher and writer, places immense value on the verification of the manifestations to the resemblances of the written strokes of the mediums and the style of writing that the spirit had, while incarnated:

> *"We have now reached an order of phenomena that should suffice to impose a complete conviction on those who could not be persuaded with the previous facts. When a medium reproduces a written form and style of a person whom it has never met in life, there is not only the intervention of a foreign intelligence, but we are in the presence of a type of photography of the personality of the deceased which is inimitable. We possess a permanent document that permits us to make much precise comparisons and remains an impeachable testament of the actions of the disincarnated being. If one of our relatives or friends had traveled abroad, and we had received a letter from them, we would without effort recognize their handwriting and form of expression, and the thought would not come to us some conjurer had been able to take their place in order to laugh at us. The communications that arrive from the spirit world, from that country separated from us by the barrier of the physical senses, are messages in all appearances like terrestrial letters and when we discover the same char-*

---

[85] GABRIEL DELANNE. *Investigaciones sobre la mediumnidad* [*Investigations involving mediumship*].Third part, Ch.III.: Escritura en lenguajes extranjeras desconocidos del médium. [Writings in foreign languages unknown by the medium]. Translated into Spanish by FÉLIX RIO. Editorial Constancia. Buenos Aires, 1948, p. 407.

acters, we have the same conviction that they are the signatories of these missives who have sent them to us. " [86]

Seeing Mediumship: The medium, with this faculty, visually perceives spirits and images in the spiritual world that may be from the present, past (retrocognition) or the future (precognition). [87]What the sighted person receives is not related to his physical sight since it can be done with eyes open or shut, in complete darkness or in full light. Almost always, the medium remains conscious during its use.

When analyzing the information given by these mediums, one must take into account that there are many variables that may intervene. Sometimes, there is involuntary incorporation of the medium's own psyche that may modify the perceived images or scenes. One must consider as well, that on many occasions the medium is responding to abstract processes. The mental projections emitted by the spirits may adopt many various forms and should be carefully interpreted since they are of a symbolic character. Figures like landscapes, flowers, animals, faces or just colors, are imagery that the spirits frequently accompany with their teachings or are an invitation for reflection regarding their interpretation.

This faculty is one of mediumship and should not be confused with clairvoyance. The former is a medium that sees scenes or objects in the spirit world. The clairvoyant (psychic) sees things through extrasensory perception and perceives objects in the material world through extrasensory perception, sometimes at great distances.

Hearing Mediumship: This medium hears the voice of the spirits or sounds produced by them. As occurs with seeing mediums, it is a form that typically presents itself in mediums that are fully conscience of what is going on. Therefore, frequently seeing mediums also have this faculty as well.

---

[86] GABRIEL DELANNE. *Investigaciones sobre la mediumnidad* [*Investigations involving mediumship*]. Third part, Ch. IV: Autógrafos de personas fallecidas obtenidos por los médiums [*Signatures of deceased persons obtained by mediums*]. p. 426.

[87] Besides seeing spirits, they may see object or scenes in the spirit world sometimes called "visions."

Many that have this faculty have it at various levels. Some hear noises and words. Others hear as much as entire conversations transmitted by the spirits to the point where the medium can have an entire conversation with the invisible spirit as if with a living person. Some of these types of mediums say they hear spirit voices in a peculiar way, different then in the way they hear the voices of living persons, clarifying by saying that they sense it internally. Others identify hearing them externally, and may recognize the particular voice of a specific spirit.

The auditory experience can be an agreeable one for the medium, in particular when the voices come from guides or elevated spirits. Sometimes, though when the voices come from inferior spirits it can become an unpleasant and disagreeable situation. One of the major events of historical relevance linked to hearing mediumship was of JOAN OF ARC, who was encouraged by the voices of the spirits to lead the struggle for France's freedom.

Intuitive Mediumship: The medium captures information and thoughts while in a conscious state from the spirit. The medium, acts as a translator or interpreter, and the spirit message is formed using words from the medium. There is a great variety of this type of mediumship. It can be difficult to separate the ideas of the medium from the suggestions of the spirit with inspirational mediumship. Among lecturers, artists, writers, sensitive persons that habitually practice meditation frequently receive inspiration, manifested in tune with thoughts offered by spirits, like the securing of subtle currents that flow in other dimensions, well beyond our own space and time. They can assimilate both of genius and of mediumship, since both are of the same essence.

Although telepathy is a paranormal ability, it has a great similarity to intuitive mediumship. In mediumship, the emitting source is a disincarnated spirit. In telepathy, the person (using their own psychic faculties) is able to tune in to the energy fields of various persons, that carry their thoughts and feelings, and that surround all living beings.

MEDIUMSHIP OF PHYSICAL EFFECTS, or objective mediumship, includes all those phenomena resulting in visible and tangible material manifestations such as noise and sounds that do not have a physical cause, like: the sudden appearance of objects, their structural modification or change of location, or even the temporary formation of biological organisms. These are acts that are produced by an exteriorized force from the medium with concurrence in obeying the psychic dynamic force exercised by spirits which works on matter and modifies it

In the same mode as intellectual effects of mediumship, its physical effects can occur naturally or be provoked. In other words, they can occur in an either spontaneous or unforeseen manner or can occur at meetings of an investigative and experimental nature involving mediumship. Spontaneous physical manifestations can have various purposes: to call attention to persons about the existence of spirits, provide advice to someone in particular, or cause disturbances to certain individuals in which there may confrontational situations. Since there are various reasons for these physical effects, one must know how to adequately manage them. For instance, one needs to offer orientation and assistance when one is dealing with disoriented and perturbed spirits, and to ignore rather innocuous phenomena when it is being produced by frivolous and mocking spirits.

These are the principal varieties of mediumship of physical effects:

Tiptology: Using to their advantage energy provided by the medium, the spirit provokes raps, blows, or sounds within an object, adapted to an alphabetical code previously agreed upon to organize words, phrases or longer messages. It is one of the oldest systems of communication with spirits, and is related with the practices of the "Ouija board" or "turning tables" or "talking tables" which drew attention and awakened the interest of the public in America and Europe in the middle of the nineteenth century, and which provided the first step to the advent of Spiritism.

This physical type of mediumship is empiric and rudimentary, and by its slowness cannot establish a fluid communication with spirits, as one can do with a speaking or writing medium. Therefore, this is not habitually practiced within Spiritist centers.

When the noise, blows and other physical effects occur with the intention to torment or cause detriment, these are catalogued as poltergeist manifestations, which could be due to mediumship or to a paranormal cause. If paranormal, it is a psychokinetic phenomena and the energy is involuntarily provided by a person or so-called epi-center. If the character of the poltergeist phenomena is due to mediumship, it is mobilized and manipulated by one or more spirits.

Apport: This includes the movement of all types of material objects, caused by spirits, utilizing the energy of the mediums. Customarily, this involves the transfer of objects from one place to another, and the subtle appearance of objects from one place to another place that is sealed, or hermetically sealed. This phenomenon can occur in the dark or in daylight.

This phenomenon have been very well observed and examined in experimental sessions under rigorous conditions and control. Physical objects that were not in the vicinity of the observers, no matter the weight or nature of the object, suddenly appeared right before those present. At times, the object was in the same residence where the session was taking place, but from another room. Exceptional cases have also been reported where objects appear from immense distances, millions of miles away and of one from another continent. The natures of the objects that are transported in this way of are an infinite variety, from inert objects (rocks, money, metal, etc.) to flowers, plants and animals that were alive. In con trolled sessions, impressive objects such as flowers, plants, and objects were obtained with English medium ELIZABETH D'ESPERANCE. In her autobiography, the medium relates the unexpected appearance of an *Ixora crocata*, a plant originating from India that was twenty-two inches tall, and it lived for three months before it withered. [88]

---

[88] ELIZABETH D'ESPERANCE. *Al Pais de las Sombras* [*In the Country of the Shades*]. Carbonell y Esteva Editores. Barcelona. s/f. p. 209

There are no, up to this time, satisfactory explanation regarding the *modus operandi* of such a potent phenomenon that incites such disconcerting questions like the "disaggregation" of matter or its "reintegration" afterwards, obeying the impulses of a special force or agent that can overcome the limitations of tri-dimensional space. The German physicist JOHANN KARL FREDERICK ZOLLNER (1834-1882), founder of German astrophysics and professor of the University of Leipzig, carried out diverse experiences with HENRY SLADE (1836-1905) of the United States in approximately forty sessions, in order to ascertain the possibility of the "penetration of matter through matter," of which he wrote about in his book *Transcendental Physics*. ZOLLNER drew an interesting hypothesis regarding the existence of a physical fourth dimensional space (four dimensional hyperspace) contiguous to three dimensional space, from where a spiritual agent or disincarnated spirit could manipulate material bodies, moving them, transfer them, or provoking modifications in structure without any obstacles.

Materialization: This phenomena is when spirits temporarily make themselves visible and tangible, in either a partial manner (fingers, hands, face) or a whole form (entire body), acquiring the appearance that they had when they were alive. In order for the spirit to accomplish this, it must avail itself of its own force in order to cover itself with a special substance, a dynamic agent that comes out of the medium, and which RICHET called **ectoplasm**. Although the medium is the principle source of ectoplasm, other persons that attend the session, release, without even perceiving it, supplemental ectoplasm. According to the authoritive opinion of HERÑANI GUIMARAES ANDRADE, expounded within his book *la teoría corpuscular del espiritu* [*the corpuscular theory of the spirit*], spirits can also utilize resources in nature, originating from animals, from plants and minerals, forming what he has called ectozooplasm, ectofitplasm, and ectomineroplasm.

KARDEC witnessed some phenomena of this type and catalogued them as "tangible apparitions," creating the neologism *"agé-
nere"* to denominate a spirit that is momentarily materialized:

> "We return to speak of the singular phenomena of the agé-
> neres that, no matter how extraordinary they may appear at
> first sight, is no more supernatural than the other [phenom-
> enon] we have been occupied with. But, as we have already
> explained in the *Revue Spirite*, on February of 1859, we deem
> it useless to repeat here its particulars. We will only say is that
> it is a variety of those tangible apparitions. It deals with the
> state of certain spirits that can momentarily take the form of a
> living person up to the point that based on the testimonies of
> belief of the phenomena its illusion is complete." [89]

Eminent researchers such as RICHET and GELEY in France,
the German ALBERT VON SCHRENCK-NOTZING, and the
English W.J. CRAWFORD, carefully studied the characteristics and
properties of ectoplasm. They described how an organic, grayish or
whitish, amorphous, variable substance, capable of exteriorizing from
the medium, of organizing itself and disappearing with rapidity, and
that upon examining a specimen under a microscope, its composition
was found to contain residuals of epithelial tissue, leucocytes and fat.

Its basic properties are: **Plasticity** – It adapts to the mental
directions of the medium and of the spirit. **Sensibility** – It reacts
favorably or unfavorably to external stimuli like light or physical
touch. **Penetrability** - It has the ability to overcome physical barriers and bring about alterations on the anatomic and molecular
composition of bodies. **Conductibility** – It can conduct any type
of physical or spiritual energy. **Variability** – It can present itself in
a tenuous form, nearly transparent, or much denser, almost totally
tangible.

---

[89] ALLAN KARDEC. *El Libro de los Médiums* [*The Mediums' Book*], Second part, Ch. VII:
Bi-corporeality and transfiguration. No. 125. Ibid. p. 144.

The phenomena of materialization, is quite rare and difficult to obtain; they are transitory and present themselves sporadically. When they have occurred in sufficient numbers, they attracted the attention of many first class investigators in America and Europe. Unfortunately, it appears their frequency has progressively declined if one compares this to the great number of physical mediums that were studied at the International Metaphysical Institute of Paris, and in other similar organizations in America and Europe during the first decades of the twentieth century. Names such as EUSAPIA PALADINO, JEAN GUZIC, FRANCEK KLUSHI, STANISLAWA TOMCZYK, EVA CARRIERE, and RUDI SCHNEIDER are widely known for their powerful faculties to provide ectoplasm during that golden epoch of physical mediumship.

They were examined with scientific rigor. Special techniques were designed to prove the authenticity of the materializations, as when molds were made of human body parts in paraffin. A mold of paraffin of an ectoplasmic materialization constituted the most objective and irrecusable proof of these types of phenomena, not only for the researchers but also for outsiders. Materializations can vanish without leaving anything of its previous existence and would allow the incredulous to believe it was a fraud or a collective hallucination. The mold remains; it is palpable, can be analyzed, and submitted to all kinds of studies. This is how they obtained it at the Institute of Paris: on the table used for the experiment a receptacle of hot water was prepared wherein was spilled in it a certain quantity of paraffin until a coating formed of a thickness of 10 centimeters. The water was kept hot by an electrical apparatus, slowly raising its temperature. At the opportune moment, which was when an ectoplasmic materialization was perceived to begin, the water was set to boiling until there was complete liquidation of the paraffin. The spiritual entity was then asked to submerge in the paraffin, whatever materialized, for instance a hand, with the intention of forming a mold and after one or two minutes the procedure was completed. When the materialized portion covered with paraffin was brought up into the air, it solidified, and the hand already dematerialized, leaving a model of an empty glove made of the paraffin. The 'glove" is then filled with plaster and one now has a reproduction of the materialized hand. Sometimes, two hands intertwined, may be involved as well.

Ectoplasm, in a solid or semi-solid state, comes out of the medium through the orifices of the mouth, the ears, or nose. Later it is mostly or totally reabsorbed. It has been stated that in experimental sessions during this process the medium lost weight, later gaining it back. At the beginning of this manifestation, the ectoplasm appears as a fog floating around the medium, of which sometimes arise small lights that sometimes become truly radiant At some sessions, the phenomena is limited to these luminous effects, but in cases of a much better quality, forms of hands, arms, faces and bodies progressively start to appear.

On rare occasions entire bodies have materialized and physiological functions have been verified. It occurred this way with the celebrated case of the spirit of KATIE KING with the medium FLORENCE COOK (1856-1904), which was registered, photographed and thoroughly verified by CROOKES; with the materializations of the spirit BIEN BOA in the Villa Carmen of Argel obtained with the medium MARTHE BERAUD (known as EVA CARRIERE) and overseen by RICHET; or, with complete materializations amply studied by CARLOS MIRABELLI (1889-1951) in at least 400 sessions for the Cesare Lombroso Psychic Science Academy produced by Brazilian mediums FRANCISCO LINS PEIXOTO (also known as "PEIZOTINHO") and ANA PRADO (1884-1923). [90]

---

[90] SIR WILLIAM CROOKES published *Researches in the Phenomena of Spiritualism* in 1874 on materializations of the spirit of Katie King. The following books also detail experiences of materializations with some of the mediums mentioned: *Las apariciones materializadas de los vivos y de los muertos* [*Material apparitions of the living and of the dead*] by GABRIEL DELANNE; *Ectoplasmía y claravidencia* [*Ectoplasm and clairvoyance*] by GUSTAVE GELEY; *Los fenómenos físicos de la mediumnidad* [*The physical phenomenon of mediumship*] by ALBERT VON SCHRENCK-NOTZING; *La mediumnismo de la Sorbona* [*The mediumship of the Sorbonne*] by JULIETTE ALEXANDRE BISSON; *marvillosas fenómenos del mas allá* [*The marvelous phenomena of the beyond*] by MADELEINE FRONDONI LACOMBE; *El trabajo de los muertos*[*The work of the dead*] by NOGUEIRA DE FARIA; *Materializaciones luminosas*[*Luminous Materializations*] BY R.A. RANIERI; *Mirabelli, un medium extrodinario* [*Mirabelli, an extraordinary medium*] by LAMARTINE PALHANO JUNIOR; etc.

Direct Voice: Spirits can make their voices heard without the use of the physical auditory system of a medium. The objectivity of this act has been established because various persons have attested to hearing the same words or phrases. (Kardec called it pneumatophonia).

The phenomena can present itself in various ways. Formerly, some mediums would put a trumpet in the middle of where the session would be held. The spirits would come and move and levitate it, as well as speak through it. Sometimes several voices manifest at the same time. Another type of mediumship is known as Electronic Voice Phenomena (EVP) or Instrumental Trans Communication (ITC) where spirits use all types of electronic equipment (phones, radios, televisions or computers) to send messages or communicate. Nowadays, there has been more interest and study being done in this particular field.

Direct Writing: In this case, writing of words and messages show up on paper, chalk boards, etc. without the use of the medium's hands (Kardec called this pneumatography).

In general, to obtain these messages one would put a piece of paper and a pencil in a drawer or compartment of a desk or table where the experiment would take place. After a certain length of time that varied according to the circumstances, writings would appear on the page; diverse characters, drawings, words and even complete phrases. At times, they would be in other languages that constituted further proof of an intelligence that was foreign to the medium and the participants.

In Western and Eastern religious traditions, there appeared phenomena that appeared to be provoked by this means. The Decalogue written for Moses and in the written words that appeared on one wall at the festival of Belshazzar (*Mene, Tekel,* and *Parsin*) in Daniel 13-31 are examples.

The first experiences of direct writing occurred in France in 1856 and were rigorously observed by Baron LUDWIG VON GULDENSTUBBE (1820-1873) in which the medium involved was his brother. They received dozens of messages in Latin, Greek, French, Italian and other languages they had no command over. The Baron published a detailed account of their experimental work that extended until 1872 in a book called *The reality of spirits and the marvelous phenomena of direct writing*. HENRY SLADE (1835-1905) in America was known for his independent writings on slate. Many sessions were held in the US and in many other countries, and the writings were investigated by researchers and apparently no fraud was found. In more recent times, satisfactory results have been obtained by the British medium MATTHEW MANNING (1955-) in whose presence direct voices and writings, as well as drawings and paintings and other psychokinetic activities manifest. From the Spiritist perspective, what permits such complex phenomena as direct voice and writing to occur are the psychic forces from spirit entities combined with those of the medium and with other participants in these experimental acts.

Levitation: By the action of the spirits and by means of the energy furnished by the mediums, there is a raising and suspension into the air of persons, animals, and objects, momentarily conquering the force of gravity. The medium is submerged within a profound trance when the medium is levitated. During some opportune occurrences, luminous ectoplasmic formations can be seen elevating and sustaining the objects or living beings.

These were called "psychic levers" by Dr. WILLIAM JACKSON CRAWFORD (1881-1930), an engineer in Belfast of Northern Ireland, who published three books with abundant photographs regarding materializations, levitations and other physical effects obtained in the celebrated Goligher Circle between 1915 and 1920.

The phenomena of levitation has been observed in the most diverse cultural and religious contexts in the world, from shamanism, the dancing dervishes, African and Polynesian ceremonial and tribal rituals, even psychic exercises of Tibetan lamas and monks. The Catholic Church officially admitted that some saints and mystics like

FRANCIS of ASSISSI, JOSE DE CUPERTINO and SAINT TERESA levitated in the presence of numerous persons and in plain daylight. For Spiritualists and Spiritists in the 1850s and 60s, the most famous medium to accomplish levitations was DANIEL DOUGLAS HOME.

Healing Mediums: Spirits intervene to produce natural physical and psychical cures, serving mediums especially gifted for this delicate activity. There exist a wide range of possibilities within this faculty, including: diagnosing various illnesses, providing prescriptions, applying magnetic passes, alleviation of certain aliments, and even amazing surgical interventions that can work at the level of the peri-spirit or on the actual physical body.

Each healing medium has its own characteristic manner that provides for action in very specific and particular ways. For example, HARRY EDWARDS (1893-1976) attended millions of persons in England for more than five decades via magnetic applications. He had said that he brought forth a curative force that was directed by disin-carnated spirits that assisted him, within a semiconscious trance. JOSE ARIGO (1992-1971) would submerge into a profound trance to allow the spirit of a deceased German doctor, ADOLPH FRITZ, to perform the healings. It was in this way, thousands of surgical interventions, both simple and serious, were performed outside official medical pro-cedures.

The classification of the effects provided by healing medium-ship may be considered as a mixed form, a combination of physical and mental effects. One has to keep in mind that there exists many healings of a psychic (animic) nature that should not be catalogued as mediumship. In those cases, the curative energies come only from the person, without necessarily any spiritual intervention, as in the applications of magnetism, in the transmission of mental vibrations, or in psychic diagnosis. KARDEC considered these two possibilities, defining them in numerous writings. In his society's journal the *Revue Spirite* of September 1865, he specified basic concepts regarding this topic in an article "Regarding the Healing Medium," expressing the following:

> *"Who says medium, says intermediary. The difference between the magnetizer, properly said, and the healing medium, is that the first magnetizes with his own personal fluid, and the second, with the fluid of the spirits, of which serve as a conductor. Magnetism produced by the fluid of a man is human magnetism; what proceeds from the fluid of the spirits is spiritual magnetism."*

There, and in relation to the economic benefit that some persons seek to obtain with healing mediumship, converting it into a paid profession, with his well-known intellect and sense of ethics, KARDEC advises:

> *"Healing mediumship is an aptitude, like all types of mediumship, inherent within the individual, but the effective result of that aptitude is independent of his will. Indisputably, it is developed with effort, and overall, by practice of goodness and of charity; but, since it has not the stability or the punctuality of an acquired talent through study of which from that one, it is its owner, it should not be converted into a [paid] profession. Therefore, it is a misuse when someone presents him or herself to the public [as such] as a healing medium."*

MEDIUMSHIP EDUCATION

Mediumship is born, it is not made. It spontaneously emerges in people, and it is not acquired through some special process nor can it be learned in schools or institutes. In conformance with the teachings of Spiritism, one should never force the emergence of the faculty of mediumship. However, when signs of mediumship appear and become evident, the medium should be educated and disciplined in three areas: in morality, in its proper orientation, and its technical aspects. All of these together, are appropriate in providing: a true knowledge of mediumship, its adequate use, and proper preparation of the medium towards an authentic spiritual growth, including all the participants in any activities involved with mediumship.

Moral Education of the Medium

Spiritism teaches that mediumship is independent of moral principles and this should be correctly understood. Mediumship is a mechanism of communication between the inhabitants of two dimensions of life, the spiritual world and the material world. Since it is a phenomena, the communication with spirits is a neutral instrument from a moral point of view, and what grants it a certain hierarchy of an ethical character are the conditions in which it is used and the intent or purposes which are pursued. According to Spiritism, it should always be practiced towards goodness, taking advantage of an incomparable method that stimulates spiritual education, self-knowledge, information about life, and the practice of solidarity and fraternity. However, unhappily, many times it is used with perverse subtlety, to cause harm, to deceive or exploit or to encourage superstitious beliefs and practices.

We cannot be held responsible for the wrong others make of the use of mediumship, in the same way we cannot be held responsible for the means of social communication of certain programs that degrade instead of ennoble moral values. Therefore, the Spiritist Doctrine puts a great emphasis on the moral education of the medium and those who participate in mediumship sessions.

The Spiritist Doctrine does not allow, under any circumstances, the receiving of any remuneration whatsoever for the practice of mediumship. Mediumship is not an official profession under the Spiritist practice and its use should always be arranged so that absolutely no monetary interest exists. All Spiritist writers have pronounced insistence concerning this, and it is a primary principle of Spiritist ethics. In our minds are engraved these words by LÉON DENIS:

> *"The best guaranty of sincerity that a medium can present,*
> *is disinterest, as it also is a much surer means of obtaining protec-*
> *tion from Up High.*
>
> *To preserve all moral prestige, to produce fruits of truth,*
> *mediumship should be exercised with elevation and without mate-*
> *rial payment of any kind; any other way, it can be converted into*
> *a fountain of abuses, an instrument of confusion of which then can*
> *serve as a malefic source."* [91]

Paid mediumship is a rapid pathway towards charlatanism by way of the attraction of inferior entities; and also, of animism (the medium's own spirit solely communicates) and actual fraud. The good spirits leave the medium, and said medium is tempted to satisfy the demands of those who are paying to receive messages from the spirits or see spirit phenomena, whether by a forced emergence of their own unconscious psychic forces or the pretending to receive a supposed spirit communication. The medium is left as to how one uses a telephone with the communication cut off; seeming to have a dialogue with an external world but the medium is left only in a monologue with its own interior world. Fulfilling a noble task to serve as bridges of communication between the spiritual and physical planes, mediums should not expect any remuneration other than the satisfaction of providing service as a great apostleship in support of the truth as well as of intellectual and moral progress.

Mediumship activity should not be treated as a diversion or a frivolous distraction. This type of thing occurs when people play with Ouija boards where attempts are made to evoke spirits to consult them for fortunetelling and absurdities. Similar practices are not only rudimentary and empiric but frequently provoke psychological disturbances and can open up the possibility for obsessive

---

[91] LEON DENIS. *En lo invisible* [In the Invisible]. Ediciones CIMA. Caracas, 1995, Ch. XXIV, Abusos de la mediumnidad [Abuses of Mediumship]. pp. 303-304.

relationships since there are inferior spirits that respond to these frivolous evocations. Those who believe they are playing with the spirits, in truth, what is happening is mocking spirits are playing with gullible humans.

Mediumship should be utilized exclusively for good purposes; with an intent that is wholesome, noble, dignified and loving. It should never be used as a tool to cause harm to another or used deceitfully to obtain personal benefits of whatever type. Those whom believe that they will have the faculty of mediumship forever, independent of its use are highly mistaken. If the person with this faculty does not conduct their life in an honest way, or uses it for mercenary purposes marketing the produced phenomena or become involved with fraud or charlatanism, they could lose it altogether or become submerged within an abyss of obsession, the victims of backward spirits. The good spirits retire from those mediums that utilize their faculty wrongfully.

KARDEC wrote extensively about this topic, examining the diverse causes that conspired against the fine and ennobling faculty of mediumship, placing ethics in the center of his preoccupations:

> *"Mediums with an interest are not only those that can exact recompense. That interest does not always translate into the hope of seeking material gain, but also in the kind of ambitious projects on which [any type of] hopefulness can be found. And, it is this fault that mocking spirits know how to take advantage of, through truly remarkable skills and cunning, fomenting deceptive illusions in those that, by this method, they have placed under their dependence.*
>
> *As a whole, mediumship is a faculty that is granted for goodness, and the good spirits leave whomever pretends to convert them into a stepping stone to advance towards whatever thing that does not correspond with the designs of Providence. Egotism is a plague of human society and the good spirits combat it. Therefore, it is not possible to suppose that they can be placed in one's service. This is so reasonable that it is needless to insist on continuing in this respect."* [92]

---

[92]   ALLAN KARDEC. *El Libro de los Médiums* [*The Mediums' Book*]. Ediciones CIMA. Caracas, 1994, Second part, Ch. XXVIII. No. 306. pp. 392-292.

Below are the characteristics of a Spiritist medium, with proper morals:

- Honest, dignified and unselfish behavior, both in private life, as well as with family and in social relations.

- Pureness of sentiments, thoughts and words. By the cultivation of virtues the medium vibrates with positive thoughts, and that produces a double effect: it attracts harmonious and elevating energies and at the same time repels harmful and vicious forces.

- Maintains a distance from a manner of ostentation, pride or vanity. The Spiritist medium comprehends that the faculty is not, in itself, evidence of moral or spiritual progress because first it is a condition inherent in the organism, and on the other hand, sometimes it is a consequence of karmic repercussions from a previous lifetime.

- In the profession or work they have elected to do, they are dignified and do not use their mediumship faculty to obtain any specific benefit or profit.

- They are not jealous or envious of the mediumship faculties of others, and are willing to share and collaborate with them as a group.

- They try to surround themselves with serene, affable, loving individuals that fortify the ambience of harmony, peace, and goodwill that should reign within a Spiritist group.

- They never deceive, provide falsehoods or fraud, or pretend regarding any alleged spirit manifestations.

- They stay away from the mental vibrations and situations that might promote mystification, deceptions or obsessions, requesting the loving assistance and protection of the superior spirits.

- They do not get involved with fetishes, superstitious or ritualistic practices. They do not participate in the practices of

those using a combination of afro-catholic-indigenous religious beliefs, of which spirit entities of a lower evolutionary nature predominate, and of whose participants generally
exploit for profit the ignorance and naiveté of the unwary.

-    And, most importantly: they should have the humility necessary to comprehend, accept and assume, that they are a human
being with faults and virtues, that they are not infallible, and
that they can become the victim of deceptions, that they can
provide animistic (or psychic) manifestations without realizing
it, and hence, should never permit or encourage any expressions
of others towards them, of idolization or of a personality cult.

The spirits were very exact in their response to KARDEC
when they said NO MEDIUM IS PERFECT:

> *"Perfect? You know very well that perfection does not
> exist upon the Earth. If it was not like that, you would not be
> here. Better said – a good medium – and that is saying a lot,
> because they are not in abundance. The perfect medium is one
> that the evil spirits would not even dare attempt to deceive.
> And the good medium, is one that sympathizing only with good
> spirits, they are deceived with less frequency."* [93]

Orientation of a Medium

It is very important not to confuse Spiritism with mediumship.
It is a natural phenomenon that is inherent in the human condition.
Meanwhile, Spiritism is a doctrine that studies it in order to determine
the laws that operate it, explain its nature, and its consequences. One
can be a medium without being a Spiritist, and obviously, one can
be a Spiritist without being a medium. However, those who properly

---

[93] ALLAN KARDEC. *El Libro de los Médiums* [*The Medium's Book*].Second part, Ch. XX,
No. p. 266.

study to be a *Spiritist medium* would more clearly know what is happening to them, they could better control their faculty and not be subject to the unpredictable consequences of uncontrollable forces.

The Spiritist medium assumes with full awareness the exercise of its faculty and studies it with love and dedication. The Spiritist Doctrine provides orientation in their lives and protection in their work as a medium. They can obtain a consistent, harmonized, complete, and comprehensive view of their physical and spiritual reality.

Many mediums without this Spiritist orientation can cause serious difficulties to those spirits that attempt to transmit their thoughts to them due to a faulty reception or shock produced by the mental interference of these mediums due to their lack of experience, knowledge and proper training. They may not be faithful instruments able to ensure clarity in the messages issued by the spirits due to deficiencies in the formation of their mediumship.

It is an error of whatever medium to suppose he or she possesses a sufficient faculty without the necessity of proper training. Mediumship experiences can cause harm by people ignorant of the laws that govern them and the necessary conditions for their manifestation, development and control.

Doctrinal study, as well as overall orientation, will develop a more complete medium, a finer instrument with more resources. Broadening the spectrum of the medium's range provides a better tuning in, to those spirits of a higher evolutionary level, and the ability to transmit their messages with much greater fidelity, establishing a more fruitful relationship without the hindrances of emotionality or animism. There are mediums that without orientation of any kind can transmit messages with refined language of a high intellectual and moral degree, but these, besides being exceptional, indicate that they preserve elements associated with this material that they acquired in past existences.

The medium, even with orientation and knowledge, needs to always be aware that this does not mean he or she will be completely immune from being deceived or obsessed, of being gullible or subject to fanaticism. Nonetheless, they will be fully aware of the value of their faculty and can responsibly assume the beautiful mission that is to be fulfilled, and be prepared to serve humanity.

Technical Education of a Medium

The practices of mediumship should not be conducted under ignorant, irresponsible or haphazard conditions. The effectiveness of the results depends on the requirement that all the participants of a mediumship session (from the mediums, directors of sessions, assistants, to the participants) possess a sufficient knowledge about the nature of the proceedings.

The practice of mediumship presents its difficulties and whomever would become involved with one should study it in depth, and be patient in comprehending its peculiarities. Mediumship sessions can be characterized by their inconstancy and variability, even in identical conditions; one day one can receive extraordinary acts and the next, the results are practically nil. It is natural that this is the way it is because the act of mediumship is a human act, and nothing is so variable or unpredictable in nature as humans.

It is not possible to identify a medium by any physical trait. There is no evidence that allows one to relate the faculty of mediumship with some aspect of anatomy or physiology. Comparative observations between different mediums confirm that mediumship cannot be correlated with any type of constitutional characteristic.

However, we can speak of **unique signs of mediumship**, when certain psychological, physiological, and behavioral expressions are present in a person that might permit us to assume the presence in particular of some type of the faculty. Among the signs frequently associated with mediumship are the following:

-   The surfacing of unexpected and spontaneous manifestations of explicit mediumship. The person says he or she feels the presence of spirits, or can see or hear them, or can enter into various stages of trance. Or, when unusual acts occur in their presence like noises, movements, disappearance of objects, unexplained lights, apparitions, etc.

- Having out-of-body experiences. The person has the sensation of leaving the physical body from an internal perspective. Although not all of these types of experiences necessarily imply mediumship, this may present itself as a first step of the faculty for many mediums.

- Recurrent dreams where the same images constantly repeat for weeks, months, or years. The contents of the dreams correspond to situations in real life or contain an authentic premonition that is verified later.

- Modified states of consciousness accompanied by strange sensations like drowsiness, vertigo, drowning, stomach pressure, perception of energies (or fluids), an invasion of strange ideas, etc.

Those that exhibit signs of this nature and go to a Spiritist center should be interviewed by the leaders with experience so that they can be correctly evaluated. One needs to be very prudent and careful before providing an opinion. In some cases these are not signs of mediumship but possibly the symptoms something of a physical or psychological nature and the person should receive attention from someone in the medical profession. It would be extremely serious for the health of that person, as well as highly damaging and compromising for the center, if the person was wrongly identified as a medium. On the other hand, it is wrong and very sad, if an authentic medium would be identified with a mental illness due to general ignorance, a unilateral materialistic approach and the biased biomedical model that prevails in our society.

It is a very delicate matter when dealing with mediumship manifestations that occur in children and it should be attended to with maximum precautions. Generally, one should not go forward in the development of the faculty of mediumship in children due to the vulnerability of their organism that is still in the process of growth, and to protect against psychic overexcitement that could put them into a trance. Now, in those cases where children have a natural mediumship that is spontaneous and unexpected, one needs to proceed with extreme care and afford the child tender attention. In a Spiritist center, the child needs to be directed and educated as much as possible, taking into account the age of the child, regarding mediumship from the perspective of morality and the philosophy of Spiritism. In addition, the child should only try to use their mediumship within an especially selected group at the center that will fervently solicit the protection and direction of superior spirits. On occasion, with the support of the spirit protectors of the child, the faculty will remain suspended until it is an adult, and it has completed its normal human development. [94]

The technical education of mediumship that some have called the development or unfolding of faculties, contains numerous aspects, theories, and practices related to all the factors that coincide with the correct realization of the mediumship session: the mediums, the support of the directors, assistants, participants, and of course, the spirits.

The Medium

- A Spiritist medium uses its faculties exclusively in a Spiritist Center. They do not participate in private sessions at home or in other private residences.

- The medium should accept or reject any contact made by the spirit world via mediumship, taking into consideration if the conditions are favorable or by following the director's instructions. A spirit should not communicate without one's explicit consent.

---

[94] In *The Mediums' Book*, KARDEC received precise directions from the spirits regarding the dangers that could occur by the use of mediumship in children, and it suggested that the parents avoid its practice by conveying it according to its moral consequences, confirming once again the scientific and ethical attitude that distinguishes Spiritism. Read in the Second Part, Chapter XVIII: Difficulties and Dangers of Mediumship.

- The medium should be able to distinguish the quality of the spirit that is approaching them, in other words its level of morality, by determination of the energy or fluids that it radiates. Previous to this, the medium has already identified with its spirit guide or "control" that assists it during the session and maintains a cooperative relationship with it.

- The medium should learn to control its physiological reactions. This means dominating and avoiding: unusual breathing, groans, contortions of the body, exaggerated movements of the arms or feet, or any other gestures that indicate loss of control or may appear false.

- The medium should maintain an atmosphere of harmony, serenity and positive vibrations during the trance. And, upon the end of contact with the spirit world, the medium should find itself in a good condition and in a normal physiological state.

- The medium should learn to conclude the trance, upon notification by the director, especially when producing manifestations linked to distressed spirits or those spirits that are a nuisance to others and may be reluctant to leave. Upon being called by the director, the medium should separate from the spirit and recover their conscious state. Each spirit possesses its own specific vibration and the medium should know how to differentiate this in order to better allow the spirit to communicate, to protect him or herself and conclude the trance with perfect normality and end in a relative state of well-being.

Director of Mediumship Sessions

- This should be a person that has a wide knowledge regarding the historical, scientific, philosophical and moral aspects of Spiritism, and of course, possess a firm and defined Spiritist conviction.

- They should be generally cultured. They should be someone who has the capacity to appropriately transmit his or her ideas, maintain a dialogue with the spirits regarding a number of diverse topics, and the power to discern the truth of their opinions, affirmations, or commentaries.

- The director should possess experience in the practice of mediumship, which can be acquired by assisting at sessions, observing development of mediums, and learning from those that are already knowledgeable. In order to be a director of the session he or she needs to have the capacity to identify the act of mediumship, know how to differentiate it from forms of animism or psychic abilities, know how to correctly lead a dialogue with communicating spirits, and know how to evaluate and analyze with good sense and critical judgment the messages received.

- It is advisable, based on experience and general sentiment, that if the director of the session is also a medium, he or she ought to refrain from the act of mediumship because of the difficulties that can occur acting in both capacities at once.

- The director should know and dominate the proceedings that are employed in the development of the faculties of the mediums, including the techniques involved in the application of magnetism ("passes" or "laying on of hands"), and everything related to the extensive and complex field of dealing with spirit obsession. (Hypnosis may be included among the repertoire of practical knowledge that the director of sessions may have that can be of great help in certain specific areas, but it is not recommended that this technique be applied to mediums in trance.)

- The director should teach the mediums all the relevant aspects, theories and practices in relation to the diverse phases of the medium experience. They need to train them so that they can be in an adequate physical and psychic state that facilitates the correct spiritual predisposition for trance, vibrating in a positive and harmonious form.

- The director should guide the sessions with firmness, but without being authoritarian. He or she should be able to correct abrupt and rude manifestations by perturbed, mocking and riotous spirits, until they are fully contained. The director should know that at all times the Spiritist practice is not based on violence, like the erroneous practices of exorcisms, but in persuasion and enlightenment. The medium's assistance to these types of spirits is based on a spiritual/moral force and not a physical force.

- It is the director's obligation to ensure that the session transpires in peace, with order, stability and tranquility. The director should correct situations when various spirits communicate at the same time that can create disorder. In the same way, positive results cannot be obtained when various persons also are speaking at the same time. Neither can one obtain beneficial results when various spirits have to struggle to express themselves or are disregarded. Solely in certain circumstances, the director can permit two spirits to simultaneously communicate via two mediums, when there is the necessity of this type of dialogue with the purpose to calm hostilities or reconcile antagonisms.

- To sum up, the management of a mediumship session requires of a director a permanent effort towards personal growth, educating with equal disposition, his or her intellect and sentiments. Intellect, knowledge of the Spiritist Doctrine, inner peace, general culture, honesty, initiative, prudence, a critical spirit, good emotional and physical health, and self-confidence are the fundamentals that define the profile of a director and guarantees the success of a mediumship session.

Mediumship Sessions

- It is recommended, that save in specific circumstances, mediumship activity be conducted at a Spiritist center and not indiscriminately in improvised places. This is even more important in sessions involving the work of spirit obsession.

- The Spiritist Center should be clean and well illuminated. There is no place for images, religious figures or other elements indicative of any type of cults or rituals. Its doctrinal study and mediumship practice does NOT involve: special vestments, alcoholic beverages, tobacco, altars, candles, hymns, talisman, amulets, baptisms, initiations or any manner of ceremonies or practices contrary to the purity and simplicity of Spiritism.

- Mediumship sessions are not indiscriminately open to all newcomers. Participants are those that attend the activities of the Spiritist center and that know the fundamental basics of the Spiritist Doctrine. Therefore, no one should participate in a mediumship session without having passed through a period of theoretical study.

- While there is no specific number of how many can attend a mediumship session or a strict limit, small groups are advised and preferable including the director and mediums, in order to better facilitate mental and spiritual harmony among the group.

- All participants should strive for unity of sentiments, maintaining a positive, mental, moral, and spiritual attitude, far from other preoccupations. It is just as harmful to be too skeptical where everything is negated as it is to be so fanatical that all is unquestioningly accepted. Everyone participating should be careful of their thoughts, avoiding influencing the mediums or the spirits with their expectations or expressed concerns. It happens with great frequency that at certain mediumship sessions no spirit manifestations occur and this should be accepted as natural, without exerting mental pressure on the mediums, or having suspicion regarding their integrity or unjustly mistreating them. The affinity among the participants is a definitive factor for the success of mediumship activity, and thanks to it, a homogeneous psychic field facilitates contact with the spirits and presents the mediums with comfort and security.

- The participants attending a mediumship session should obey the criterion of rationality, general agreement and efficiency. Taking into consideration the functions that they fulfill, the director and assistants and the mediums in accordance with their particular type of faculties, should be situated at the places that facilitate their particular tasks. Obviously, the director should be centrally located. The mediums that receive spirit communications via their person and also see and hear the spirits should be near the director. Writing mediums should have tables to receive the spirit messages. Assistants should be near the mediums in order to assist them pertinent to any instructions received.

- In conformance with the needs of the Spiritist center and the convenience of the mediums, specific days should be established for the mediumship sessions that should be rigorously obeyed and respected by everyone. Equally important is punctuality, as the time set is an indispensible requisite for the proper fulfillment of the activity. Once the session has begun, no persons should be admitted. All of these provisions are for the sole purpose of order and discipline and not for any mystical reasons. This has nothing to do with the naive belief to "obey the mandates of spirits" or the superstitious belief that in order to make contact with spirits, sessions must be conducted on certain days or hours. The reliability and regular occurrence of mediumship sessions helps establish affinity with the spirits and on many occasions, serves as a base to establish a commitment for their appearance.

- The duration of a mediumship session varies, on average, between one and two hours. Each group of mediums freely establishes the time of their reunions according to their objectives, striving not to prolong the end unnecessarily in order to prevent weariness, fatigue, or boredom.

- Participants should arrive some minutes before the fixed start time, sit in their corresponding seat and adopt an attitude of concentration, distancing any thoughts or preoccupations from them that have nothing to do with the purposes of the mediumship session.

- The ambient that surrounds a medium exercises a decisive influence on the results of a session. The medium is a sensitive person, highly susceptible to the mental radiations of all the participants, of whose thoughts and attitudes, concerns and expectations, can cause in a certain manner for the mediums to feel hesitation or distress with an influence so powerful within their psychic structure that it can provoke difficulties, hinder or make it impossible for them to attain a trance. The medium needs a harmonious, tranquil, uplifting, and fraternal atmosphere in order for their faculties to emerge dynamically. It is this reason that it is recommended that mediums should abstain from attending sessions when they find they are indisposed or their psychic state is altered.

- The session should start with a moral pronouncement that invites all the participants to elevate their thoughts towards the Creator. This is used as a spontaneous prayer that expresses a state of transcendence from worldly thoughts and of positive spiritual vibrations, without implying any specific sacramental or religious formula. This continues with a solicitation from the director to the spirit world for their assistance and protection for the unfolding of the spiritual work at hand. As a factor to unify everyone's thoughts, not only for its excellent educational potential, one can read a paragraph from a Spiritist book, those of ALLAN KARDEC or any others of known doctrinal value. The practice of mediumship without an elevated objective and without proper spiritual protection is filled with uncertainty and risks, for without this a door can be opened to influences that can have very harmful results. On the other hand, mediumship when in harmony with Up High is a fountain of light and of love.

-   With the intention to aid in the establishment of major concentration and to facilitate the mediumship process, one can dim the intensity of the lights, without total obscurity, and also, if desirable, one can listen to some piece of melodic and harmonious music.

-   It is convenient to remember, that in the general sense we are all mediums; so in some special circumstances some participants may feel the presence of a spirit. Human beings emit and receive mental waves and the interrelationship between some and others vary according to their frequency. Mediumship is an interchange of mental waves where incarnates and disincarnates participate, and where the perispirit plays a fundamental role.

The mediumship trance can be differentiated in three principle phases. Initially, the medium perceives the radiating fluids of the spirit that wants to manifest, and discriminates its qualities.

A psychic connection is produced between the spiritual entity and the medium by means of an interrelationship between their respective perispirits. The spirit projects a magnetic action over the centers of force of the perispirit of the medium, and through this exercises influence over the nervous center, unchaining psychic and physical changes. Depending on the intensity that is produced with contact of the perispirit, the medium can remain conscious, or gradually adopt a semi-conscious state, or a totally unconscious one. The perispirit of the medium acts as a receptor for the emanating vibrations of the perispirit of the disincarnated spirit, and as a conductor of the spiritual currents towards cerebral structures.

A distinguished scholar of Spiritism and of mediumship, the Brazilian doctor JORGE ANDREA, has offered a valuable contribution to the knowledge of the mechanisms of the phenomena of mediumship that is indicated by his plentiful bibliography. From one of his books we extract this enlightening concept:

> *"We think and have as logical, that the perispirit (vibratory emanations from the zones of the unconscious), by means of the energy discs or chakras, from the neuro-vegetative (system of equilibrium and emergence of the physical body) and the pineal gland (gland of the greatest expressions of the human psychic), constitute a triad, par excellence, of the highest expression of the mechanism of mediumship, selecting, analyzing, transforming and adapting the energies so that the conscious zone, the final thread of these manifestations, are in condition to translate the communication. The unity of the nervous system of the cerebellum, with its characteristic energetic charge, is an element of high importance in the process of the coupling adjustment and accommodation of mediumship."* [95]

In its third phase, the spirit is present with the emergence of mediumship due to an effect of an intellectual and physical character in accordance with the dispositional mode that determines the type of faculty that predominates in the medium.

PURPOSES OF SPIRITIST MEDIUMSHIP

Nothing advances with just spirit phenomena if there is no study of it. The principle body of work to do this is the Spiritist Doctrine. Mediumship serves the doctrine; the doctrine is not subordinate

---

[95] JORGE ANDRE. *Nos aliceres do inconscientes* [*On the foundations of the unconscious*]. 2a. edición, Rio de Janeiro, 1980. Ch. V. Consideraciones sobre el trance [Considerations regarding the trance], p. 122.

to the act of mediumship. It is convenient to state here the wise observation of ALLAN KARDEC:

> *"To suppose that Spiritism derives its strength from physical manifestations, and that it might therefore be put an end to by hindering manifestations, is to form to oneself a very false idea of it. Its strength is in its philosophy, in the appeal it makes to reason and to common sense."* [96]

The true purpose of Spiritism is to orientate humanity reading its intellectual and moral progress, demonstrating the reality and immortality of the spirit, and teaching it the profound consequences that can come forth from this truth. Communication with spirits is a means that concurs with such an elevated purpose, and not an end in and of itself.

Continuing with this premise, one can consider the following principles as the purpose of mediumship:

Experimental demonstration of immortality

The most outstanding limitation that has marked classic spiritualism throughout the centuries, is due to its inability to offer determinate proof regarding the continued existence of a spirit after death of its physical body, of which, certainly, is its first and foremost postulate. Mediumship is an instrument that takes care of this deficiency. And, thanks to mediumship, Spiritism obtained the certainty of the immortality of the soul and the afterlife, using the same methodical resources that the natural sciences employ. Mediumship is to Spiritism, as the microscope is to microbiology or the telescope is to astronomy; it is the essential elemental tool for the observation and the confirmation of the facts that are studied.

The manifestations of the spirits constitute the convincing proof of the existence and continuation of life after the grave. Certainly no one better than the spirits, can prove the existence of the spirit, since they themselves constitute the best confirmation of their own reality.

---

[96] ALLAN KARDEC. *El Libro de los Espíritus* [*The Spirits' Book*]. Ibid. Conclusion, Part VI, p. 366.

Spirit communication via mediumship sits at the base to rectify the false religious beliefs that hold spirits as "ghosts" or "troubled souls" or "souls in purgatory" which have generated so many myths and superstitions. This has produced in a great majority of people, states of anxiety, fear and panic, and has led them to shun relationships with their beloved families and friends that have parted the earth.

Control of a Natural Faculty

The phenomenon of mediumship has been produced in all ages and it was not discovered or invented by Spiritism. However, a Spiritist study of it permits the medium to comprehend it, understand it within nature, and discover the laws that regulate it.

It is one of the vital resources derived from the constitutions of humans and it needs attention, comprehension, and discipline. Mediums need proper orientation, technical knowledge of the faculty, and knowledge of its moral implications. Suppression, obstruction, or its misuse can cause disruption and alteration of the medium's psychic and physical equilibrium, caused on the part of ignorant, superstitious or ill-intentioned individuals.

Many persons that spontaneously exhibit mediumship faculties, without any knowledge of it, usually go through a terrible ordeal as a consequence of ignorance, lack of understanding, disbelief or rejection, and suffer within their families and society. When they are taken to the doctor, generally they are labeled as neurotic or psychotic, and condemned to a long term treatment with drugs which in this case is inappropriate. At other times, they are attended to by priests or religious pastors that are determined to submerge the mediumship faculty with prayers, litanies, ceremonies or exorcisms, convinced that any contact with spirits is naturally demonic. In the worst of cases, persons developing their mediumship may fall into the unscrupulous hands of those who presume to have magical powers, and carry on all manner of superstitious rites and rituals causing them grave harm, not only of their faculty but also to their physical and mental health. All of these circumstances can create tremendous confusion and anguish.

It is Spiritism that plainly provides an educative role, lovingly supplied and fulfilled, within the protective environment of the Spiritist Center. It is there, when persons exhibit the beginnings of mediumship, where they are educated and their faculties are properly oriented. However, this does not constitute an alteration of their health, their emotional stability, or their normal development in life.

The enfoldment of the faculty of mediumship, guided by the standards of Spiritism, is part of a natural process of normal personal growth; of physical, mental and spiritual adjustment; and, the ordered, prudent, and systematic exercise of mediumship faculties. This is perfectly compatible with the compliance of daily activities, corresponding to and within, the context of personal, familial, and social life.

Instrument of spiritual assistance and protection

Those that find themselves afflicted by the physical lost of their dear loved ones receive through mediumship helpful and appropriate consolation. Grief and pain is calmed by offering the surety that our deceased loved ones still live and that they maintain close mental proximity to us. This knowledge consoles, inspires and lovingly encourages us to continue forward in life and to overcome and conquer higher goals.

By way of mediumship, we can also find unhappy and tormented spirits that are suffering the consequences of their poor choices. These are spirits that we should attend to with indulgence. We should help them become aware of their situation, to resolve any issues, and to assist them along on their pathway towards moral and spiritual recuperation.

Utilizing the faculty of mediumship is how we can obtain success in the work of obsession. This is done by reeducating the obsessing spirits that have wrapped themselves in the darkness of hate, vengeance, and various types of interpersonal conflicts, until they are liberated from the chains that hold and torment them. One cannot, without the practice of mediumship, act effectively in the difficult and complex field of dealing with spirit obsession. And, that is why mediumship imposes upon all those that participate in this type of work, a spirit of sacrifice, an inclination of service to others, tremendous patience, and most of all, a great deal of love.

Stimulus for moral reform of the human being

The Doctrine of Spiritism sheds light on the fact that mediumship has a superior and transcendent objective: to encourage the moral transformation of every individual, and by extension, society itself, as a direct and natural consequence of the firm conviction in the existence of the spirit and its evolutionary continuity through multiple material existences.

We would like to close this topic, relative to the purpose of mediumship with the words, always beautiful and edifying, that LÉON DENIS placed in the last chapter of his book *En lo invisible* [*In the invisible*], called **Glorious Mediumship**:

> "*The constant and profound study of the invisible world, that is also the world of causes, will become the grandiose sea and the inexhaustible spring of which will nourish thought and the life of man on earth, and mediumship is the key. By way of that study, man will arrive at the science of truth and the truth of belief, one that does not exclude the one or the other, but unites them for mutual productivity; so likewise a much more intimate communion will be established between the living and the dead and more abundant assistance will descend over us from space. The man of yesterday will better comprehend and bless life; now he no longer fears death... Then, he will have realized, that by his own effort, the kingdom of God over the Earth, that is, of peace and of justice [has arrived], and, finally he has come to the end of the road, his last day will be bright and tranquil, like the setting of the celestial constellations at the moment the morning dawn appears on the horizon.*"

EVALUATION OF MEDIUMSHIP

Necessity of evaluation

> *"By submitting all communications to scrupulous examina-*
> *tion, scrutinizing and analyzing thoughts and expressions, as we do in*
> *judging a literary work, and rejecting without vacillation when it runs*
> *counter to logic and good sentiment, all that disproves the personality*
> *of the spirit that is thought to be manifesting; proceeding in this way,*
> *we repeat, we discourage the deceiving spirits, that end by leaving,*
> *when they are persuaded completely that they cannot deceive us. We*
> *insist that this is the only valid method, and [with] infallible results,*
> *for there is no bad communication that can defend against a criti-*
> *cal examination. The good spirits are never offended by this, for it is*
> *them that have counseled us to do so and because they have nothing*
> *to fear from undergoing scrutiny of their messages. Only the bad ones*
> *resent it and try to dissuade us from working this way, for they have*
> *everything to lose. And by this conduct they prove what they are."* [97]

This categorical declaration by the Codifier of Spiritism relieves us from having to produce other arguments in order to justify the obligation that is incumbent upon all those that attend mediumship sessions. One has to examine the content of all messages that are received, pass it though the sieve of reason and evaluate it with a critical mind, both in regard to its origin and the ideas expressed.

We would just like to add that with a permanent, serious and honest evaluation of mediumship activity in all its involved aspects is how you can:

- Avoid fraud and spirit deception.

- Distinguish animism (medium's own spirit communicating through itself and/or psychic abilities) from actual mediumship (disincarnate spirit communicating).

---

[97] ALLAN KARDEC. *El Libros de los Médiums*. [*The Mediums' Book*]. Second part, Ch. XXIV, No. 266. Ibid. p. 311.

- Attract good spirits and repel spirits of evil intent.

- Elevate the intellectual and moral level of spirit communications.

- Encourage the participation of serious, cultured, honest and sensible persons in Spiritist groups.

- Dignifying Spiritism; by gaining social respectability through the seriousness and elevated practice of mediumship and other activities.

TWO PRIMARY PRINCIPLES

The evaluation of mediumship contains obstacles of diverse complexities all originating with ignorance due to lack of proper education and orientation. These warn about the conditions required to obtain good results in the experimental field of mediumship. Ignorance leads to attitudes and behavior that may be identified with gullibility, fanaticism, and superstition. Ignorance about what the spirits truly are, regarding their source and the human condition, knowledge of the relative value of spirit's opinions according to their evolutionary level has much to do with this.

If one wants to participate in a mediumship session and obtain positive results within an ambient dominated by seriousness, rationality and critical discernment, it is convenient to have a thorough understanding of these two basic concepts:

Spirit Hierarchy

Spirits are the souls of deceased beings. They are humans without a physical body. They form, provisionally, the invisible population of the Earth, just as incarnated beings form, temporarily, its

visible inhabitants. In successive interchanges, within the evolutionary laws of reincarnation, the disincarnate will return to the physical
plane, and we will pass to the spiritual world. Hence, spirits are not
angels or demons, or special beings that know everything or can do
anything; their level of wisdom and morality is proportionate to their
evolutionary grade.

Death does not substantially change the spirit. Each one is,
as a disincarnate spirit, what he or she was as an incarnate human
being; having the same virtues and defects, beliefs, habits, tendencies and inclinations. It should not be believed that the soul of a
human can instantly acquire exceptional knowledge solely by passing from the material world into the spirit world. Generally, spirits
do know much more in the other world than they did in this one.
Progress is realized, in this world as well as in the next, only by our
own self efforts through study and work, and by experience and the
practice of love.

The spirits with which we enter into contact with, occupying
the different grades of knowledge and morality that they do, may be
truthful or lying or without being deliberately misleading, may discuss topics they believe they have mastered but in reality are ignorant
of, or know little, or are erroneous.

Even the more advanced spirits do not know everything; they
teach us much, but within their own limitations. It is essential to know
and to assume that the value of the opinion of a spirit originates from
itself and not from another source. If this is understood well, and this
knowledge is put into practice, one can eliminate credulity that is a
fountain of so much disappointment and deception.

Therefore, knowing that disincarnated spirits differ among
themselves in intellectual values and ethics the same as incarnates,
it is imperative that each person that wants to become involved in
mediumship sessions should know the system of **SPIRIT CLASSI-
FICATION** that KARDEC presented. It is considered "the key of
Spiritist Science; for solely through it can be explained the anomalies

that present themselves in the communications, illustrating to us the intellectual and moral differences of the spirits." [98(1)]

It is a classification, that in accordance with KARDEC, "is not absolute," yet offers a panoramic vision of the diverse categories wherein one can place each spirit according to its advancement by the qualities they so far have acquired and the imperfections they still have to overcome. It is distinguished by three orders, and within them are ten classes. *Imperfect spirits* are essentially characterized as those where material interests predominate over spiritual ones. This order includes those spirits that are: impure, frivolous, pseudo-wise, neutral, and bothersome spirits. *Good spirits* are those that have already reached higher levels of progress and strive for the practice of goodness. They are distributed within four classes according to what their dominate quality is: benevolent, learned, wise, and superior. The last order is of that of the *pure spirits*. They have reached the last level of intellectual and moral superiority.

This spirit hierarchy is a magnificent instrument to use as a tool for the correct evaluation and identification of spirits during mediumship, based on the content of the transmitted spirit messages and the language used. Those who are involved in mediumship sessions should know and apply it.

Principle of Concordance

The doctrinal bases of Spiritism are united within Kardec's Codification. They are solid bases that not only have endured with use and the passing of time, but have been reaffirmed by scientific development and culture in general. Of course, it should also be well understood that in light of the progressive and evolutionary character of Spiritism, it should be open and always favorably disposed to revision, refinement and actualization in conformance and pursuant to progress, as needed.

---

[98] ALLAN KARDEC. *El Libro de los Espíritus* [*The Spirits'Book*]. Second book. Ch. I, No. 100. Ibid. p. 77.

Therefore, the progressiveness of Spiritism should be assessed by the use and incorporation of all new ideas that have received the sanction of science, and also, certain knowledge that has been provided by the spirit world via mediumship.

It needs to be very clear that the Spiritist Doctrine cannot admit as truths, much less incorporate them within it basic principles, certain ideas that are presented as innovations or superior revelations, often linked to certain spirits, mediums or leaders presumptuous enough to want to be recognized as new teachers or redeemers. Generally, such ideas are unverifiable, constitute confusing, tedious, and meaningless concepts and terminology, and frankly, commit an outrage against the most basics of commonsense.

There are deplorable situations, wherein certain persons, many times acting out of good faith but with little wisdom, proclaim themselves as the reincarnation of celebrated historical figures dependent on the "revelations" that have been offered by spirits through certain mediums. This is lamentable behavior, showing a lack of good judgment and violates the basic principles of prudence, logic and good sense. This also discloses the sinking of these individuals into the abyss of pride, vanity, and self-centeredness. These aberrations have not only occurred with people who lack even the most elemental instruction, but even directors of groups, writers, orators, and even founders of Spiritist or Spiritualist institutions have also succumbed as well.

Therefore, legitimate recognition for messages should be given to information showing characteristics of seriousness and verisimilitude that is transmitted by various spirits, employing different mediums unconnected to each other, that proceed independently from diverse places, and that significantly coincide in their teachings. *This is the sanction of concordance, objectivity, and universality that is required by Spiritism.* This stands in opposition before the fantastic speculations and trickery with which people seek to "save" the world when they find themselves lost in psychological disturbances or submerged in the dark drama of an obsession or their own self-delusion.

It is for this very reason that KARDEC insisted upon the necessity that spirit messages be evaluated and verified. Also, that they be in accord with the principle of concordance, as a general guarantee that the source of the communication is good and safe, and that the transmitted teachings are consistent in scientific, cultural, doctrinal, and moral quality.

IDENTIFICATION OF SPIRITS

The identification of spirits is convenient, but not absolutely essential. As a rule, if one knows the identity of the spirit that is communicating one can work from a much firmer base in the activity of mediumship.

It is recommended that the spirit be invited to provide a name, but without pressure or an obligation to do so. If the spirit voluntarily provides a name, one can and should solicit any dates or details that can confirm this. However, if the spirit prefers to remain anonymous or use a pseudonym, what remains is to evaluate the content of the message, keeping in mind the aim of the message and language used. *The primary importance is the content of the message.*

However, one can rationally and objectively infer, with respect to the identity of a spirit by determining its corresponding grade based on the scientific, philosophical and moral quality of the message, and by its personality. Frankly, it is obviously not acceptable to identify a spirit as Aristotle ignorant of formal logic, as Darwin who has forgotten the basis of evolution, or that Léon Denis cannot expound on the principles of the Spiritist doctrine with the endearing and elegant prose that distinguished him during his incarnation on earth. It is precisely for this reason that one should be cautious about spirits that provide illustrious names or names of famous people from history. Sometimes frivolous spirits or those pretending to know more they that do, like to deceive and impose their opinions.

In some cases, if one is trying to identify a spirit based on a written communication, and the trance is deep, one may be able to identify the spirit by its writing or signature, comparing it to writing that the person's spirit left behind. This field has ample possibilities for investigation and experimentation in the identification of spirits and as a consequence can be a formidable scientific proof of survival of the afterlife. An expert in this area is CARLOS AUGUSTO PER-ANDREA, a professor in the area of the identification of fingerprints and handwriting analysis at the University of Londrina in Brazil. He has written about this subject in an original and well-documented book regarding the scientific methodology that permits verification of authenticity in a comparative analysis that can be done between the automatic writing by the medium with that of the spirit author when he or she was alive.[99] Also in this book is an examination made of various written spirit messages received by the medium FRANCISCO CAN-DIDO XAVIER, some written in Portuguese and some in Italian, which after handwriting analysis was concluded, specific common elements in the writings were found, of the spirit from its previous incarnation and after its disincarnation, and were sufficient to confirm authenticity.

In the mediumship phenomena of transfiguration, wherein facial features of the medium are modified and are similar to the spirit that is communicating in trance, there are elements that permit one to make precise identifications. This is almost the same as in material-izations, when the spirit makes itself visible and tangible making use of ectoplasm as a covering. Sadly, these are isolated phenomena that present themselves sporadically and spontaneously.

One sort of recognition of spirits can be made by the study of the reactions observed in the face and body language of the medium

---

[99] CARLOS AUGUSTO PERANDREA. *A psicografia a luz da la grafoscopia*. [*Automatic writing in the light of handwriting analysis*]. Editora Folhla Espírita. Sao Paulo, 1991.

during trance. Generally, it can be pointed out that vibrations emitted by spirits that are good, modest, intellectually and morally elevated, are received with welcome by the medium and it makes him or her feel tranquil, comforted, and protected. Spirits of an inferior nature can transmit disharmony, restlessness, as well as produce sudden or jerky movements in the medium.

The assistance of other mediums not in a trance can also be a factor of primary importance in the identification of spirits. Depending on their level of development, they can see the spirits prior to their communicating via the trance mediums. They can also verify if the spirits are correctly identifying themselves or if there is any deception since they can determine their true intentions. These mediums can confirm the end of the trance and the effective separation of the spirit from the trance medium. They are, hence, a key piece to mediumship activity that is practiced with order, proper method, seriousness, and elevation of purpose.

Content of Spirit Communications through Mediumship

The two essential elements that should be analyzed in all spirit communications are: language and quality.

Language Used

At various opportunities KARDEC said that the language of the spirits is always in accord with its level of moral and intellectual elevation. There are cases where a spirit disguises its language and appears to be at a higher evolutionary level than what truly corresponds to it. However, it is also true that the imposter and these appearances, sooner or later, are unmasked revealing its genuine nature.

In response to the importance that the mode of expression of each spirit has, we present some patterns that can assist directors of mediumship sessions in recognizing the moral and intellectual conditions of a spirit. We will use the names "superior spirits" and "inferior spirits" only for convenience of expression, and in no case, as absolute or definitive categories. Spiritists know full well that each spirit occupies a temporary place within the evolutionary scale that is in proportionate to its major or minor inclinations toward goodness and truth, and that this varies constantly over the course of time throughout its successive existences. Created simple and ignorant, all spirits march inescapably towards an eternally superior destiny.

- Superior spirits always express themselves with goodness, cordiality, simplicity, and modesty. They do not provoke hatred, resentment, or vengeance. They do not boast or display excessive pride in one's knowledge or power. The teach humility and forgiveness. They urge for the practice of virtues. Inferior spirits transmit messages full of aggression and violence. They are vain and boastful with their supposed powers. The stimulate vices and debauchery of the passions.

- Superior spirits only speak about what they know. They recognize their limitations and prefer to remain silent about what they do not know. Inferior spirits speak about everything. They believe (or pretend to believe) they know everything and that they are the absolute possessors of the truth.

- The messages of superior spirits reveal an excellent capacity for synthesis and are coherent and clear. Superior spirits say much with few words. Meanwhile, inferior spirits go on and on, getting lost in redundancies and inconsistencies

- Superior spirits never give orders or make impertinent requests. They solely advise and educate. Inferior spirits are demanding and controlling.

- Superior spirits appeal to reason and good sentiments. They accept disagreement and dissent. They do not aim to persuade or impose their views. Inferior spirits require that you believe them and obey them.

- Superior spirits do not flatter or foster servitude. They recognize the merits of everyone, in serene and restrained terms. Inferior spirits excessively praise those they seek to manipulate, encouraging pride and vanity.

- Superior spirits show reserve and prudence in relation to intimate questions that pertain to the private life of individuals. They can provide orientation of a general moral character, so that from there each one can extract from the lesson what they consider adequate. Inferior spirits love frivolity and they intrude in domestic affairs and enjoy disrupting personal, family, and social relationships.

- The style of language of superior spirits is of a higher quality; their noble words stimulate good sentiments and assist people to progress. The vocabulary of the inferior spirits can be confusing, indecent, vulgar, and full of profanity.

- The main thing is that the language of the superior spirit is always in concurrence. There is one basic type of guidance, independent of the epoch, the place or the circumstances. Superior spirits express themselves in terms that are relatively similar when referring to God, life in the spirit world, or of moral spirituality. The same occurs with inferiors spirits, since this coincides totally with their negative tendencies.

Quality of Spirit Messages

In his excellent book *Investigaciones sobre la mediumnidad* [*Investigations regarding mediumship*], GABRIEL DELANNE, dedicated extensive chapters in examining numerous communications received from all parts of the world by diverse mediums, with the intention to demonstrate that the spirits are the first interested in determining the true value of messages of a truly spiritual origin. The illustrious French researcher says:

> *"We should not be hesitant to set one's effort in critique of the methods concerning communications, because only through that path will we build the true science about the relations between the living and the dead."*

A recommendation that is common among all thinkers and scholars of Spiritism, and that provides a barrier keeping in check ignorance, deception, incredulity and fanaticism.

Taking into account that each spirit possesses different intellectual and moral levels that distinguish it from the rest, and that their psychological and psychic conditions in the spirit world are also different as a direct reflection of its evolutionary stage within the reincarnation process, we can establish that the spirit messages come from:

Spirits that appear of their own freewill:

***Encountering Errant spirits*:** These are spirits that enter within the ambient of the medium. They wander about in the spirit world not knowing when, why, and what they are there for. Many times these are lost souls, confused and afraid, because the situation in which they are now living, are in contradiction to the expectations that were already in their minds due to their materialistic or religious beliefs. They find neither heaven nor hell or find they have not disappeared upon their death. They continue living as before, although they have no physical body. For this reason, they communicate via mediumship without having a clear idea of their situation and need much guidance in order for them to adjust and orient themselves to continue on their evolutionary journey.

Spirits of family and friends: At many mediumship sessions, spirits having familial ties and/or who were united to the participants as friends when alive, surprise those in attendance by expressing the continuation of their feelings of connection. This mediumship interchange is the best confirmation that the "dead live," and that our dear disincarnated loved ones are enthusiastic when we are happy, and also worry over the problems that we may be having.

One should not force the contact with these familiar spirits, exercising mental pressure or demands on the mediums. These contacts occur when the conditions are favorable, and it is precisely when they are unexpected that these types of spirit communications provide a special touch of authenticity. For example, this is confirmed by the materialized apparition of the mother of the eminent Italian criminologist CESAR LOMBROSO that he described in his book *Los fénomenos hipnótocos y espiritas* [*Hypnotic phenomena and spirits*]. LOMBROSO could converse with his mother in their common dialect and it was possible to observe her face, countenance, her body and the extension of her hands. It was a decisive experience in his life that caused him to abandon his materialistic visions and embrace Spiritism.

Necessity in transmitting a message or a request: There are certain spirits that feel compelled to communicate, using mediums that are willing, by an intense desire to fulfill a promise, make known the existence of some document, to draw attention for some action to be taken on their behalf or express something left undone that upsets them. At times, in order to make their presence known, they may resort to bringing about noises, raps, or other physical effects so that their requests for assistance may be fulfilled.

In different epochs throughout history many cases of this type have been recorded of a spirit creating noises until it is attended to. Frequently cited, is an incident relayed by the Roman PLINY the Younger (to distinguish him from his uncle) in one of his Epistles which are valuable historical texts because they describe in great detail the customs of those times. In this particular occurrence, he tells of a house in Athens that no one wanted to live in because it was frequented by noises and an apparition which started with the inexplicable disappearance of the last tenant. The philosopher Athenodorus acquired the house not believing in such a fabulous story. However, on the very first night he stayed there, he heard noises that sounded like chains. Shortly thereafter, he saw an old man making gestures that indicated he wanted to be followed (and the philosopher did so) to a place in the courtyard, whereupon the apparition then disappeared. Athenodorus marked the spot and the next day he notified the magistrates. Excavations were made and a skeleton was found that was bound up by chains. Apparently, this man had been murdered. A respectful and proper burial were performed, and afterwards there was no more noises or appearances in the house.

Spirit Guides: They are loving spirit benefactors, superior in wisdom and morality. They use mediums to transmit beautiful messages that bring knowledge to us of spiritual realities taught to bring forth the practice of goodness and our moral transformation.

Spirits Brought to Mediumship Sessions by Other Spirits:

Spirits in a confused state: Generally, after physical death and during the soul's transition into the spirit world, it enters a phase of confusion which clouds its consciousness, and lasting a few hours up to a period of many years. In violent deaths involving accidents, homicides, and other tragic events, the level of perturbation that the spirit may suffer can be grave. Time is needed so that it can be clear to them that they are no longer in the physical plane because of these types of upsets and by so sudden a change. They need to comprehend and accept their new situation. They should not desperately cling to the persons they had maintained relationships with, whether relatives or through affinity, or with any objects or material benefits that pertained to them. If their thinking proceeds and/or continues in that direction it can lengthen the discomfort and suffering they are experiencing. These spirits are brought to sessions so they can be helped and instructed. They need the necessary well-balanced energies that can calm their physical and moral pains, discipline their reactions, and so they can orientate themselves in their new situation. Directors of sessions, mediums and spirit benefactors should unite their efforts to offer this effective aid that permits the calming of these suffering spirits and prepare them so they then can continue their evolutionary journey in new incarnations.

Spirits of obsession: These are viciously attached, as much as with incarnated as with disincarnated spirits, by a desire for vengeance or by immoral thoughts, blinded by hate, envy or by immoral passions. They require moralizing instruction that will allow them to pardon the offenses of their current victims and to desist from their present conduct. It is obvious that directors, mediums and any assistants need to have an adequate preparation in dealing with the work of spirit obsession. This is not where spirits, treated as criminals, appear as if before a court in order to be compelled to lay bare the intimate details of their soul, or to be sentenced or condemned. It is a work of charity, and it is worth saying, one of solidarity, directed at helping not only the victims but also the obsessing spirits to comprehend and overcome the unhealthy situation that is affecting the both of them.

Basic Criteria to Evaluate the Quality of Spirit Messages:

- Devotion to reason, logic and a common sentiment.
- Coherence of ideas and the absence of contradictions.
- Their moral quality.
- Their literary, artistic, historical, philosophical or scientific value.
- The contribution they offer in originality, new ideas and reflections.

Any group involved in mediumship is in a condition to realize an exhaustive and honest evaluation of the spirit messages that they are receiving by taking these criterion as a primary reference, reaffirming in this way its seriousness and objectivity and protecting itself from any attempts of trickery or manipulation.

Chapter Six

REINCARNATION

"When I lie down in my tomb
I could say as so many others: I have finished my
journey! But I would not say I have finished my life. My
journey will commence another day, in the tomorrow.
The tomb is not an alley without an exit; it is an avenue
that closes at dusk and returns to open again at dawn." \

Victor Hugo (1802-1885)
Celebrated French Poet and Novelist – Author
of *Les Misérables*

GENERAL AND HISTORICAL CONSIDERATIONS

The word **reincarnation** literally means a "return to the flesh." It is the return of the spirit to a new material existence. Therefore, to reincarnate is to be born again, in a new organism starting from the moment of conception.

Reincarnation is a natural law of life, a means by which the spirit progresses intellectually and morally, striving through its own effort to superior states of evolution.

The spirit reincarnates innumerable times, without losing its individuality. In each existence, the basic traits of personality are definitively retained and remain distinct by its spiritual component nuanced by the biologic characteristics of its new physical body, and the influence of the surrounding social and cultural conditions of its new environment. This includes a new family, other friends, and its insertion within the general process of socialization. In the material world, the human being configures globally as a very complex and dynamic biological, psychological, sociological, and spiritual entity in constant evolution.

Reincarnation should not be confused with **resurrection**, the dogma of some religions like Christianity and Judaism. That concept provides that the soul lives only once, and after death, following a certain period of time, it will eventually occupy the same physical body to receive the ultimate sanction of God's Final Judgment. This thesis has numerous difficulties when being presented or defended. It gives to the soul the attribute of survival after physical death, but denies its preexistence before birth. That is perplexing because if it is supposed that life begins at birth, it would seem it would end at death, and that, inevitably results in a materialistic perspective. If life does not end with death and the soul survives it, it should necessarily preexist birth. On the other hand, how can each soul use its old physical body again, if its molecular decomposition has experienced numerous transformations due to integration with other physical bodies?

Reincarnation is also not **metempsychosis** (or transmigration of souls). This is an ancient Eastern belief that accepts the possibility of a human soul that can be reborn into the body of an animal species as punishment for its faults and wrong-doings. It is an absurd idea that deforms and contradicts the vision of incessant progress that the theory of multiple lives implies. Reincarnation is synonymous with evolution; in its biological sense as well as progression on a spiritual level.

The following are equivalent expressions of reincarnation: palingenesis, rebirth, plurality of existences, and successive or multiple lives because they employ the same sentiment and transmit the same idea of the eternal progress of the spirit animating different material bodies.

Reincarnation is the most significant principle of the Spiritist doctrine, as in some other spiritualist schools of thought. Although it is obvious that it was not discovered by Spiritism, it is within Spiritist studies and confirmations, obtained through mediumship where the concept of reincarnation has been placed within a rationalist and scientific context, free of any dogmatic notions as well as any mythical, magical or superstitious ideas arising mostly from religious or esoteric doctrines. The plurality of existences is the principle upon which the anthropologic vision of Spiritism is based: the soul incarnates, disincarnates, and reincarnates to fulfill its individual unfolding within a general history. Thus, forging a new consciousness among humanity, a new spiritual and historical understanding, where the present, past, and future are interconnected by an eternal being, that is born, dies, and is reborn without end.

The arguments that substantiate the reality of reincarnation and give reason to declare it as a principle law of life and of evolution can be found in these three categories:

Scientific: The favorable evidence that has been accumulating as a result of worldwide research, give it a solid base which is in complete harmony with natural laws and does not contradict any established scientific principles.

Philosophical: The concept of reincarnation can respond with great consistency in answering the numerous questions humans have asked throughout eternity. Who are we? Why, and what are we here for? Where do we come from? Where are we going to? How does free-will and responsibility reconcile with each other? Are we free or is life predetermined? These are questions of serious importance and of great interest, and of which this doctrine can explain with clarity, simplicity, and objectivity.

Moral: The unhappiness, pain, suffering, injustices, inequalities, and all the evils that afflict humanity, in general, can be reconciled within the moral aspects of reincarnation. It provides an explanation that allows an understanding as to why these afflictions occur, and it also encourages a dynamic attitude to overcome them. When there is true comprehension of the implications and consequences of the law of cause and effect, humans feel compelled to make a tremendous effort in their intimate and personal reform, which will in turn provide for the social transformation that humanity requires in order to achieve a more complete, just, and dignified life.

In the following terms, the eminent French physician and paranormal researcher GELEY summarized his conviction on the certainty of this universal law:

> *"I am a reincarnationist. I am for three reasons:*
> *Because the palingenesis doctrine appears to me:*
> *1) from the moral point of view, fully satisfactory;*
> *2) from the philosophical point of view, absolutely rational, and*
> *3) from the scientific point of view, credible and, better yet, probably true.* [100]

It can be affirmed with total accuracy that belief in reincarnation has occupied a conspicuous place in all ages and among all cultures throughout the long history of civilization. It is the most ancient and widespread conception of life and of human destiny on the entire planet. It has had different names and been understood under diverse forms, and has been transmitted either directly or allegorically. This noble idea appears in the diverse stages of the historical development of humanity up until today, where we find it knocking with insistence upon the doors of academia, demanding its definite recognition.

In the most primitive societies belief in reincarnation was extensive; having a profound influence over the life and the institutions of its people, and this has been confirmed by contemporary social scientists. Rumanian author, philosopher, and anthropologist

---

[100] GUSTAVE GELEY. *Estudios sobre la Reencarnación y la Mediumnidad* [*Studies regarding Reincarnation and Mediumship*]. Ediciones CIMA, Caracas, 1994. P.17

MIRCEA ELIADE (1907-1986), author of numerous studies about ancient religious traditions and customs, states that the majority of these people accepted it very naturally. Making reference, for example, to the charungas, sacred objects of the Arandas and other Australian tribes that have survived, he states:

> *"Known is that these ritual objects, made of stone most of the time and ornamented with diverse geometric themes, represent the mystic body of the ancestor. They are kept hidden in caverns or buried in certain sacred places and are shown to the youngest after their initiation. Among the Arandas, the father speaks to his son in these terms: 'This is your own body, you came out for a new birth.' Or this: "This is your own body, the ancestor that was you when, during your previous existence you traveled. Later you descended to the sacred cavern to rest there.'"* [101]

The doctrine of successive rebirths appears, in explicit or allegoric forms, in the basic works that give support to the fundamental religions of humanity: *The Book of the Dead* of the ancient Egyptian civilization; the *Bardo Thodol* or *Tibetan Book of the Dead*; the *Vedas*; the *Upanishads*; the *Zend-Avesta* of the Persians; and the *Koran*; the *Talmud*; the *Zohar*; and the *Bible*, etc.

The majority of the Asian peoples of the world live with this belief, and if in the Western world reincarnation has not had the same acceptance, it may be due to the decisions and pressures made by official or traditional religions and the skepticism of a widespread materialist culture. Among the Greco-Latin civilizations, it had ample dissemination and enjoyed great sympathy among the early Christians until it was anathematized by the Church authorities at several Councils between the 4th and 5th centuries. Reincarnation was a simple and clear concept of destiny understandable by the most humble, and that harmonized with Divine justice and was able to explain the disparity

---

[101] MIRCEA ELIADE. *Historia de las Ideas y de las Creencias Religiosas* [*History of Religious Ideas and Beliefs*] Editorial Cristiandad, Madrid, 1978. Volume I. p. 47

of human conditions and human pain. Nevertheless, the Church raised in its place a whole monument of dogmas and mysteries, like the concepts of eternal punishment, the resurrection, and the Final Judgment. Happily, in spite of these Councils and all their theological subtleties, the churches could not distort the profound reincarnationist truth set forth by JESUS before NICODEMUS, "You must be born again." [102]

Whatever type of historical review is made, it will show that belief in successive lives has been accepted by notable figures in history that had a universality of thought. Forming a true gallery of honor, we present some names with the intention of showing their tremendous influence upon human history, and that reincarnation could be found in their teachings: BUDDHA, CONFUCIUS, LAO TSE, HERMES, HERACLITUS, PYTHAGORAS, PLATO, PLUTARCH, ORIGEN, PLOTINUS, PARACELSUS, GIORDANO BRUNO, THOMAS MORE, BENJAMIN FRANKLIN, DAVID HUME, EMMANUEL KANT, ARTHUR SCHOPENHAUER, FRIEDERICH HEGEL, FRIEDERICH NIETZSCHE, MOHANDAS GANDHI, to name only a few of the moral and philosophical reformers of ancient and of modern significance.

It has also been reaffirmed by the following authoritive writers and intellectuals of recognized prestige: VICTOR HUGO, HONORÉ DE BALZAC, ALEXANDRE DUMAS, THEOPHILE GAUTIER, GUSTAVE FLAUBERT, CHARLES FOURIER, JEAN RAYNAUD, MAURICE MAETERLINCK, AMADO NERVO, RAINER MARIA RILKE, JOHANN WOLFGANG GOETHE, LEON TOLSTOI, WILLIAM BLAKE, RALPH WALDO EMERSON, HENRY LONGFELLOW, EDGAR ALLAN POE, WALT WHITMAN, ALFRED TENNYSON, HENRY DAVID THOREAU, SAMUEL TAYLOR COLERIDGE, FEDOR DOSTOEVSKY, HERMAN HESSE, and JACK LONDON.

In addition, these outstanding researchers and scholars of the psychic sciences have considered it a fundamental law of life, that guarantees biologic and spiritual continuity within the evolutionary process: ALLAN KARDEC, CAMILLE FLAMMARION, GABIEL DELANNE,

[102] Gospel of John 3:7

GUSTAVE GELEY, ANDRE PEZZANI, JOSE MARIA FERNANDEZ COLAVIDA, ALBERT DE ROCHAS, CARL DU PREL, ARTHUR CONAN DOYLE, OLIVER LODGE, ERNESTO BOZZANO, HELENA BLAVATSKY, ANNIE BESANT, CHARLES WEBSTER LEADBEATER, GERARD ENCAUSSE, RUDOLF STEINER, MAX HEINDEL, ALEXANDRIA DAVID-NEEL, WILLLIAM JAMES, KARL GUSTAV JUNG, PIETRO UBALDI, ERNESTO MOOG, KARL MULLER, JOSE S. FERNANDEZ, HATMENDRA NAT BANERJEE, IAN STEVENSON, EDITH FIORE, GINA CERMINARA, MORRIS NETHERTON, HELEN WAMBACH, JOEL WHITTON, THORWALD DETHLEFSEN, DENIS KELSEY, PATRICK DROUOT, JOHN BJORKHEM, ALEXANDER CANNON, HANS TEN DAM, BRIAN WESS, ROGER WOLGER, HERNANI GUIMARAES ANDRADE, HERMINIO MIRANDA, and MARIA JULIA PRIETO PERES.

This list is quite significant and constitutes a categorical demonstration in favor of the universality and widespread consideration of the doctrine of reincarnation, and for the same reason, it cannot be ignored or underestimated. We could make a longer list of names of famous personalities, but we consider this enough. In any case, we recommend to those who would like more information on this topic to consult a work that presents a very ample compilation of short texts related to belief in multiple existences, in all epochs and cultures, and the book is, *La reencarnción en el pensamiento universal* [*Reincarnation in universal thought*] by JOSEPH HEAD and S. L. CRANSTON. [103]

PROGRESS IN THE RESEARCH OF REINCARNATION

For many centuries reincarnation was proclaimed as a religious belief, as a "revealed truth." For hundreds of millions of Buddhists,

---

[103] Editorial Diana, Mexico, 1976. The English version is *Reincarnation in World Thought*. New York, Julian Press. 1969. Another book compiled by the same authors is *Reincarnation - an East-West Anthology*. The Theosophical Publishing House. Wheaton, IL. 1985.

Brahmans, Jainists, and the followers of other Eastern religions, the certainty of the rebirth of the spirit constitutes an unquestionable dogma that does not require proof since it is a matter of faith.

On the other hand, for the ancient Greeks, this seductive idea that had arrived from India and Egypt could and would be examined from a rationalist perspective. The Italic school of thought leaded by PYTHAGORAS had placed reincarnation as a central postulate in the conception of man and of life, alongside other scientific concepts very advanced for that time, like: the spherical nature of the earth, the heliocentric system, geometric theorems, or the proportionality of musical notes. He, himself, spontaneously remembered some of his previous lives. The third century biographer DIOGENES LAER-TIUS, wrote that the philosopher had in other times been: Aethalide, and then later he had been reborn successively as Euphorbus, Hermotimus, Pyrrhus, until he was reborn as Pythagoras. [104(2)] At his philosophical school at Croton, PYTHAGORAS taught his more privileged pupils certain procedures in order for them to be able to access their past lives (information guarded deeply within the soul), as he had done himself.

It is to the merit of SOCRATES and PLATO for attempting to prove the plurality of existences using a theoretic and rational demonstration. In *Phaedrus, Meno, Gorgias, Phaedo*, the *Republic* and other works, we find their famous eschatological dialogues directed to stimulate the imagination and the reflection of each person, opening roads that facilitate one towards self-knowledge and that one can "learn by the remembrance of that of what one has lived before" and causing to bloom forth "the reminiscences of those previous lives."

For many centuries the idea of reincarnation was condemned by the major religions. Catholic Bishops and Protestant pastors exerted all their influence to impede its diffusion and they did not curtail any efforts to prosecute its followers. Academic rigidity united

---

[104] DIOGENES LAERTIUS. *Vidas de los mas ilustres filosofos griegos* [*The Lives of the most illustrious Greeks*] Vol. II. Book 8.

with that hostility, progressively covered the world of scientific and philosophical knowledge with the shadow of a stale materialism.

In the middle of the nineteenth century, ALLAN KARDEC gave a forceful momentum to the study of reincarnation when he received from the spirit world information that confirmed it, and this concept was included as one of the central principles of the nascent Spiritist doctrine. Its books contain solid arguments and verifications regarding life after death. It explains the conditions that the disincarnated spirits found themselves in the interval between one material life and another, as well as the preparation needed to begin a new existence. It is due to the Spiritist method that the mediumship interchange was incorporated as a practical tool in the experimental investigation of reincarnation. GABRIEL DELANNE, a paranormal researcher and an outstanding representative of Spiritist Science, published in 1924 the book *Documentos para el Estudio de la Reencarnación* [*Documents for the Study of Reincarnation*], with 50 cases related to the remembrance of past lives, that was, at that time, the most relevant and major work on the subject.

At that same time, a follower of Spiritism, JOSE MARIA FERNANDEZ COLAVIDA from Spain, became a pioneer involved in experimental procedures for verification of reincarnation by way of employing hypnotic techniques directed at past life regression. COLIVIDA accomplished his work with excellent scientific criteria, adopting precautions that were considered essential: hypnotizing various subjects of different sexes, ages, and levels of culture and beliefs; he modified the experimental conditions to contrast the results; one particular person was hypnotized by various persons unknown to the subject, to avoid the factors of inference of a suggestive or imaginative character; and, he also verified the information (names, dates, places and other objective references) that surfaced throughout these regressions.

Shortly thereafter, ALBERT DE ROCHAS (1837-1914), Director of the Polytechnic School of Paris, used hypnotic procedures similar to COLIVIDA assisting many subjects to relive their past lives. In his book *Las Vidas Sucesívas* [*Successive Lives*], considered a classic on this material, he describes in detail his experimental works that also included investigations into other areas; those that had the opportunity to corroborate the existence of the astral body or perispirit, and the exteriorization of sensibilities outside the limits of the physical body. In order to overcome the objections of critics regarding his work, who said that his subjects were the victim of unconscious falsehoods and that suggestions had made them believe in past lives, COLIVIDA as well as DE ROCHAS resorted to a distinct procedure. First, an experimenter hypnotized the subject and transmitted suggestions so that the subject would acquire within their subconscious the idea that reincarnation did NOT exist and whatever personality that emerged was solely the product of their imagination. In another session, a different hypnotist would proceed with the regression. They corroborated that, independent of the subject's beliefs, and even with suggestions in contradiction of them, information regarding past lives emerged as objective proofs that did not depend on imagination or their will.

Throughout the twentieth century, there have been well-known books having to do with work in hypnotic past life regression well known for their scientific quality and the professional competency of their authors, among many we mention the following: Swedish physician JOHN BJORKHEM (1910-1963); Welsh hypnotherapist ARNALL BLOXHAM; British physicians DENIS KELSEY, JOE KITTEN, ARTHUR GUIRDHAM; German psychologist THORWALD DETHLEFSEN; Canadian psychiatrist JOEL WHITTON; and in the United States, psychologist EDITH FIORE, and psychiatrists HELEN WAMBACH and BRIAN WEISS.

In the United States, MOREY BERNSTEIN created a sensation impacting public opinion with his book, *The Search for Bridey Murphy* (published in 1956 by Doubleday), provoking intense debate among journalists and scientists. The story is the result of a series of hypnotic past life regressions between November 1952 and August 1953 with VIRGINIA BURNS TIGHE a housewife in Pueblo, Colorado that appears in the book with the pseudonym of RUTH SIMMONS. Based on the descriptions given by Ms. TIGHE under hypnosis, she was born in Cork, Ireland in a past life in 1798. Her name then was Bridey Murphy, and her death occurred in 1864. The memories were thorough with respect to details of her life, family, and the information regarding places, customs and historical references. These were investigated by WILLIAM J. BARKER, a columnist of the Empire section of *The Denver Post*, who stayed three weeks in Ireland, and then published an essay on the subject. The book was made into a movie and served to awaken popular and scientific interest in reincarnation.

The studies made by psychiatrist IAN STEVENSON, M.D. (1918-2007), born in Montreal, Canada, are well-known throughout the world. He was Professor and Chairman of Psychiatry at the University of Virginia. He founded the Division of Personality (now Perceptual) Studies, where this research still continues. He methodically dedicated his life to the study of the investigation of memories of past lives which lead him to travel all over the world over a period of 30 years, studying and documenting well over 2,700 cases. This included, especially, recording the spontaneous remembrances of past life information from children, from the most diverse places on the planet. STEVENSON was the author of hundreds of publications in medical and parapsychological journals and 14 books. He was known for his attention to detail, his objectivity, accumulation of documents and corroborating evidence, and scientific rigor in all his research. His most famous book was *Twenty Cases Suggestive of Reincarnation* (1980). Two others were: *Unlearned Languages: New Studies in Xenoglossy* (1984) and *Children who remember Previous Lives: A Question of Reincarnation* (2000).

Working along the same lines of research as STEVENSON, investigating cases of children that had spontaneously remembered various aspects of past lives, was DR. HEMENDRA NATH BANERJEE (1931-1985), professor at the University of Rajasthan and researcher at the India Institute of Parapsychology in Jaipur, India. He was one of the first precursors in the scientific study of reincarnation, that he called "extra-cerebral memory." BANERJEE lived his last days in California in the United States. In over 30 years of patient searching, he found more than 1,000 cases that are suggestive of reincarnation as the most logical explanation, of which he made known in specialized journals and in the seven books that he wrote. [105]

An American from New York, Dr. GINA CERMINARA, wrote several instructive and rational books on the topic of reincarnation and on Edgar Cayce. She became interested in the possibility that some psychosomatic disorders could be adequately explained when one takes into consideration the nexus that exists between the present life and a past one. She became interested in this subject when she learned about the life and work of EDGAR CAYCE (1877-1945), the very sensitive American that became famous for his successful diagnoses that he obtained in a paranormal trance state. By performing a "reading of past lives" he could ascertain the reason for the illness that afflicted a patient, establishing a cause-effect relationship between the actual symptoms and past life behaviors. By the time of his death, he had written nearly 25,000 instructions and protocols due to his psychic observations and in providing recommendations with surprising precision and accuracy.

A highly recommended book published in 1970 entitled *Reincarnation based on the Facts*, was written by KARL E. MULLER (1893-1968), born in New Orleans of Swiss parents, who had a great knowledge of parapsychology and Spiritism. He belonged to several psychical organizations and was also the president of The International Spiritualist Federation. His book has 8 chapters and covers 58 topics; the historical background of the idea of reincarnation, the spontaneous and experimental character supportive of the evidence, the hypotheses and theoretical explanations, illustrating each situation with historically verifiable cases, totaling 176 throughout the whole book. Of prime importance are the practical consequences that are derived from the reincarnationist theory, and the replies he provides for objections against it.

Since 1966, the pioneering activities have been known of the Association for the Investigation and Therapy of Past Lives (now The

---

[105] One of these books was *Americans Who Have Been Reincarnated.* MacMillan, New York, 1980.

Association for the Alignment for Past Life Experiences) in Los Angeles, California founded by Dr. MORRIS NETHERTON. Past life therapy is a therapeutic method that is utilized for the regression of a subject to remember personal information and events from the past in a current life and/or past lives. The latter situation reveals that some emotional or physical problems may have their origin in conflicts or trauma from prior existences. Actually, numerous physicians, psychologists, and therapists are employing this alternative procedure in their clinical practice which has continued to be perfected by the contributions of numerous professionals that have obtained additional experiences. The National Institute for the Therapy of Past Lives, founded in 1987 in Sao Paulo, Brazil, has received therapeutic results of great significance under the competent direction of Dr. MARIA JULIA PRIETO PERES, assisted by a group of physicians and psychologists. Dr. PRIETO PERES, who is well respected as a doctor and Spiritist leader, has realized praiseworthy work regarding the scientific dissemination of this curative method, with its exclusive use in the clinical area within strict ethical parameters.

Special mention should be given to the significant work accomplished by the engineer HERNANI GUIMARAES (1913-2003), past president and founder of the Brazilian Institute of Psychobiological Investigation, who is considered to have been a very significant academic researcher in the field of Spiritist science. He united, methodically and with great patience, a good number of identified cases wherein reincarnation was the best explanation for those particular situations. His book *Reencarnación en Brasil* [*Reincarnation in Brazil*], contains fundamental bibliographical references for the study of this subject due to its attention to detail and the rigorous methodology employed; considering all alternative hypotheses such as fraud, extrasensory perception, and criptomnesia, until recognition of reincarnation was the most complete explanation and was in full agreement with the facts.

In the last decades of the twenty-first century, throughout the world there have been widespread indications of acceptance for reincarnation. Although some live in nations of Western cultures where the traditional religions are opposed to it, a good percentage of the population supports the idea. [106]And, even from the proper world of science, there are emerging modern trends that consider it viable and perfectly adaptable to a new vision of mankind and the universe, just as it gave way to the revolutionary concepts of quantum physics, of psychoneuroimmunology, and transpersonal psychology. Parapsychology has incorporated within its investigations the phenomena known as *Theta*, referring to the eighth letter of the Greek alphabet which stands for Thanatos or death, to place within this category all paranormal manifestations having to do with, or caused by, beings that have died, that is to say, by spirits. Prior to this, parapsychology only worked with phenomena *Psi-Gamma* (extrasensory perception or PSI) and *Psi-Kappa* (psychokinesis or PK), in that psychic processes were verified coming from incarnated beings. In Theta phenomena, is included the study of reincarnation, with names such as extra-cerebral memory or remote memory.

PRIMARY EVIDENCE IN FAVOR OF REINCARNATION

Direct Evidence

Spontaneous Remembrance of Past Lives

These recollections are more common in children than in adults. In children, memories present themselves more vividly between the ages of 2 and 6 years of age and later on they gradually fade. This effect may be related, in part, with the complex process involving the integration of the spirit and the structure of its perispirit with the developing biological organism that is establishing itself, and also with the family and cultural influences that the child is receiving during the first and fundamental phase of its socialization. Curiously, when these

---

[106] In the United States alone, the Pew Research Center reported on December 10, 2009 (based on a 2009 nationwide phone survey) that it found "24% of the public overall and 22% of Christians say they believe in reincarnation -- that people will be reborn in this world again and again." www.pewresearch.org/

memories surface at the adult stage they are permanently remembered by the person throughout their life and are difficult to erase.

There are cases when these remembrances are imprecise and fragmentary and are not sufficient to confirm. In these situations, when the recollections are fairly complete it is convenient for family or friends to document the information without distortion, that is, without pressuring the child or exaggerating or modifying the content, and if possible, to solicit a specialist in this area of study.

The methodology used by Dr. IAN STEVENSON was very meticulous and objective, proceeding cautiously, without affirmation or negation a priori. It is required, at the least, to have six evidentiary details that permit the exclusion of chance, coincidence, or other causes such as fraud or the possibility that the memories were obtained through extrasensory perception. Some of these details, in addition, must clearly be a remembrance of a past existence with concrete and precise quotations, names, places and dates; that the person relates to the individual, possibly in gestures, peculiarity of voice, likes and dislikes, opinions, similar or identical handwriting; and, the data permits a detailed profile for comparison of personality and behavior.

Frequently, the amount of cases to study is considerably reduced by certain obstacles. Many times, the children do not relay these memories or keep them to themselves, especially when they are rebuked or ignored. These are difficulties that originate in the religious prejudices and/or customary beliefs that prevail in many societies that are against the idea of the possibility of reincarnation; the antagonism against it in the general culture sustained by a conceptual model based on materialism, and the ignorance or indifference of the children's parents that do not attach value to their recollections or dismiss them as simply fantasies due to their young age.

Among spontaneous experiences of reincarnation, one early case received worldwide attention due to the objectivity and precise details of the remembrances which were fully confirmed after being rigorously and objectively examined. It had to do with a young girl named SHANTI DEVI who was born in October of 1926 in New Delhi, the capital of

India. Starting at 3 years of age, she started to speak of a past life saying her name was LUGDI, and that she was born on January of 1902 in Mathura (Muttra), in the state of Uttar Pradesh. She plainly remembered her previous parents' names, and that she was the second wife of KEDAR NATH CHOUBEY, a prosperous business man. In addition, she had a son with him by the name of NABANITA LAL, and that she had died a week after the birth, on the 4 of October of 1925. A year later, she was reborn in New Delhi, as the daughter of RANG BAHADUR and PREM PYARI. She perfectly remembered the customs of the other family, the food they ate, and the names of the persons who were her neighbors.

Her parents tried to persuade her against the reality of these remembrances. However, she insisted that she be taken to Mathura, about 150 kilometers from New Delhi. It was on September of 1935 when the verification of all the information began. A relative of a retired school principal answered the insistent requests of SHANTI, and wrote to the address she indicated. Mr. CHOUBEY responded confirming the exactness of the details and sent a relative to meet the girl. Then, Mr. CHOUBEY went to New Delhi to find her, with his son NABANITA, and all reports were substantiated! [107]

Information Obtained via Mediumship

Innumerable communications have been received by way of mediumship, obtained at different epochs and countries, containing messages transmitted by spirit entities, where they have relayed situations that they have experienced different lifetimes. They have also explained the relationships, pleasant or unpleasant, that there is between one existence and others. On other occasions, they announce it to certain persons who will have a child, and provide information about the spiritual path of the being that is to be reincarnated. In addition, some cases are known that spirits predict their

---

[107] Available is a 1998 edition of a biography and interview of SHANTI DEVI, by Sture Lonnerstrand, translated from Swedish into English by Leslie Kippen, and published by Ozark Mountain Publishing.

next incarnation and give some details that would permit them to be recognized.

From a purely scientific perspective, and in order to proceed with an investigation, the messages received by the mediums should contain the following information:

- Complete personal information of the person alluded to by the spirit, including name, place and date of birth, profession, next of kin, and cause of death.

- Significant knowledge related to the cultural, geographical, and linguistic features linked to that of the previous life.

- Other obvious details that permit one to rule out other alternatives such as fraud, heredity, pantomnesia (an imagining of an experience because of something one has seen before), or extrasensory perception.

The history of mediumship records many cases that meet these requirements and which can be considered as direct evidence proving the reality of successive lives. GABRIEL DELANNE presented various experiences of this type in his books: *Documentos que pueden server para el estudio de la reencarnación* [*Documents that can serve for the study of reincarnation*] *Las vidas sucesivas* [*Successive lives*], and *La reencarnación* [*Reincarnation*].

Obsessions

Within the context of Spiritism, obsession is defined as the pernicious influence that a spirit exercises over another, for various reasons. Depending on the gravity and psychopathological consequences, it can be classified as: *simple obsession* (slight spiritual influences); *fascination* (when the spirit deludes the thoughts of its victim, deceiving and paralyzing the victim's reason regarding his or her situation); and, *subjugation* (when the obsessing spirit totally controls its victim, leading to severe disruptions that alter the victim's physical and mental health).

A high percentage of the processes concerned with obsession are intimately linked to reincarnation, since the origin of many of these cases are due to a conflict between the obsessing spirit and the victim going back to one or more lifetimes.

Through proper diagnosis, one that goes beyond the symptoms and social components, and takes into consideration the spiritual factors, one can determine the origin with precision, identifying the root of the problem. Once the particulars of the past life dynamics are understood, one can proceed to solve it through educational and moralizing techniques recommended by the Spiritist doctrine. This permits the separation of the unhealthy ties that keep these beings attracted to each other, as a consequence of hate, of envy, or the desire for revenge, that can corrupt the soul.

The failure of traditional psychiatric therapies in situations of this nature is due in good measure to the unintentional or deliberate ignorance of reincarnation as a factor. In contrast, the many successful recoveries obtained in caring Spiritist institutions provide proof in favor of palingenesis, and demonstrates its extraordinary possibilities and scope within the medical, psychological, and scientific fields, in general.

Indirect Evidence

Birthmarks

This is when scars, patches of discolored or unusually textured skin, or any physical deformities that a baby is born with, exactly corresponds with lesions or wounds that caused the death of a person in a previous life, and also, coincides with information obtained by spontaneous remembrances the child provides of the previous existence or are obtained through experimental techniques.

Dr. IAN STEVENSON, foremost researcher regarding cases suggestive of reincarnation, wrote three books documenting over 200 cases where such physical evidence correlated with the necessary pertinent information. They are: *Reincarnation and Biology: A Contribution of the Etiology of Birth Marks and Birth Defects, Volume One* (1997), *Reincarnation and Biology: A Contribution of the Etiology of Birthmarks and Birth Defects Volume 2: Birth Defects and Other Anomalies, Volume Two* (1997), and *Where Reincarnation and Biology Intersect* (1997). The third book provides a summary and conclusion of the two other voluminous works.

The presence of these congenital markings, and the like, causes one to contemplate that perhaps the perispirit acts as a Biological Organizing Model with the facility to translate into the new physical organism, dominant structures that it brings with it, imprinting them upon the genetic code.

In his documented work, *Reencarnación en Brasil [Reincarnation in Brazil]*, HERNANI GUIMARAES ANDRADE reports on eight cases (selected among 70) that were exhaustively studied by the Brazilian Institute of Psychobiological Investigation (IBPP), objectively and completely, which concluded with the sole hypothesis being that of reincarnation.

Patricia (a fictitious name to protect her and her family) was a woman who was born in the city of Araraquara, in the state of Sao Paulo, Brazil, on November 14, 1939. A member of the Justice department, she held a high position in the state. Her parents are Brazilian of Italian heritage.

She started to express her recollections of her parents and family practically from the moment she started talking, when she was 2 1/2 years old. She remembered many aspects of her life in France; that she was born in Vichy and had lived at the port of Le Havre, and many details of her previous parents, with geographical, social, and historical information of that epoch. She also remembered that she had died when she was 15 years old being shot by a soldier which injured her heart. She was examined by equipment at

IBPP and two marks were found on her body, one of them in front, below the left breast, and the other, on the underside, at the level of the left kidney. ANDRADE states,

> "The first mark had the aspect of a scar coming from a wound caused by a perforation. The second one was bigger, a little more visible, and gave one reason to think of a wound caused by something that came out, lacerating the tissues of the flesh. The two marks gave the impression that the wounds were produced by a projectile that had transversely pierced Patricia's body. The profile of the marks, side view, formed an angle of 15 degrees, approximately, with the horizontal, displaying that the alleged projectile was discharged by a much taller person than the patient. This detail adds more evidence to the assumption that these are the marks of a bullet that would have killed Alexandra.
>
> The mother of Patricia became surprised, at that moment, for she always noticed these marks since birth, but never associated them with the recollections of her daughter, since two years of age
>
> The tendency of these marks is to disappear with time. Although Patricia was 35 years old at the time of the interview, the scars were sufficiently clear in order to be photographed." [108]

In fact, there appear four photos showing the scars on Patricia's body, and the correlation that there is between them and the entry and exit of the projectile.

Persons with Extraordinary Skills and Knowledge – Prodigies

Small children that have displayed incredible intellectual aptitudes, exceptional knowledge, artistic, and scientific skills are well known, which cannot be fully explained as being acquired by genetics or through sociological or cultural influences.

---

[108] HERNANI GUIMARAES ANDRADE. *Reencarnacion en Brasil* [*Reincarnation in Brazil*]. Casa Editora O Clarim, Matao, 1986, pp. 237-286.

ANDRÉ-MARIE AMPERE, one of the greatest French physicists, at four years old and without knowing his letters or numbers, performed impressive mental calculations. Another French physicist, FRANÇOIS ARAGO, was a child prodigy in calculus the same as KARL GAUSS, whose talent was revealed at age 3. LOPE DE VEGA wrote verses at 5 years of age. GIOTTO was a shepherd boy when he was discovered by CIMABUE, who found him so perfect there was no definition to describe him. He took him to his workshop where he became one the greatest of Italian painters. MICHELANGELO so amazed Italy at age 13 that his teacher DOMENICO GHIRLANDAIO told him, "We have nothing left to teach you." GOETHE, at the same age, could write in several languages. PASCAL, since a very young child was distinguished by his genius. Possessing a background in the geometry of EUCLID, he wrote a book at age 16 dealing with the mathematical investigation of cones, and provoking such admiration around him that DESCARTES could not believe he was so young. JOHN STUART MILL, celebrated philosopher and English economist, at the age of 3 could read and speak Greek, and at age 6 discussed ancient philosophy with various professors. JOSÉ RAUL CAPABLANCA, a native of Cuba, from 4 years old played chess with the experts of his time and eventually became a world champion.

What child prodigies demonstrate is that their gifts are not hereditary or a product of instruction, but appear "spontaneously" without outside stimulus. It forms a part of the unique heritage of the spirit, as a consequence of the level of progress achieved in past lives, regardless of the physical body. How can we comprehend a MOZART writing menuets, violin sonatas, and a symphony before 8 years of age? What can we say about TASSO already writing verses at age 7? And, what of HANDEL, who had mastered several instruments by age 12? What about the precocious abilities of CHOPIN, BERNINI, BERNOULLI, and ALEXANDER POPE? The list is too long and includes children of all epochs, from numerous countries, and with abilities in the most diverse artistic, literary, and scientific fields. Furthermore, we only know the cases that have become publicly known. How many more are there who are known only by their close relatives?

Intelligence is of the spirit and not of the physical body, which is solely an instrument. Genius is not the consequence of the determinate configuration of the nervous system, but the demonstration of the presence and actualization of an evolved spirit, manifesting its various unique characteristics because of having acquired in past centuries a respectable accumulation of knowledge and intelligence.

Innate Tendencies Reflected in Personality and in Behavior

Reincarnation jumps out at us as an obvious and most appropriate explanation to understand with ease the tendencies that lie dormant and hidden in our innermost world; that can be creative and constructive as well as disagreeable and pathological.

Brilliant ideas, just as a certain vocations, can remain dormant in the unconscious, that is, the remote memory of the spirit where information is preserved throughout the process of palingenesis, and can emerge before a powerful stimulus bursting forth in positive achievements.

The sudden consciousness of a soul, until then ignorant of itself, when acquiring its innate ability or calling, at times, is accompanied by receiving a shock that reverberates in the deep roots of the moral life, in its most innermost Being, where the spiritual and the physical merge. When MALEBRANCHE felt the calling for working in metaphysics, it was upon reading Descartes' *Meditations on First Philosophy.* WAGNER knew nothing of his musical vocation, before hearing for the first time at Dresden, a symphony by BEETHOVEN. Disturbed by the intensity of his emotion, he arrived at his house ill, and it took several days before he returned to a normal state, meanwhile becoming fully aware of what his vocation would be and determined to pursue it.

Among human beings, there has always been a surfacing of inclinations or strange aversions of which frequently no reason or origin can explain. Like fears that can become phobias; diverse manias and compulsions; sympathies and antipathies between certain persons, situations, or places, without us knowing why. Many people have recognized a time in their life or on various occasions they have experienced a feeling of attraction for someone, that at that very moment upon meeting them it appears they have known that person their entire life. The opposite also holds true; the instant and inexplicable feeling of repulsion one has for a particular person from the very first moment upon meeting. Official psychological explanations of these vivid attractions and revulsions allege concurrent and complicated psychological mechanisms, where physical and social variables intervene, related to pre-established patterns of familial, educational, and cultural values. However, they fail to explain the significance of the unusual experiences of profound feelings of attraction or repulsion for people one does not know and have just met. The depths of our unconscious are full of such impulses that condition our physical and psychological states. Why are they there? When and how do they start? Where do they come from? These are questions that the current science of psychology cannot answer, but have clear and simple, logical and rational explanations in the process of reincarnation.

Déjàvu

Coming from the French, this expression signifies "already seen" or "already lived" and applies to those situations for certain individuals, that although finding him or herself at a place for the very first time, have the feeling of having already been there. Persons have recognized streets and even small specific corners of a city, where they have never been in their life, as if they are remembering them.

Also, on seeing the presence of certain persons or objects, with a strange sensation of recognition, hidden memories are liberated. At times, they parade though our minds, both in dreams and during wakefulness, images that we cannot decipher at those particular instants, and then later recognize them before the occurrence of certain events, and even as part of them. We feel that we have lived in another time, or that we recognize a certain area, a city, a building, although we are seeing it for the very first time in this lifetime. Revealing his past life reminiscences, in his *Voyage en Orient [Trip to the Orient]* (1835), French writer and poet, ALPHONSE de LAMARTINE stated:

> *"When I visited Judea, I scarcely found a place or thing that for me was not a memory. Have we lived twice or a thousand?"*

There are many explanations, but under circumstances like these, reincarnation becomes the most complete one to explain in a most rational and fitting manner the question of the remembrances of past lives.

Experimental Evidence

Hypnotic Regression

Applying the techniques generally used for hypnosis, having a good subject united with the appropriate circumstances, one can regress the memory of a person, touring the diverse phases of their life; arriving at their childhood, during the period of gestation, while observing their gestures, impressions, and psychophysiological reactions corresponding to the different stages of which can be analyzed with certain clinical evaluations. And, one can also pass beyond the limits of the current memory of the subject, beyond the fetal stage, arriving at a phase before birth into this life, and reaching the threshold of the unconscious or spiritual memory, to retrace the course of one or more of the subject's past lives.

At times, one obtains information that refers exclusively to the life immediately previous to the present one, but in other cases one can recognize situations associated with other previous lives. The possibilities of this system and the results depend on several factors related to the abilities of the hypnotist, the receptivity of the subject and their willingness to cooperate without restraint or inhibitions.

The experiences achieved by COLAVIDA and ROCHAS, as well as by those that have been made in more recent times by professionals in psychology and medicine, like: GINA CERMI-NARA, EDITH FIORE, HELEN WAMBACH, JOHN BJORKHEM, ARNALL BLOXHAM, ARTHUR GUIRDHAM, ALEXANDER CANNON, DENIS KELSEY and BRIAN WEISS, [109] are sufficient to note that hypnotic regression, employed with precautions in each case, and within clinical and scientific parameters, is a valid method that can experimentally demonstrate reincarnation. These researchers and therapists did not start this process with philosophical motives, yet their work resulted in them becoming convinced of the plurality of existences when they could not find in the present life of their patients, the focus of conflict that affected them and whose origin was found in one or various past lives, through past life regression.

So-called Past Life Therapy has developed and become improved with new criteria by competent professionals in medicine like: MORRIS NETHERTON in the United States, HANS TEN DAN in Holland, THORWALD DETHLEFSEN in Germany, PATRICK DROUOT in France, or MARIA JULIA PRIETO PERES in Brazil, that comprises a set of procedures that can realize memories from the present and of past lives without recourse to hypnosis. There are clinical procedures that nevertheless acquire new cumulative information with evidence in support of reincarnation.

In general, past life regression is a therapeutic procedure that successfully confronts diverse existential problems that have repercussions involving both the mind and the body, bringing from the unconscious data which provides the key to both interpreting and

---

[109] BRIAN WEISS, M.D. is a graduate from Columbia University and Yale Medical School. He is Chairman Emeritus of Psychiatry at Mt. Sinai Medical Center in Miami. He maintains a private practice, but also conducts seminars, workshops, and training programs around the country. His first and most well-known book on past life regression and reincarnation was *Many Lives, Many Masters*, however, he has written six others.

expressing problems that are present, reconstituting it, and healing the trauma and suffering that has its origin in a past life within the reincarnation process. The process includes two crucial moments: that of the *action of awareness*, raised when the patient emotionally relives the conflicting situations from the past that are now surfacing into the area of consciousness, and, the moment of *transformative action* when the patient proceeds to modify his or her mental state of mind, by being provided the tools to make positive changes in their current life, overcoming conflicts, and establishing a certain equilibrium.

Modified States of Consciousness

Some persons possessed with particular spiritual conditions (mystics, sensitives) can attain knowledge of their past lives developing intimate experiences that lead them into various states of trance. In actuality, groups proliferate that teach techniques that include exercises of concentration, physical and mental relaxation and meditation, and it is by these means that the train themselves to access information from their previous existences. These experiences can offer positive results for reflection and self-knowledge, but they lack objectivity and do not provide much possibility for scientific research.

Some experimenters have tried to provoke remembrance of past lives through the administration of pharmaceuticals or other drugs. ALPHONSE CAHAGNET, a French scholar in the field of magnetism, somnambulism, mediumship, and other psychic phenomena, stated that he was able to obtain revelations on previous existences on some subjects provided with narcotics. Similar experiences were obtained in Germany in 1936 with injections of mescaline, an alkaloid containing peyote, a cactus of Mexican origin. Some physicians did this to prisoners in penitentiaries with the intention of obtaining confessions, but found that they transferred them through time and space to other scenarios that related to other lives.

It is well-known that in more modern times, experiments were conducted utilizing hallucinogenic drugs in order to obtain other states of consciousness. In some cases, it appears that one of the effects was the momentary opening of spiritual memory and the emergence of memories of past lives. Dr. STANISLAV GROF, Czechoslovakian psychiatrist, carried out experiments at the Psychiatric Institute of Prague. In 1955, he administered LSD or lysergic acid, a powerful hallucinogen that modifies visual and auditory sensations. He could observe that some subjects entered into trance with regression of personality until infancy, intrauterine life, and including past lives. The investigations at Prague, as well as other places of research replicated these particulars, and were confronted with the possibility of reincarnation. We say, however, that this should only be conducted under rigorous methodology for the health and equilibrium of the patients, and keeping in mind the results are rather uncertain.

OTHER ASPECTS IN CORRELATION WITH REINCARNATION

Interval or Period In Between Material Lives

This is understood to be the stage between physical death and the moment of a new birth. It is the period where the spirit lives when it is disincarnated, developing in the spiritual plane. It has been established that the duration of these intervals are variable, it can extend from a few minutes to many, many years. In the studies conducted by KARL MULLER the average amount of time was about 70 years. There is no set duration. It appears to depend on the psychic condition of the spirit as well as the level it has attained in its moral evolution that determines the more or less promptness as to when there is the necessity to reincarnate.

The situation of those beings of an inferior morality, if we may express it this way, provides for a more rapid return to the material world; and, once again we see the infinite wisdom of the Divine, that provides them with more opportunities towards their rehabilitation.

When disincarnated spirits are at a more advanced moral level, if they have reached in the material world a clear notion of their immortality and try to act as a consequence with rectitude and kindness they reach a faster re-adaptation, remember their past existences, they reflect over the progress they have accomplished, and plan their future life with an aim towards further self-improvement and advancement. For them, reincarnation can be more at their convenience, with longer intervals between one material life and another. This is not the case for spirits not so advanced, that reincarnate with an imposing necessity, without their being involved in planning, subjected to a certain psychic and biological determinism.

The knowledge of the conditions of the spirit in the spiritual plane is of great importance for the comprehension of the evolutionary process that involves every human being. Already, in the book *El Ciel y el Infierno* [*Heaven and Hell*], KARDEC advanced this knowledge regarding the individual situations that spirits are found in, one of happiness or suffering, knowledge or ignorance, and this was told by the spirits themselves in the communications that they dictated to the mediums. In various books, the spirit communications received by FRANCISCO CANDIDO XAVIER, dictated by the spirit ANDRÉ LUIZ, provided valuable information relating to life in the spiritual plane. We will close this subject with the final words from the book *Life between Lives* that has the subtitle "*scientific explorations regarding the interval that separates one reincarnation from the next,*"[110] and we fully recommend it for those who desire to explore more fully this topic:

> "*While much has been achieved, the life between lives, is a human resource hardly utilized, that remains in the preliminary stages of its comprehension. Solely an investigation on a massive scale will be able to reveal the profound secrets of this other world and its potential for human development. This book is a record of*

---

[110]   JOEL L.WHITTEN M.D., Ph.D. and JOE FISHER. *La vida entre las vidas* [*The life between lives*]. Editorial Planeta Venezolana, Caracas, 1991, p. 181. The book in English is entitled *Life between Life*. Published by Warner Books. New York, 1986. This book was based on thirteen years of research and thirty medical case histories.

preliminary explorations. Consequently, as scientists advance and penetrate into [the study of] this intermediate [state of] existence, surely a major comprehension of our incorporeal heritage will surely come about. The study of meta-consciousness[111] with its capacity to pass the barriers of birth and of death, may apply, with all its importance, for the betterment of the human condition. It prompts us to understand why we are here and what we should be doing."

Changes of Gender

Each spirit has lived a myriad of material lives, as a woman and as well as a man. This change of gender within the palingenesis process is definitively confirmed. A spirit does not have a certain sexual category in the context that there are no feminine spirits or masculine spirits. However, in each material existence, or in each cycle of incarnation that includes various existences, it shows signs of a predominant tendency, that is, it polarizes towards one sex or the other.

In question number 200, in *The Spirits' Book*, one reads:

"Do spirits have sex?" Followed by the following response: "Not as you understand it, because the sexes are dependent on the [physical] organism. There exists love and sympathy, but based on the similarity of sentiments."

There is no defined or definite gender, but once the spirit has incarnated, its gender will be expressed in the physical body. However, within the spirit itself there are sexual tendencies inasmuch as there is a sexual energy inherent in the spiritual being, in its essential dynamic. The true seat of its *sexual identity* is not found in the physical vehicle (its human body), but within the spirit.

In certain cases, the condition of masculine or feminine gender immediately changes after each subsequent reincarnation. Meanwhile,

---

[111] The term "meta" is a prefix derived from the Greek meaning, "after or occurring later."

on other occasions, the spirit reincarnates time after time in the same gender, and then later changes to the alternate gender. The change of sexual polarity preserves connections with all the experiences the spirit has lived in the exercise of its sexuality. This can explain some of the tendencies of sexual behavior of masculinity in women, of femininity in males, or of homosexuality that can occur upon a spirit reincarnating. These situations did not go unnoticed by KARDEC, when he dealt with this topic in the *Revue Spirite* (January of 1866):

> *"A change of sex, may then, under that impression in its new incarnation, conserve its tastes, its inclinations and the inherent sexual character of the sex it just left. This explains certain apparent anomalies, observed in the character of certain men and of certain women."*

Some curious data was derived by some studies made by KARL MULLER that alludes to the influence of certain cultural or psychological factors, involving inhibition or of confidence, regarding the remembrances of past lives. He found that the women in their regressions, spontaneously or induced, remembered 24% of their experiences that they had lived as men. While one the other hand, among the men, only 4% remembered being a woman. This is another reason why all researchers should be very careful in the area of past life regressions, evaluating the information with tremendous objectivity and taking into consideration human reactions, whether voluntary or involuntary.

Forgetfulness of Our Past Lives

One of the strongest objections frequently raised against reincarnation is the generalized forgetfulness of previous existences. There is much that can be argued about this. The fact that we do not remember our past lives does not summarily discount the truth of reincarnation, in the same way that we cannot limit the dimensions of our actual life to what we have in our current memory of it. And, in the ultimate instance, our objective or real existence is not dependent on whether we have or do not have a memory of it.

Besides, there are very powerful moral reasons that justify this law of forgetfulness, of this "blessed forgetfulness" that AMALIA DOMINGO SOLER spoke about in her book *Hechos que prueben* [*Acts that prove*], symbolized by the Greeks in the mythical waters of Lethe. A formative "forgetfulness" that stimulates the progress of the soul through the experiences of a new life, with renewed energy, free from the failures produced by the same or similar situations of the past. The blocking of this information from the physical memory facilitates a totally new approach to the same type of problems, that in some way held back the advancement of the soul in the past and that still remains unresolved. Easily, one can understand that between two persons there could have occurred strong disagreements, that carried to the extreme could have caused serious damage to one or both, and even death itself. Looking far ahead, we find that the definitive solution of this conflict, which could have lasted during various existences, was to link these souls through ties of the flesh as blood relatives, where the force of love would set the basis for a constructive relationship and for the particular growth of each being. This task would have lasted much longer and would been more complicated without forgetfulness.

From a systemic perspective, the spirit and the physical body constitutes a system that needs to find its state of homeostasis or state of equilibrium so that it can act with efficiency. And precisely, it is the distinct forgetfulness of its past material existences that is a mechanism of balance preventing any tensions provoked by remembrances of conflicting natures, so as not to psychologically violate the person, and their family and social relationships. This forgetfulness permits the spirit to continue to advance on its evolutionary trajectory, without remorse or pangs of conscience that would haunt it or cause it relapse into the same errors, enveloping it within a vicious cycle.

The consciousness of past lives sleeps deep within the soul. The soul incarnates into a new body, and these memories, far from being useful in the new life, can cause enormous difficulties. Solely in special circumstances may the spiritual memory appear, permitting a contact with its past. Forgetfulness of past reincarnations is the law; remembrances constitute exceptions and should have a reason and explanation.

Many cases are known that involve persons of historical relevance who affirm that they possessed fragments or complete memories of their past lives. The Indian philosopher KAPILA remembered that he participated in the writings of the *Vedas* in previous centuries. PYTHAGORUS recalled having been at Troy as EUPHORBIUS. EMPEDOCLES, that he was a woman in another age. PONSON DU TERRAIL remembered that he lived four centuries earlier during the times of HENRY IV. THEOPHILE GAUTIER, ALAXANDRE DUMAS and WALTER SCOTT, maintained their beliefs in memory of their past lives as well as intimate personal details that they reported in their autobiographies.

One has to keep in mind that information processed by the spirit in other lives was accomplished with other brains, and so cannot be accessed by the current one; besides, it is housed and synthesized in the unconscious spiritual memory. In point of fact, our physical organism does not possess the complexity or the necessary brain development that can permit the conscious registering of experiences that have not been registered by our physical senses in the current life. We function with two processing structures of information: the cerebral memory intimately associated with the nervous system, related to psychic activities of the conscious level, and an extra-cerebral memory, that is the archive of the spirit, and is related thereupon, to the unconscious world. In a current lifetime, to ask the brain in a conscious form to remember past lives, we are demanding for information that it simply does not possess. That is why, in regressions and other experiences, when the unconscious is accessed and the channels of information are opened, the memories appear.

There is no moral injustice in acts that affect all of us due to the consequences of situations that originated in lives we do not have a current memory of. Since, as well as establishing a universal principle, this ignorance of the law does not justify its failure or preclude its direct effects. Furthermore, although the conscious past life personalities are obliterated by the coupling of the spirit with a new body, there is always expressed, in a synthesized form, certain aptitudes and vocational inclinations, tendencies and habits, and the moral and intellectual acquisitions conquered throughout the spirit's evolutionary journey. There is temporary forgetfulness of these memories, but this does not mean that they have been extinguished (as has been proven with the techniques of regression) and they are there recorded for those who would seek to plunge into the spiritual unconscious.

Famous People

A rational and beautiful an idea such as reincarnation is not always properly understood and assimilated by all who believe in it. It is well know that in certain religious sects of India, the evolutionary and ascendant sentiment that is involved has been distorted with the supposition that the soul can retrogress and incarnate in the bodies of animals as a punishment for wrongdoing. And, it is also there that some sects contradict the progressive and egalitarian character of successive lives, maintaining a backwards and arbitrary system of social division of superior and inferior castes.

Another false idea that undermines the coherence and logical position of the thesis of palingenesis is the affirmation that various persons make that in their past lifetimes they have been famous persons. They imagine they have been MOSES, ARISTOTLE, CLEOPATRA, JOAN OF ARC, SIMON BOLIVAR, or ALLAN KARDEC, and engage in real paranoid delusion, or in the majority of these cases, it is a demonstration of pride and vanity. We know personally certain persons that, in different countries and at the same time, self-proclaim themselves to be the reincarnation of JESUS OF NAZARETH! And, to make the situation even more absurd, these are people that do not even remotely exhibit in knowledge, tendencies or behavior, the moral or intellectual traits that distinguish these famous personages of history, of who they say they are the reincarnation of.

And, it is not true that in past life regressions, whether through hypnosis or other procedures, subjects remembered that they were celebrated men and women of the past. In practically all serious works that were conducted for clinical and experimental purposes, the personalities that appeared were of common and ordinary human beings, that carried their strengths and weaknesses, like all of us, struggling to overcome them and advance within the vicissitudes of life.

Reincarnation, like all true ideas, is not responsible for the mythologies that can be improperly created in its name.

SPIRITISM, REINCARNATION, AND THE LAW OF CAUSE AND EFFECT

The law of spiritual causality (of cause and effect) is a superior principle of justice that involves all human beings in their evolutionary process. It is understood that all behavior absolutely carries with it, its consequences inasmuch as each person harvests what he or she has sown. This law has been identified with the Eastern concept of "karma," which is a Sanskrit term that signifies action and reaction. Karma does not necessarily denote something negative, but refers to a function of balance and compensation; to collect on the consequences, pleasant or unpleasant, of our actions. The concept of karma has spread widely in our Western culture, although many times it is not used properly because it is separated from its close relationship with successive existences. It is not proper to refer to karma if one does not allude to reincarnation, since both concepts are directly interconnected.

The notion of personal responsibility that is derived from our acts is one of the most transcendental teachings of the Spiritist doctrine, and we are continually reminded of it by the sobering spirit messages we receive. Therefore, a man, in association to what he does, forges his own freedom, or clasps shut the chains of his own moral and social enslavement. Each occurrence is tied to previous causes and subsequent effects; making the present the result of the past, and with the present currently sowing the seeds of the future. Regarding our existence, it is worth saying, we essentially find ourselves in the state we have created, in accordance with our thoughts and behaviors that we have cultivated throughout numerous previous lives. The future will be the situation that corresponds to the degree that we have evolutionary attained in this life.

Upon disincarnating, we will not find paradises or hells, or eternal fires or demons. Each spirit will come across the spirits of other human beings previously disincarnated, and will come face-to-face with the effects of its own works, reaping what it sowed. Those who on Earth were generous and fulfilled the commandment of love to their fellowman, will receive the same, and enjoy a fraternal and harmonious ambience. Those who forgot their fellowman in their self-ishness, retained hypocrisy or succumbed before avarice or covetous desires, will find the same bitter fruit. The thoughts, sentiments, and actions of each spirit projects an energy like a magnet, whose lines of force are curved and then return upon having been discharged, so they return to their owner, with positive or negative effects.

Within the law of spiritual causality resides the solution to the ancient and complex philosophical dilemma between determinism and freewill, options that seems to run counter to each other in explaining the meaning of existence and the destiny of mankind. However, the solution is clear and convincing: there is liberty to act and determinism regarding its consequences. Freewill is a primal faculty that character-izes all conscious individuality in order to freely use his or her thoughts, desires, and acts, and is the constant measure of a spirit's progress. Noth-ing restricts its action, just as there is no escape from the responsibility derived from it. The Spiritist approach does not pretend to explain all acts by means of the absolute freedom of individuals, being that incor-porating factors that compel us to the acquisition of superior states of consciousness teaches that freewill does not solely consist in the free-dom to do all that we want to, but, within a more elevated category, the freedom to want all that we do. Neither does Spiritism participate in a fatalistic vision that marks a rigid predetermined destiny, but presents reincarnation from a natural and dynamic perspective, as a useful and necessary process to enable the progress of beings.

No establishment of facts have been found for the reasons of the universal evil exhibited by the horrible inequalities and injustices in this world, which cause religions inextricable difficulty in trying to explain the dramas of material existence in relation to the idea of a just providence. This is, encircled by materialism, a doctrine that reduces all of life to a single existence, with each human's destiny condemned to the vagaries of chance, gratuitously providing to some: health, riches, and precious abilities. Meanwhile, others sink into misery, sickness, and cruel anguish. However, Spiritism comes with its message of evolution and reincarnation, which reconciles mankind with a rational and hopeful conviction about the infinite presence of the Creator in the vast plan of the Universe, and offers a perfect comprehension of what happens in mankind's daily experiences and opens immense possibilities to finding the path of its liberation. In the Spiritist philosophy, we cannot make a binary division, absolute and static, between good and evil, since evil is not a punishment or goodness a reward, but are the consequences of an evolutionary grade reached. Evil is the measurement of our ignorance, goodness is the measurement of our spiritual richness, and by the same evolution, evil becomes good conforming to the process of palingenesis.

Spiritism promotes the simultaneous transformation of man and of society, facing in a dynamic form the law of cause and effect, and in that respect considerably distances itself from other spiritualist interpretations with its Eastern and esoteric notions of karma. Continuing with GELEY, we can say that there are two approaches: the supporters of a primitive or simplistic reincarnation, and the supporters of an elevated or dialectic reincarnation. For the first group, the law of cause and effect becomes mechanical and fatalistic as if it serves as a divine instrument of punishment for faults committed before, which one is only to be resigned to. According to those criteria, humans are divided into "bad" and "good" as if there were absolute ethical categories. In contrast, the dialectic character of the palingenesis vision considers that the law of causality must be assimilated within the relativity of the continuous moral variations imposed by the process of advancement experienced by each human being. It is not considered as divine punishments or rewards to be accepted passively, but the consequences of one's own actions which must be understood and responsibility assumed, so it will be addressed by a moral determination inevitable towards change, progress, and evolution. The essential finality of the law of cause and effect is not to punish, but to educate and to help us so that we live in harmony with nature.

There are those who are accustomed to present the law of spiritual causality in terms like "payment of debts" or of "terrible expiations" within a simplistic criteria and inherited by cultural religious traditions. They believe that if someone is suffering it is automatically because they made someone suffer in that same way, enclosing the reincarnation process within a vicious circle and ignoring the multiple factors that affect an incarnated being, whether biological or social. Why are they like that, what is the finality of that suffering? Who benefits with more suffering? It is much more useful, noble, and rectifying, that we direct our energies to alleviate the sufferings of others and come together with those that suffer. One has to say in a very loud and clear voice, we do not reincarnate because we have sinned, we simply reincarnate because we live. We do not reincarnate to repeat the past, but to overcome it!

It is within this dynamic and progressive conception that the problems of man and of society, and coincidentally in all of what KARDEC, GELEY, DELANNE, and PORTEIRO as well as many other scholars have taught, that reincarnation can be understood in all its redemptive potential and the plentitude of its beautiful morality, and not as a justification to advance moral miseries or to calm the consciences of those who cross their arms before social inequities. Reincarnation, and the law of cause and effect that represents its natural correlation, are thus a powerful force that will boost and accelerate efforts in pursuit of the cherished ideal of universal fraternity, which will strengthen the law of all laws: LOVE.

In one of his magnificent books, the psychologist and Spiritist writer JACI REGIS concluded one of his chapters, especially well entitled, "Learning how to be a Spiritist," and with the below inspired words. We also use it here to close this topic:

"Does not God want a smile, happiness, the best?

The Kardecist doctrine opened the doors of hope. No one will be left outside the kingdom, because God loves everyone, although we do not have the

conditions to understand the mechanisms of his wisdom. Reincarnation consolidates the solicitude and wisdom of the divine. In it is reflected the grandeur of the Creator and of his Natural Law.

And how can I be sure of this?

First, because history and life, belie each hour the terrifying prophecies, the pessimistic prognostications.

Goodness overcomes. Man will be victorious. He has life and needs to learn to live it. He has time and he needs to take advantage of each reincarnation segment so as to grow and overcome his own obstacles.

Joy is the natural goal in life. Suffering is transitory, contingent.

We need to construct a happy conscience; that loves, that looks for joy in living, of building, of enjoyment, to use sexuality to grow and self-realization with mutual respect.

What model do we have?

Look at JESUS; JESUS of NAZARETH, born in Nazareth, son of Mary and Joseph, as was stated by J. HERCULANO PIRES in Revisión del Cristianismo [Examination of Christianity] and not the Jesus Christ, born of the constellation of the Virgin, in Bethlehem, the city of David. From that JESUS, is where ALLAN KARDEC only and exclusively looked for morality, above the sects and the interpretations." [112]

---

[112] JACI REGIS. *Introducción a la doctrina Kardecista.* [Introduction to the Kardecist Doc-

Chapter Seven

OBSESSION

> *"All those who are reasonably knowledgeable with the Spiritist Doctrine understand the terrible dramas of obsession that torment the great multitudes of incarnated and disincarnated spirits.*
>
> *These spiritual illnesses cannot be treated with drugs or electrical shocks, not with psychoanalytical therapy. The conscious utilization of spiritual methods could liberate a considerable part of the immense and growing population in psychiatric hospitals, as well as the many tormented beings who roam the streets in various obsessive states."*

Herminio C. Miranda
Brazilian Spiritist Researcher,
Author and Translator

THE EVOLUTION OF PSYCHIATRY IN THE UNDERSTANDING AND TREATMENT OF MENTAL ILLNESS

The manner in which human beings have dealt with mental illness has been conditioned by the cultural, moral, religious and

trine] Ediciones CIMA, Caracas, 1998, p. 47

scientific criteria that have been dominant in each moment of history. Since antiquity, and even in relatively recent epochs, mentally ill patients have suffered the ignorance, apathy or hostility of a society that considered them to be savages or possessed by the devil, and that they should be dealt with by way of seclusion through imprisonment, social isolation, cruel deprivations or torture, and even death. Moreover, in some countries, this included the utilization of certain procedures like cerebral trepanation so that through the hole that was bored, the demons could escape.

The Greeks, with a much more benevolent and understanding attitude, built temples where the sick were attended to with loving care, received proper nourishment, and were administered baths and massages while listening to harmonious music. One of the most important physicians of the Greco-Roman civilization had already outlined some theories to arrive at a rational explanation of mental disorders. HIPPOCRATES (circa 460-377) considered to be the father of scientific medicine, organized and classified these disorders, thereby creating the first classification manual of psychiatric diseases. He used designations like childbirth madness, phrenitis, mania, melancholy, epilepsy, etc., associating them with imbalances in the bodily fluids. GALEN (129-201), compiler of all the medical knowledge accumulated by his predecessors, thought that their source lay in cerebral lesions or alterations.

Prevalent during the Middle Ages was a type of irrational thinking due to a tendency towards the supernatural, as well as superstition that revolved around belief in the influence of the devil.

Mental illnesses, in and of themselves, because of their characteristics and dramatic qualities heightened common superstition, and the "psychiatry" of the times inflicted brutal and punitive "therapies" to patients.

The Renaissance period has extraordinary significance for medicine, psychology, the sciences and the arts in general, and also for philosophy because the human being became the focal point, one to be acknowledged and appreciated as a person, in who reason has a fundamental place. The concept of the sick person as a victim of demonic possession gradually vanished thanks to the contributions of anatomists like ANDREAS VESALIUS (1514-1565), pioneers of psychology like JUAN LUIS VIVES (1492-1540) and altruistic physicians of great sensibilities like PARACELSUS, CORNELIUS AGRIPPA and his disciple JOHANN WEYER (1515-1588), whom courageously denounced the horrors that were being committed in the name of Christianity to combat demons. They compelled reforms in the hospitals and prisons so that mental patients could receive more dignified treatment.

They launched the beginning of what is known as the First Psychiatric Revolution, whose main thrust was to overcome the standpoint of demonic influence. Mentally ill patients went from being the responsibility of the clergy to that of the physicians; monasteries turned into hospitals and houses of refuge. Two centuries later, a scientific and humanitarian trend would have a staunch defender in PHILIPPE PINEL (1745-1826), who removed the shackles and chains that restrained the patients of the Parisian asylum of Bicêtre, thereby transforming it into a true psychiatric hospital. PINEL started by making the place physically healthier so that he could immediately liberate these alienated beings, thus becoming the founder of modern psychiatry and social service that was geared to the study, understanding and treatment of the mentally ill. The revolution that was prompted by PINEL was continued by prominent physicians like ANTON MULLER (1755-1827) in Germany, VICENZO CHIARUGI (1759-1820) in Italy, JOSEPH DAQUIN (1733-1815) and JEAN ETIENNE DOMINIQUE ESQUIROL (1772-1840) in France, all of whom were distinguished physicians animated by an elevated spirit of goodwill and enthusiasm, as well as outraged by the deplorable manner in which mentally ill patients were treated. They worked towards the transformation of social service, clinical and therapeutic criteria.

The culmination of psychiatry continued in the nineteenth century with the painstaking work of German-born EMIL KRAEPELIN (1855-1926), who developed a descriptive system of the classification of psychiatric illnesses. Other important influences would come from SIG-MUND FREUD (1856-1939), KARL GUSTAV JUNG (1876-1961), ALFRED ADLER (1870-1937) and other distinguished representatives of psychoanalysis. In addition, the existential ideas of KARL JASPERS (1883-1969), which give a wide perspective to the understanding of mental illness as a set of classifiable diseases and of the patient in his or her particular condition; and, more recently, to the technological progress made in the fields of pharmacology and biochemistry.

The prevention of mental disorders in psychiatry, clinical psychology and psychosomatic medicine has intensified progressively, offering an integral form of care to the patient, starting with an extensive study of his or her infancy and adolescence, as well as family history and the social environment where the patient lives, being that the influence of environmental factors is highly important in the configuration of the patient's personality.

Recognizing that psychiatry has run an extensive and enriching course that has currently steered it towards a prospect of synthesis, making possible the integration of the social with the psychological and biological, it is important to point out that it is still far from linking one essential aspect relative to the acknowledgement of the naturally spiritual and transcendental nature of human beings.

THE MAIN CAUSES OF MENTAL ILLNESS

Psychiatric pathologies constitute a very complex and diverse world, and in the quest to determine its causes, a variety of interpretations have surfaced that come from different levels and distinct points of view. Generally speaking, the current scientific panorama of psychiatry is dominated by categories that we can identify as: biological, behaviorist, psychodynamic and sociogenic. Each has a particular notion concerning the causes of mental problems and the therapeutic procedures that should be followed.

The biological view comes from the position that establishes an organic theory as the main cause of mental disorders, including heredity factors and alterations in neural activities and in the biochemistry of the brain.

The focus of the behaviorist, whose primary point is the observation and recording of the subject's behavior, place these disorders in the context of the interaction that exists between the individual and his or her surrounding environment, and designate them as pathologies that are produced within learning processes.

In the psychodynamic perspective, the unconscious world plays a determining role. Here mental imbalances originate from states of anxiety that are released as a result of the eternal conflict between the pleasure principle and the repressions that are triggered by censorship, which obey the reality principle.

The sociogenic position stresses that family relationships, and social, cultural, political, and environmental factors are the main determinants of mental health disorders. Followers of this inclination have grouped themselves into what has been called anti-psychiatry; taking a course that espouses the integral care for the patient, one less dependent on medical recourse and more dependent on the understanding of the problems resulting from certain social circumstances.

Admitting that an appreciable percentage of the causes of mental disorders (for in their origin and evolution a combination of factors may present themselves) are as yet unknown, and that many people do not respond to solely one of the above approaches, the causes that set off mental illnesses may be summarized, in general and in light of clinical practice, in the following list of factors:

Exogenous factors:

Cranioencephalic trauma or Severe Traumatic Brain Injury – Various blows to the head can produce states of unconsciousness, even coma, leaving an aftermath of multiple disorders.

Radiation - Permanent exposure without appropriate protection to X-rays, lasers and nuclear medicine can produce amnesia, confused states, spatial and time disorientation.

Drugs – Drug addiction; including ethyl alcohol, barbiturates, stimulants, hallucinogens and other substances immediately produces severe psychiatric and somatic disorders that gradually disorganize the personality in an irreversible manner.

Viral and bacterial infections – Diverse infections or contagions can affect the central nervous system, causing hallucinatory states, lethargy, depression, and depending on their complexity, states of confusion and progressive general paralysis.

Deficiencies:

Vitamins - Vitamins are organic substances that are indispensable in small doses for the growth and well-functioning of the entire organism. Some high levels of certain types of vitamin deficiencies can cause confusion, hallucinations and psychotic episodes.

Oxygen - Especially in newborn babies, this can cause major deterioration and mental retardation. Not enough, as well as too much oxygen can bring about disorders of consciousness or dissociative states.

Hormones - For example, in the case of hypothyroidism there can be episodes of depression, energy loss and memory disorders; hyperthyroidism produces states of agitation, disorientation and delirium. Hyperglycemic shock can result in irritability and certain delirium disorders. An increase in the secretion of certain hormones can bring about a series of psychiatric symptoms.

Sleep - After 72 hours without sleep a person may experience a great variety of disorders, accompanied by states of delirium and confusion.

Sensory stimuli - When someone is subjected to prolonged periods of sensory deprivation, the person can react with fears that become more acute, have hallucinations, amnesia, and can even suffer severe psychotic reactions.

Stress:

It is a situation where demands are placed on an organism, provoking a rupture in its internal equilibrium. It is expressed in a person with a manifestation of anxiety due to the demands of the person's social, biological and psychological environment, which tends to be excessive. Stress is associated with a wide range of organic, mental, and emotional ailments. For example, prolonged and heightened levels of stress can produce many psychiatric problems and psychotic states, even dementia.

Biochemical agents:

There is clear evidence that links psychiatric disorders with alterations in the brain's biochemistry. Neurotransmitters play an important part in all psychological processes, since they are the messengers of nervous impulses. These neurotransmitters are synthesized in the neurons and afterwards are stored within them. When the neuron is stimulated, the release of the neurotransmitter is activated, which at the same time stimulates the nearest nerve cell. The main substances that act as neurotransmitters are catecholamine, serotonin and acetylcholine. It has been proven that in cases of depression, there is a decrease in neurotransmitters, while there is a great increase of them in manic states.

Besides the above, the following must also be added to possible causes: **cerebral tumors** and **lesions**, and **degenerative processes** such as cerebral arteriosclerosis and senile dementia; and, **hereditary factors**.

It should be in the interest of science and in the deepest concerns for humanity to delve into the knowledge regarding the causes of mental illness, and in so doing this, it is asked that one should abandon all type of prejudice and be open to the study of any prospects or alternatives. It is imperative to have a vision of synthesis wherein all of the positive and established elements of the different schools are collected and incorporated. And, within these possibilities, Spiritism, which relying upon its vast experience stemming from the study, consideration and the satisfactory solution of countless cases, incorporates within the etiology of these mental disorders, the element of spirit obsession. It should not be confused with any other disorder, for it has specific roots and specific symptoms, and its treatment requires a special focus.

CLASSIFICATION OF MENTAL DISORDERS

The traditional diagram previously provided for two categories of mental disorders: **neurosis** and **psychosis**. Neuroses were considered less serious than psychoses because the neurotic patient acknowledges the pathological nature of his or her ailment and does not dissociate from the objective reality that surrounds him or her. However, persons who suffer from psychosis are unable to develop self-criticism because they only consider their own perceptions as reality and cannot be brought to reason by logic. Nowadays, the use of the term neurosis has been discontinued although psychosis is still utilized.

A basic reference book was finally adopted to serve as a guide for psychiatrists and clinical psychologists. It is published by the American Psychiatric Association and called *The Diagnostic and Statistical Manual of Mental Disorders* (the DSM has a wide and comprehensive listing of mental disorders that undergoes periodic revisions).

Some different types of psychiatric disorders can be grouped under the following headings:

Anxiety Disorders - Anxiety forms a part of a repertoire of responses everyone faces in specific situations, like loneliness, darkness or the unknown. The "normal" type of anxiety is different from those considered a disorder, which is characterized by the presence of constant recurring reactions of anguish. This can occur in anticipation of something, while the situation is occurring, and even after the anxiety-related situation or event has passed. In addition, it can be brought on by even an unidentifiable threat.

Phobic Anxiety Disorder - Phobia is an intense irrational fear of an object or situation that normally does not produce that reaction. Certain phobic reactions (fear of the number 13, walking under a ladder, opening an umbrella indoors, etc.) are the basis for superstitious behaviors. They are considered phobic in nature when they interfere with the normal course of the lives of people. Among the main symptoms of phobic anxiety disorders are fear, restlessness, rapid heart palpitations, and a sensation of drowning, trembling, psychomotor inhibition and loss of consciousness.

Conversion Disorder or Dissociative Disorder – Previously known as hysteria, it is a nervous disorder characterized by a variety and multiplicity of symptoms. It occurs more frequently in persons who are very sensitive and who do not dare to manifest their need to attract attention and their desire to be taken into account. They repress those personality traits in their unconscious, which they later externalize by way of somatic or convulsive crises. Sometimes it can be a reaction to very remarkable stressful situations. It is manifested in two ways: one in which the patient symbolically expresses conflict by translating it into bodily symptoms, as it is likely to occur with pseudo-blindness, pseudo-hearing loss, pseudo-paralysis, pseudo-anesthesia; and, as dissociative where there is a strong alteration in the consciousness, characterized by short or long-term amnesia, twilight states with tightening of the consciousness, sleepwalking, and can even reach a level of pseudo-dementia.

Obsessive-Compulsive Disorder - In this type of disorder, patients become obsessed with fixed thoughts or actions and even though they resist it, they feel a compulsion to act upon it, exhibiting specific behaviors in a determined and repetitive manner, for example, washing their hands a number of times because they feel extremely worried by the thought that they are full of germs. These impulses cause conflict with the person because they are always fighting them, though they have difficulty resisting their influence.

Depressive Disorders - The main symptoms are: profound sadness, pessimism, feelings of guilt, slow thought and speech patterns, lack of appetite, insomnia, drastic loss of interest in sex, anxiety, chronic fatigue, and in certain cases, suicidal tendencies. Social factors may precipitate depression because of a loss; it is perfectly normal for any person who is faced with the death of a loved one or the break-up of a relationship to become depressed, but what turns that normal reaction into a more serious situation is the disproportionate intensity and duration of the reaction. Heredity as well as changes in neurotransmitters in the brain and in endocrine functions may also be factors.

Depersonalization Disorder - It occurs when the patient reacts with feelings of strangeness with respect to his or her own personality and physical structure. Patients who have this disorder feel that their ego is dissolving because they "no longer feel like themselves." When they look in the mirror, even when there is self-awareness, they feel like they are staring at the face of a complete stranger. In its most pronounced phase, it can trigger situations of double or multiple personalities.

Derealization Symptom- Patients who suffer this condition are under a high level of anxiety because they feel that their surroundings, including other people, are totally foreign or unreal to them. Depersonalization, as well as derealization is accompanied with symptoms of anxiety, depression and obsessive thoughts.

Somatoform Disorder - Patients exhibit an excessive preoccupation with any sign or symptom occurring in their body, attributing these symptoms to serious diseases that in reality do not exist. This unjustified fear persists despite medical explanations. They imagine that they have illnesses that they have read or heard about and desperately seek professional care or self-medicate themselves. The worries of these imaginary ailing persons lead to personal, family, social, work-related breakdowns, as well as to deterioration in other important areas of their life.

Psychotic Disorders are more severe disorders that disorganize the personality and impede persons from correctly assessing the reality of the external world and their personal situations. There can be disorganized thinking, hallucinations, delusions, and bizarre speech and behavior.

When organic psychoses are present, structural lesions are evident in the nervous tissue. They are referred to as chronic when they are irreversible and incurable. The greatest deterioration occurs in the intellect. The different types of organic psychoses are established from the onset by the factors that trigger them: substance abuse related (including drugs and alcohol), syphilis related, by brain tumors, intracranial infection, head trauma, cerebral arteriosclerosis, epilepsy, senility, pre-senility, etc.

Psychotic Disorders are divided into two groups: 1) mood and bipolar disorders, and 2) schizophrenia.

In the case of mood disorders, they are marked with excessive sadness or joy over prolonged periods of time, in many cases, of an undetermined origin. The main characteristics of bipolar disorder are varying degrees of depression and mania.

Schizophrenia includes a group of severe psychotic disorders that deteriorate the patient's relationship with reality. For EUGEN BLEULER (1857-1939), the Swiss psychiatrist who coined the term in favor of "dementia praecox" proposed by KRAEPELIN, the main symptom of this illness is the displacement or splitting apart of mental functions and of the psyche, whether affective or intellectual.

Schizophrenia is characterized by: loss of reality, loss of interest in the surrounding world and withdrawal into oneself, delusions, disorganization and confusion of ideas, limited range of emotions, contradictory and changing reactions towards people and objects, as well as cognitive deficits. In progressive stages of deterioration, patients show symptoms of diminished psychomotor skills and affect displays until they experience paralysis. They also progressively lose their intellectual abilities and memory, refuse to be fed and clothed, and ultimately may succumb to death.

There are two main types of schizophrenia. Type I (positive schizophrenia) main symptoms are delusions and hallucinations. Those with Type II (negative schizophrenia) show little emotional response, poverty of speech, lack of interest in taking care of personal needs and grooming, become apathetic, unable to maintain interpersonal relationships, and feel unable to work. The five subtypes of schizophrenia are: Disorganized, Paranoid, Residual, Catatonic and Undifferentiated.

Disorganized schizophrenia - It appears early on, between the ages of 15 or 18. It is marked by disorganized thinking and weak willpower. It produces extreme regressions towards infantile behaviors. The patient's behavior becomes childlike and silly, characterized by continued restlessness, inappropriate laughter to a situation, incoherent speech and hallucinations.

Paranoid - The main disorder is manifested in cognitive functions (reasoning, judgment and memory). Patients report hearing commands or insults that "steal" or "intercept" their thoughts. They express delusional thoughts of being persecuted or harmed by others or exaggerated opinions of their own importance. Their behavior is marked by hallucinatory states. On occasion, they exhibit absurd behaviors, like taking a slight interest in philosophical and scientific matters and consider themselves great inventors or benefactors of humanity.

Residual - This type of schizophrenia shows itself in patients who have had prior schizophrenic episodes and some symptoms have remained, as if they were secondary or residual. It is characterized by emotional ambivalence that disturbs the patient's interpersonal relationships.

Catatonic – This type is characterized by disturbances (inhibition or exaltation) of movement and a high level of disorganized behavior. Patients may oscillate between states of stupor or agitation and are unable to be responsive to their surroundings; they adopt disorganized mannerisms and exaggerated speech.

Undifferentiated - It presents itself when diverse symptoms, characteristic of other types of schizophrenia come together; patients exhibit behaviors that fluctuate between depressive and manic (bipolar).

SPIRITUAL OBSESSION

To every cause of mental disorders already described, duly recognized and studied, the Spiritist doctrine incorporates its own, one whose comprehension and understanding and acceptance is indispensable so that mental illnesses may be treated completely and in a more integrated and efficient manner. Spiritism treats: OBSESSION OF A SPIRITUAL ORIGIN.

The term obsession is usually used in the context of psychopathology to indicate a mental disturbance that is characterized by persistent thoughts that dominate and torment a person, who cannot escape them even when that person knows that these thoughts lack a logical reason. This term acquires a profound meaning within Spiritist terminology because it encompasses all symptomatologies which extend its etiology even to a spiritual cause. This offers a more effective therapy, inasmuch as it does not offer simply a temporary palliative, rather it delves into the deep-rooted causes of the problem, whether from in this and from other lifetimes, and definitively solves it.

It is true that the long list of somatic, genetic or environmentally based causes must not be ignored, lest the psychiatric disorder be treated from a unilateral perspective, but it is also true that official psychiatry makes a grave error when it does not take into account the possibility of the intervention of a spiritual agent, in certain cases where no organic or other factors have been identified as responsible for the disorders.

Spiritism teaches that besides the social context in which the lives of incarnate men and women evolve and the changes that the physical organism endures, one must include among the factors that produce mental disturbances the disincarnated spiritual entities that proliferate around them who may harbor harmful intentions. That is why the best scientific and ethical attitude that should be adopted consists in considering these illnesses as a result of a combination of causes, material and spiritual, which can be intimately linked. Spiritist science does not oppose any of the medical scientific fields; its purpose is to complement them with Spiritism's discoveries and confirmations.

In the light of Spiritist teachings, obsession is defined as the harmful influence that a spirit exercises over another for various motives and using a variety of actions and methods, thereby provoking in their victims a number of physical, psychological and moral disturbances which affect their health and alter their behavior. This is how KARDEC defined it, with the precision that characterized him in everything he wrote:

"Obsession is the persistent action that an evil spirit exercises upon an individual. It manifests with different characteristics, from a simple moral influence without any notable outward signs, to the total disequilibrium of the organism and of the mental faculties." [113]

We live submerged in an ocean of vibrations, even though we are only aware of an infinitesimal fraction of the realities to which they belong. Above and below human sensory ranges are numerous dimensions outside of our reach, and which are accessed by mediums and those with paranormal sensitivities with the aid of their faculties. Spirits, that is, disincarnate souls, surround us everywhere influencing us in multiple ways. We are all more or less sensitive. Consequently, we are susceptible to a certain extent to being influenced by the spirits that surround us, for better or for worse, in accordance to how we live or behave, whether for good or bad. Allan Kardec became aware of this from the moment of his first contacts with the spirits, and when these confirmed that these influences are frequent. He made note of it in the first of his great works:

"Do spirits influence our thoughts and actions?
"In that respect, their influence is greater than you believe, because often times it is they who direct you." (Question 459) [114]

As it can be gathered, spiritual influences can come from loved ones, which because of their goodwill, are desirous to transmit to us a worthwhile message or to encourage reflection, or inspire a beautiful thought. However, the same sort of influences can be exercised by spiritual beings that resonate from an inferior moral level that are motivated by rancorous and vengeful impulses that propose to do harm to those that oppose them or that they

---

[113] ALLAN KARDEC. *La Génesis* [Genesis], Ch. XIV, La obsesión y posesión [Obsession and Possession]. p. 243.

[114] ALLAN KARDEC. *El Libro de los Espiritus* [*The Spirits' Book*]. Ch. XI: Intervention of spirits on the material world. N. 459. Ibid. p. 189.

are jealous of. When spiritual influences are poisoned with these harmful characteristics, this is when, and with all likeliness we are dealing with obsession.

Psychic influences move in all directions. The same way that disincarnate beings influence those who are incarnate, so too does the latter influence the former; in reciprocity, in step with certain processes of similarity and harmony that link the participants. In a like-minded work that stands out for its functional orientation, as well as for its appeal, the well-known Brazilian writer WILSON GARCIA clarifies:

"Of one thing we can be certain: spirits influence our thinking in the same manner that we influence theirs, in other words, the reciprocal is true. Just as we act upon fluids and give them a quality, spirits do this also. If we have the power to influence other people, to transmit to them our thoughts and along with them fluids of equal quality, it would be fair to acknowledge that spirits have the same power. Well then, only one thing needs clarification: well beyond giving a quality to fluids, our thought defines the type of spirits that should live with us.

There is a popular saying that affirms this in the following: 'tell me who you keep company with and I'll tell you who you are.' In Spiritism we can say, 'tell me who you are and I'll tell you what company you keep.' That is the way it is because through our behavior and way of thinking, we can determine the class of spirits that live together with us. A person, who is accustomed to bad-mouthing others, will certainly keep company with spirits that are known for their indiscretions. An individual that is resolved to commit a robbery will attract the influence of villainous spirits, capable of encouraging him to fulfill that wish and even assist him in committing it.

Functioning here is the law of affinity. Kindred spirits that share the same types of thoughts and the same inclinations end up attracting and living together with each other. That phenomena is not unknown, for we know that, in our society, that also happens;

persons are attracted to each other according to common factors: professions, their tastes and through their interests, no matter what these are." [115(1)]

Not in the area of obsession or in its doctrinal vision does Spiritism acknowledge the existence of the devil or demons, which some religions blame for many mental disorders, primarily those concerning obsession. What there is are spirits lacking moral evolution; that act wickedly or are of a mocking character with the intention of tricking or manipulating their victims. Obsession is a natural and not a supernatural fact that is related to certain physical and spiritual pathologies whose roots lie in the lowest moral levels of the majority of the people who make up humanity. Kardec established well that concept with simplicity and truth when he stated, "If bad men did not exist on Earth, there would not be evil spirits around the Earth."

CAUSES OF OBSESSIONS

Obsession is a two-sided relationship: on one hand, there is someone who owes, and on the other hand, there is someone who feels entitled to collect. It is a relationship that exists wherein, despite the difference in the levels of responsibility, a reciprocal bond splits the blame between the aggressors and the assailed. To a great extent, victims psychologically and fluidically facilitate the penetration of their mental field by the obsessor, be it through their thoughts or actions.

---

[115] WILSON GARCIA. *Vocé e os espiritos* [*You and the spirits*]. EME publishing, Capivari, SP, Brazil, 1993, pg. 28 (As mentioned previously the word "fluids" is in keeping with Spiritist terminology, but the word "energies" can be substituted).

Moral imperfection is generally the basis why obsessive processes develop.

This is further reaffirmed when the factors involved in every obsessive process are analyzed. It is true that there are obsessing entities that appear for no specific reason, only for the morbid pleasure to bother or harm. However, most of the time that such pathologies of a spiritual origin appear, there are concrete and specific causes that link the persons in this unhealthy drama.

These are the principal causes of spiritual obsession:

Revenge - The eager desire for vengeance can plunge any human being into a whirlwind of negative and harmful vibrations that are clearly displayed with all their destructive weight within the obsessive process. The source of the conflict can be located in the current life, as well as in past lives. Its main theme has to do with the intention of settling a wrong committed by the current victim against the current obsessor, who at the same time was a victim in a former time. Displaying its moral deficiencies, the persecuting spirit seeks to find relief for its suffering by making the one who harmed it, suffer, thus involving both parties in a situation of unhappiness and desperation. In addition, there are also spirits that are very distressed when they are prevented from reincarnating because they want to live with or among specific individuals.

Disordered Thoughts - Pride, vanity, selfishness, envy, oppression, ill-treatment and manipulation of others, addictions (to alcohol, nicotine, illicit drugs and other substances), lack of sexual control (deviations, perversions, immoderate or vilified use of pornography), as well as the imbalance and poor use of mediumship faculties (using mediumship for commerce and profit, casting supposed spells or hexes to harm third parties, frauds, etc.) are behaviors that attract inferior spirit entities. They resonate with the lowest and meanest passions and desire to place those who are morally weak under their influence and power. They find in those actions the psychic gaps where they can penetrate, and then become linked to their victims.

The inhabitants of the spirit world are certainly the very same human beings who lived in the material world; they are disincarnated beings or spirits. They continue to have the same personality traits and the same positive or negative habits and tendencies. Some continue to resonate with the same negative inclinations that they displayed in their last material existence, approach certain persons to influence and control them, especially if these persons allow it or make it easier on account of their inferior behaviors. They turn into intrusive personalities that are parasitical in their mental sphere. They intercept a person's thoughts, weaken his or her willpower and take ownership of a person's actions, provoking great suffering and becoming the source of a wide range of mental disturbances.

It is necessary to emphasize that just the opposite occurs when highly developed spirits, or our spirit protectors and friends, radiate to us their loving thoughts, transmit to us messages of hope and enthusiasm as well as encourage us to take a virtuous path in life. Those elevated psychic emanations comfort us and contribute to our physical, moral, and spiritual health.

Negative, Immoral or Malevolent Thoughts - Thought is a vibration that has profound repercussions which can have an effect on people, animals or plants, as well as being able to produce alterations in physical bodies. Thought is a form of electromagnetic energy that can become objectifying, as in the phenomena of ideoplasty, or the shaping of mental images into concrete forms, which may be observed by psychics and may even cast an impression on a photographic plate.

Each thought is a psychic wave that becomes synchronized with whoever is on that same vibratory frequency. In this manner, an idea, where certain thoughts and feelings are being transmitted by a being, whether incarnate or disincarnate, ends up being fixated into the mind of another being, again whether incarnate or disincarnate, as long as there is an affinity between them. These ideas are attracted or rejected depending on the type of thoughts that are being radiated, thereby establishing a circuit of mental synchronization.

Our mind acts like a station that transmits and receives ideas that come from other minds. If there is an affinity, synchronization is established; and, within mental fields a process of reciprocal feedback occurs. From the moment that our thoughts and feelings, with their subsequent conversion into words and conduct, are dominated by moral inferiority (infected by hatred, envy, pride or of the lowest of passions), we attract entities that identify themselves with our vibrations and these entities turn into troublesome guests in our mental household. An unhealthy symbiosis begins to take shape, in which we end up being relegated to the rule of their commands, thereby developing into an obsessive process. The law of affinity is relentlessly fulfilled: by our good thoughts and feelings we become joined together with friendly and protective spirits, but with detrimental and destructive ideas, we attract frivolous and obsessive spirits. *Similia similabus*: like attracts like!

Other Causes

Besides those already mentioned, which are the most common, obsession can be the product of other causes that often surface in mediumship sessions. These involve cases of disincarnate spirits who cling to persons in the material plane with whom they shared a romantic or sexual relationship and do not accept for those people to begin new personal relationships. They have not adapted to life in the spirit world. In addition, obsession may develop among those people involved in cases of indiscriminate spirit evocations, whether among groups of friends who "play games" with a Ouija board, etc. or in social groups that are governed by religious and mediumistic syncretism, where African, indigenous and Catholic rituals are fused and confused with practices of witchcraft and sorcery. These situations are teeming with inferior spirit entities anxious to showcase their psychic powers and keep under their whimsical commands the greatest number of their victims. Cases of obsession can be found where people have superstitious behaviors and with those involving gullibility and religious fanaticism, which lead individuals to psychologically depend on amulets and talismans or ritualized prayer and miracles, instead of having a serene and rational trust in God. Cultivating values of education, work, and love are what constitute the paradigm that should be guiding human beings toward the mastery of a greater destiny, as free and conscientious creatures that are in a permanent process of evolution.

At times, some situations occur that more appropriately should be considered as unsatisfactory or negative spiritual influences and not cases of obsession. This may happen when a spirit approaches a living person without intentions of harm, because it feels that it has something in common with that person, because it enjoys being around him or her, or because it finds solace in that person's company. However, it unknowingly or unintentionally transfers the signs or symptoms of the illness that caused its death. It can also transfer any psychic disorders that affect it and that still leave a mark and trace on its perispirit; acting like a bioenergetic matrix where all of the consequences of its physical and mental states are reflected. The U.S.-born psychiatrist KARL WICKLAND (1861-1945) proved incidents of this category in numerous cases in a great number of patients that he treated in his Chicago clinic (The Psychopathic Institute). There he used innovative techniques with the intention of freeing them from their obsessive disorders, such as the application of small doses of electroshock and the assistance of his wife's mediumship faculties. He recorded the clinical experiences he applied toward "disobsession" [116(1)] in a book entitled *Thirty Years Among the Dead* that strongly attracted the attention of psychiatrists and investigators around the world who were interested in the subject. In addition, Dr. IGNACIO FERREIRA (1904-1988), a pioneer in spirit-oriented psychiatry and Director of the Sanatorio Spirita de Uberaba [Spiritist Sanatorium of Uberaba], a city in the Brazilian state of Minas Gerais, studied and treated many cases having to do with the harmful consequences that ailing spirits cause, even if unintentionally, when they latch on to the mental spheres of persons with whom they feel safe and comfortable with.

---

[116] The new term "spirit release" has recently come into use in England and the United States.

If the pathological consequences that could affect any person involved in the schemes of an obsessive process are serious, think of what could happen to mediums, considering that their hyper-sensibility places them in a more direct and frequent relationship with spirits. That is why the Spiritist doctrine is so insistently concerned with the education and moralization of mediums, for they can become easy prey for obsessive spirits if their thoughts and behaviors slip down the slope to frivolity, pride, fraud or commercialization of their faculties.

VARIETIES OF OBSESSIVE ACTIONS

Spiritual obsession is a very complex process, having multiple causes. There are many types of obsessive actions. They can occur when:

A spirit influences a human being: This is the most common type of obsession because the spirit obsessor is invisible. This allows it to come into close proximity with its victim without detection and enables it to project its morbid thoughts, images, orders, and mental suggestions.

It can happen for a variety of motives, among which prevails the thirst for vengeance, where the obsessor resonates typically at the level of its moral backwardness. In addition, due to the predisposition of a living person to develop and transmit sinister or perverse thoughts, these find resonance among spirits in the spiritual plane that resonate in a similar way through attraction and affinity.

A spirit influences another spirit: The same impulses that lead a spirit to try to dominate or harm a living person are the same that precipitate obsessions among spirits in the spiritual domain. Conflicts take place in the spiritual world, as on earth, like the sequence of the same play that enfolds in several acts.

The yearning for vengeance to settle the score and to complain about unfulfilled promises, prompt the obsessive action of one spirit against another. Often times it involves the continuation of an abnormal bond that was originally established in past epochs when one of them or both were living persons in other existences.

A human being influences a spirit: This can occur when there is a mental fixation by people in the material world that desperately cling to memories and images of loved ones who have preceded them in disincarnation. They have not accepted the reality of the situation and consequently they may sink into the throes of depression. This causes the spirit to become frustrated and extremely upset.

In the midst of bitterness and inconsolable expressions of grief, these persons transmit mental vibrations that make the spirit suffer, keeping it magnetized to them within a state of confusion and emotional turbulence.

This unfortunate situation, almost in protest of the spirit having disincarnated before them, to a degree, reflects the erroneous religious or materialist misconceptions about death. These circumstances, many times unintentional, becomes a strong obsession that hurts the deceased, who, on the contrary, is in need of harmonious, serene, consoling, and guiding vibrations to help overcome its state of confusion and find the right path to continue to evolve in the spiritual plane. It is necessary to make clear that this type of obsession can have a much more disturbing side when the thoughts and emotions of those in the material plane are saturated with resentment, discord or evil.

A human being influences another human being: This situation occurs quite frequently in the family and social circles of people, as a direct consequence of selfishness that rules and makes them act in a way that makes others revolve around them and their whims. Kardec placed selfishness at the heart of all human weaknesses:

"A child of pride, it is the source of whatever miseries abound on earth. It is the denial of charity and, consequently, it is the greatest obstacle to the happiness of mankind." [117]

There is obsession between living persons when a domineering father tyrannizes his children, exploits them financially or interferes with their development by arbitrarily bridling their initiatives or imposing decisions on their studies or vocations. On the contrary, it is present in the inconsiderate attitudes of children who abuse the love of their parents and subject them to their every whim and fancy. In the relationships between a man and woman, those who have strayed from the important values that should unite a couple, like love, respect or solidarity, and who succumb to the torments triggered by uncontrollable jealousy or possessiveness and domineering love. These obsessions can reach very deep pathological levels and can even produce suicides and murders. When the sexual component cannot be channeled within feelings of love and respect for the dignity of one another, it becomes distorted to the point of turning into an instrument that unleashes all sorts of subjugating passions. Genuine obsessions can occur in the scenarios of social life that enchain living persons when pride, wickedness, slander or the thirst for money and power, prevail in the relationships they establish.

Self-obsession: A person can become his or her own victim of psychological and spiritual imbalances. Self-obsession, therefore, fits within the complex framework of mental illnesses, whose main pathological symptom is as a result of acute single-mindedness that makes persons focus on one word, thought, or subject, and which propels them to behave in strange and disconnected ways.

[117] *El Evangelio según del Espiritismo* [*The Gospel According to Spiritism*]. Ch. XI, N. 11 Ibid., p. 151

This complex and overwhelming situation can be the result of physical, mental, social, or other changes that occur in the current life, or which can be attributed to older causes that can date back to one or more past lives, when the particular conflicts, traumas, and anxieties may have began; and, which disincarnation and life in the spirit world did not resolve.

Degrees of Severity of Obsession:

There are some signs and symptoms that indicate that what is at hand is a case of obsession and one must pay attention to them. They are: a constant bad mood without a justifiable cause; aversion to or dislike for others who have not warranted such behavior; inappropriate, unprovoked and uncontrollable laughter; habitual physical or verbal aggression; people who repeatedly tell lies, and become linked to one another to deceive or to feign wealth, social status, or academic degrees that they do not have; beliefs that they are the reincarnation of great historical figures; manias, imbedded fears that become exaggerated and different phobias; personal neglect; job or family abandonment; social isolation, etc. Those kinds of thoughts and behaviors are frequently associated with obsessions and reveal the bond that exists between them and mental disorders, because they share common symptoms. Their difference lies in the investigation of their cause.

Spiritual obsession has multiple and very different characteristics, relative to the degree of aggressiveness in which it is manifested and the consequences it releases. Following Kardec's classifications, there are three levels of obsession:

Simple Obsession – This is the type that a spirit exhibits when it meddles in the mental sphere of a person, causing psychological or physical discomfort. The obsession interferes in the thoughts of its victim and opposes the victim's will. Generally, the victim is aware that he or she is under the effects of a negative influence and feels discomfort, although the obsessor may not cause severe disturbances.

We all have been exposed to suffer obsession at this initial level, if we have experienced the already mentioned situations, which have to do with the way we are, think, and act. Naturally, we can overcome it and regain normality, if we humbly show the disposition necessary to remedy it.

Fascination – The obsessor fills the senses of its victim with illusions, deceives his or her victim, and persistently seeks the victim's cooperation until it obtains it, deprives the victim's ability to be self-critical, with excessive praise, keeps the victim far away from those who can make the victim aware of his or her faults, and makes the victim act the way it dictates. The deceit is so great that the victim grows to fanatically believe the absurd ideas of the obsessor and becomes upset with anyone that tries to make him or her come to reason.

When mediums become fascinated, the situation is much more serious and dangerous, because their mediumship abilities become distorted, and they are only in tune to the meddling and mocking spirit(s) and block the good spirits that wish to help them. The obsessor deceives the medium in many ways, even by manifesting itself under different guises to make the medium believe that there are different spiritual entities involved. Once the domination is complete, the obsessor excites the medium to act in a ridiculous fashion. Many mediumship communications that come from fascinated subjects contain the most extravagant ideas, and once they are spread by gullible persons or fanatics, they can cause great harm to the prestige of mediumship and of Spiritism.

Subjugation - It is the most complex degree of obsession. It is sometimes referred to as "possession," but this is not the most appropriate word. Here, the obsessor completely controls its victim, morally as well as physically, to the extent of triggering severe pathological disturbances that could lead the victim to insanity.

The subjugated victim makes the most absurd and incoherent decisions and behaves in the most aggressive, extravagant, and ridiculous manner. His or her mind succumbs to every sort of paranoid delusion and slowly loses touch with reality. The obsessor does not really "enter" the body of its victim; rather it exercises absolute mental control, taking over the victim's willpower, rather similar to what occurs during a state of deep hypnosis.

In his book, *The Psychic Evolution*, Gabriel Delanne devoted many chapters to the study of obsession and its relationship to madness and other mental disorders, highlighting the need for Spiritists to have knowledge of psychiatric criteria and for physicians to become more familiar with spiritual factors. The great French master stated:

> "Spiritism offers a logical explanation to certain states of the spirit that have been classified as insanity, but that are not. There are certainly among them false perceptions and mental disturbances, attributed to an obvious action; however, it is analogous to which suggestion produces among living persons and its causes should be sought in the spiritual world. What makes it very difficult to distinguish spirit obsession from insanity is the fact that the senses are exposed to hallucinations without external intervention, after certain nervous system disorders. Therefore, it requires great practice and discernment to be able to distinguish whether the illness is due to one or the other cause, and that is why it is desired that specialists that normally treat [persons having] hallucinations, would consent to approach the matter from the point of view just described: we are inclined to believe that this would result in great progress for this offshoot of medicine." [118]

Having vast knowledge of the theoretical and practical aspects of Spiritism and of psychic sciences in general, Delanne brings to the forefront a theory of great importance to the understanding of the mechanisms of mental and spiritual health that occur in cases of obsession, considering that they are similar to the procedures in hypnosis:

> "Many persons who are obsessed are treated as if they are insane because what they acknowledge being the result of

---

[118] GABRIEL DELANNE. *La Evolucion Animica*, Editorial Victor Hugo, Buenos Aires, 1948, pg. 204

irresistible spiritual suggestions is attributed to simple hallucinations. When one sees a subject under hypnosis laugh, cry,
experience pleasure or pain, become astonished or seized with
fright, passively perform the strangest, most foolish or dangerous actions, according to hallucinatory scenes being suggested,
one can understand obsession. One can see that the action of
the spirit upon the obsessed person is similar in nature to that of
what the hypnotizer exercises on his or her subject, with the only
difference that in cases of obsession, there may be more than
one spirit that is suggesting these actions, and because they are
invisible, they are impervious to regular medical procedures." [119]

Spiritist Treatment of Obsession

In general, obsession is not easy to cure, in some cases those
with deep seated roots are not curable in the current lifetime of the
person involved. Fortunately, for the majority of cases, a treatment
that is geared to the spiritual aspect of the problem and its sources
achieves results that are efficient and long lasting.

The Spiritist doctrine, with its focus on therapeutic practices to
treat obsession, rejects the practice of exorcism, which is a ritual that
is sanctioned and practiced by many movements within Christian religions. First of all, this is due to the fact that Spiritism does not allow
or promote rituals of any kind, nor does it utilize material objects or
substances that are presumed to be miraculous. Secondly, because exorcisms uphold the belief that it is the devil that is causing the problems
and Spiritism does not accept the existence of such a personage; it attributes the cause of the obsessive process to morally inferior spirits, those
of human and not superhuman, beings. Finally, because exorcisms are
based on actions that seek a violent expulsion of the perturbing entity,
meanwhile those that apply the Spiritist approach seek to understand
the causes that give rise to the problem. The Spiritist practice proceeds
in the moralization and education of all parties involved in the complex

---

[119] GABRIEL DELANNE. Ibid., pg. 199.

obsessive machinations, until by means of persuasion, contrition, and pardon, the longed for solution to the conflict is achieved.

Spiritist groups that in a beautiful expression of having assimilated the ethical values of this doctrine, set to work on the task of dealing with cases of obsession, will find in the following guidelines useful tips on how to obtain the best results:

- It is convenient to advise a person who has come to a Spiritist Center in search of assistance, with a supposed situation of obsession, to first undergo any necessary medical, psychological, and/or psychiatric testing to determine if there are any organic or psychological factors that may be causing the disturbance. Spiritists do not indiscriminately attribute spiritual or mediumship type causes to all disturbances that

- alter a person's mental faculties. That is why it is prudent for the person to be duly examined before receiving assistance at a Spiritist Center; that way a mistaken interpretation of symptoms may not be attributed to a spiritual source, when in fact they have a medical explanation.

- The person will be interviewed. A disorder as complex as obsession requires as much information as possible, such as a personal history and the particular circumstances involved. The spirit, which is behind this unhealthy situation, must be found, as well as the subjective meaning of the same, the conditions by which it established itself, the factors at hand and remote ones that have contributed to its appearance, and all of the elements that could influence its development. Without a personal focus of the person's suffering; it would not be possible to fully analyze the inter-relationship of the physical, social, psychological and spiritual aspects and the degree of participation of each one in the investigation and source of the situation.

- The person under obsession is advised to perform a self-analysis in order to evaluate his or her own behavior and life in general. He or she is encouraged towards moralization and personal reform for the benefit of spiritual growth; to request to be forgiven for his or her transgressions or offenses, with humility; and, to elevate his or her thoughts towards the Creator and superior spirituality.

In essence, the cure for obsession is a process of self-healing.

Therefore, it is up to the victim to become free from the harmful influences that are tormenting him or her by closing the doors of his or her mind and soul, through profound moral transformation. It must be kept in mind that each human being is his or her own master, who has absolute jurisdiction over him or herself, and that no one can invade his or her psychic space if he or she does not allow it. Obsession is a state of synchronization between one's mind and other minds in various types of disequilibrium. It is everyone's duty to sever that bond and to instill a constructive direction to one's mental processes by thinking and transmitting healthy, good and optimistic thoughts and deciding to strengthen one's willpower. Family members play an important role in the patient's re-education and recuperation by providing a healthy household that is teeming with vibrations that shelter and protect a patient from harmful influences.

Therefore, we can see that awareness and moralization are the most effective resources against obsession.

- The necessary mediumship sessions are held to determine the cause of the obsession, its origin and any others that may be involved in it, whether directly or indirectly. Participation of mediums that are appropriately trained for this sort of activity, establish a dialog with the obsessing spirit entity in order to re-educate and lead it to a favorable psychological state, thereby breaking the chains that bind it to its victim. It is important to remember that forgetting and forgiving of offenses is the best therapy in every task regarding cases of obsession.

The utmost discretion should be used in mediumship sessions designed to deal with obsessions. These meetings should be private and only involve the participation of those persons sufficiently experienced and prepared to deal with this type of work.

In addition, Spiritists are well aware of the great value of enlisting the aid of morally enlightened and superior spirits because of the wise counsel they offer and for their valuable assistance, and therefore, Spiritists always solicit their help and joint participation with love and humility. The higher moral development of the persons working with cases of obsession, the more effective the results obtained. Moral authority is the most important tool that can be exercised upon undeveloped spirits and that is the one thing they will most yield to.

Chapter Eight

MAGNETISM

"They shall lay hands on the sick, and heal them."

Jesus
Gospel of Mark 16:18

HISTORICAL OVERVIEW AND DEFINITIONS

First, it is necessary to clarify that the word *magnetism* possesses various definitions and many different meanings have been attributed to it. Generally, it is used to describe that force a person exerts over another by the use of certain distinguishing physical or psychological attributes. In the field of science, it is studied in that part of physics dealing with the properties of magnets or the movement of electrical charges. However, in our study, we will refer to this term from a spiritualist perspective, and specifically from a Spiritist point of view, to designate a psychic fluid, force or energy inherent in all human beings that can, at will, be utilized for external purposes.

The knowledge regarding the existence of this special force has been known since time immemorial. Its practical applications were fairly common among earth's ancient inhabitants. The Egyptians, Chaldeans, and Chinese, among others, practiced the art of healing by a special means of the placing of the hands on individuals as part of their sacred ceremonies. JESUS OF NAZARETH fervently recommended to his disciples the use of their hands on the sick with the intention of healing, or for the liberation of the obsessive actions of inferior spirits.

A pioneer in the methodological study of magnetism was PARACELSUS (1493-1541), who was a distinguished Swiss physician, an alchemist and proponent of hermetic philosophy. He attributed the human body with magnetic properties that acted for two purposes: first, the attraction of astral radiation for nourishment of the soul, and the other, the externalization of fluids for the benefit of other people. This idea would inspire numerous studies in this area in the centuries that followed.

The Belgian physician, JEAN BAPTISTE VON HELMONT, was a devoted disciple continuing in the tradition of Paracelsus, and has been recognized for his valuable contributions to physics, chemistry, medicine and the psychology of his time. Knowledgeable in the characteristics and possibilities of magnetism, he said in his book, *De magnetica vulnerum curatione*:

"Magnetism operates everywhere, and there is nothing new about it except for its name. There is within man an energy that solely through his will and imagination can work outside of him and provide a long lasting influence over a distant object."

He applied his magnetic force over newborns and toddlers healing them of various ailments, with the intention of setting apart magnetism as an objective agent, thus demonstrating that imagination was not an intervening factor.

The German Jesuit ATHANASIUS KIRCHER (1601-1680), developed important experimental demonstrations with his magnetic applications in humans and animals, provoking lethargic and cataleptic states.

But, it was with FRANK ANTON MESMER that magnetism obtained more recognition and popularity. In 1766, he presented his doctoral thesis on the topic before the Vienna medical faculty. The theme of his investigation dealt with the influence of the planets over the human body, and from there he expounded his theories regarding the reciprocal actions produced among celestial bodies, the earth and living beings, establishing that an omnipresent fluid of extraordinary subtlety served as a vehicle for such influences.

That subtle fluid, a general agent of all transformations, appears, due to its properties, as a magnet, and for that reason he called it animal magnetism. Through his own work, Mesmer brought back and updated the traditions of the past, surpassing the Egyptians and the teachings of Paracelsus and Van Helmont that had presented similar principles.

Thirteen years later in 1779, he made known in Paris his famous dissertation entitled, *Memoir on the discovery of Animal Magnetism*, wherein he reiterated his conviction that all human beings emit a magnetic fluid, a type of invisible and imponderable element, that by its effects, appears to be within the substance of the nerves manifesting with properties that are analogous to those of a magnet; and that, by the application of magnetic passes or the act of laying on of the hands, achieves effective cures of all types of physical and mental illnesses. Initially, Mesmer applied a magnet on the unhealthy organs of a patient, but he later was convinced that the magnet was not necessary, since the human operator acted as an accumulator and propagator of the fluid, and could direct it through rhythmic hand movements:

"The operator [is] positioned in front of the subject, in such a way that is in opposition to the magnetic poles, and one begins by putting hands over the shoulders [of the sick individual], continuing after a while to the arms until the tips of the fingers; the operator should have in his hand, for a while, the subject's thumb. Do this two or three times, until the operator establishes a current from head to the feet, and in this manner, looks for the cause and location of the illness and of the pain, and even its cause. Provided by such indications, the operator constantly touches the origin of the illness and maintains the symptomatic pain until they become critical. One must touch, within the mentioned posture, with the thumb and index finger, or with the palm of the hand, or with a finger reinforced by another finger, and following when possible the direction of the nerves, or finally with the five fingers open and curved. Touch at a short distance is more powerful because there exists a current between the hand or conductor that is being used and the sick..."

In his *Memoirs*, in these explanations presented by Mesmer, it is important to keep in mind that what he meant by "conductor" (besides the use of hands alone) was a slender glass rod, of gold or silver, through which the fluid emitted from the magnetizer, would spread, reaching all the parts of the body in which the rod made contact with.

Finally, Mesmer took up residence in a Parisian hotel, and as his fame rose rapidly in a few months, it transformed into a sanatorium confirmed by the crowds of people, that went there from all social classes and with illnesses of all kinds. Unable to attend the numerous patients who sought his help, he adopted the procedure of magnetizing objects or water, especially with the creation of the popular *baquet* or tub-like object in which various pointed iron rods stuck out, so many patients could touch the unhealthy parts of their bodies to it. This then created a great variety of nervous and hysterical reactions en masse, but with effective cures in many cases. It could be stated that with his excess of patients and work, Mesmer introduced group therapy. Mesmerism (as his concepts and system came to be known) caused a great furor in Europe, and became the central topic of conversation of the day which caused conflicting reactions, with enthusiastic followers as well as fierce enemies. In France, a scientific commission in 1784 was appointed by King Louis XVI to investigate the situation. A number of sick who had been treated with Mesmer's system were interviewed and the facts of the effects were recognized, but these were attributed to people's imagination. There were disagreements, and the decision of the commission was not unanimous. [120]

[120]   EUGENE BLISS, M.D. *Multiple Personality, Allied Disorders, and Hypnosis.* Oxford University Press, New York. Ch. 1, pp.11-14.

After this, two theories formed: those in favor of the positive results that could be obtained through the application of animal magnetism (the fluid hypothesis) in opposition to those who were convinced that all the effects were the product of suggestion (the animist hypothesis). This disparity continues to the present day.

Among those who continued Mesmer's work, the most distinguished was Marquis ARMAND DE PUYSEGUR (1751-1825) who is recognized as the discoverer of artificial somnambulism (magnetic sleep) and a pioneer of investigational parapsychology, and who foresaw a relationship between magnetism and the phenomenon of extrasensory perception. Around the same time, the German chemist KARL VON REICHENBACH (1788-1869), after the realization of numerous experimental and ingenious experiences, admitted the existence of a psychic force, he called the Od, equivalent to the magnetic fluid of magnetism. Based on the results of his studies, he affirmed that the odic force manifested itself in the form of colorful emissions that radiate around people forming an aura. [121]

Other researchers that gave emphasis to the study of magnetism were: JOSEPH PHILLIPPE FRANCOIS DELEUZE (1753-1828), librarian of the Museum of Natural Sciences of Paris and author of one of most important books on this topic, *Critical History of Animal Magnetism*; JEAN DE SENNEVOY, better known as the Baron DU POTET, who attended the patients at the General Hospital of Paris with the use of magnetic applications for numerous years, where he recognized the great possibilities that could be derived by magnetic applications; JOHN ELLIOTSON, (1791-1868), an English physician founded and directed the first mesmeric hospital of London; and, JAMES ESDAILE (1808-1859), who developed his medi-

---

[121] The term "Od" as coined by REICHENBACH, has the following origin: "Va" in the Sanskrit language means breath; in Latin "vado" and the word "vada" from the ancient Nordic signifies "travel rapidly" or "flow." Wodan proceeds from the ancient Germanic language and means "Penetrating all." In the different languages, its meaning is modified taking on the significance of the "power that penetrates all," adopting the forms of "wooden," "odan," "odin." Reichenbach indicates that the word "od" is a phonetic symbol used to designate all that is in nature that has an incessant power, a penetrating force that flows from everything that exists.

cal career in Calcutta and there founded a mesmeric hospital. In different reports that he sent to medical societies in India and in

England, he relayed how he performed more than 2,000 operations, including 300 major surgeries under the effects of anesthesia obtained through the use of magnetic applications. In addition, HECTOR DURVILLE (1848-1923), General Secretary of the Magnétique Société [Magnetic Society] of France, was also a notable researcher and enthusiastic disseminator of magnetism and its therapeutic applications.

The history of magnetism branches definitively into two with the publication of the book: *Neurypnology: or the Rationale of Nervous Sleep*, where magnetism is considered to be a form of "nervous sleep," by Scottish medical physician JAMES BRAID (1795-1860). He reaches the conclusion that the same results obtained through the use of magnetic passes may be also achieved without their application, instead, while making a patient focus his or her sight on a shinny object or through the use of verbal suggestions. Thus, hypnotism was born, and it followed different historical pathways than those of magnetism. Obviously, there are some similarities between the two, but since the basic definitions used within the two fields of study as well as the procedures used to induce the psychical and physiological changes are very distinct, and generally utilized for different purposes, one can affirm that both are two independent phenomena.

Throughout the twentieth century, spectacular cures have been known to occur around the world in different countries by the laying on of hands and other magnetic applications. SERGE LÉON ALALOUF (1905-1982) was one of those healers who reached an extraordinary level of prestige. When he was being accused by a French court for "illegally practicing medicine" the judges were obliged to absolve him, when he was able to demonstrate that he had produced 327,000 effective cures of which he had documented testimonies, along with a great many letters written by physicians who knew of his work. AMBROSE WORRAL (1910-1972) in the United States, cured successfully thousands of sick people by imposing his hands over the affected areas, and there are many well documented cases where there was reduction and disappearance of malignant tumors. DZHUNA DAVITASHVILI became very famous in the old Soviet Union, during the decade of the eighties because of her success treating president LEONID BREZHNEV with magnetic applications that the Soviets called "bio-energy." Pertaining to DAVITASHVILI's faculties, the Spanish reporter Enrique De Vicente commented in one of his books:

"Dzhuna affirms that she limits herself by 'listening' to her hands which perceive the body's unbalanced zones and her hands direct themselves there. One of the academic researchers that studied her confirmed that the energy emitted by her hands inexplicably accelerated the slow "drying" process of a subcutaneous ulcer; to the extent that, twenty minutes after initiating the experiment, it was observed that the cells of the skin were beginning to regenerate. In successive experiments, Dzhuna has been able to psychically alter the blood pressure of frogs and humans beings. Another study appeared to indicate that she was able to beneficially influence the nervous systems of sick individuals." [122]

The magnetic force that is emitted from living organisms, and particularly from human beings, presents interesting analogies with the forces understood within the physics of magnetism. In the same way, in light of the science of physics, to magnetize is is to saturate, as in the lines of the magnetic force of a chunk of steel or other appropriate alloy, and will produce effects of attraction or repulsion solely when it finds itself in the presence of another magnetized body. Consequently, one can establish through analogy, that to magnetize on the level of human being interactions, this consists in that one person transfers his or her magnetic energy to another person's organism or to a specific part of it until obtaining its particular effects.

It is well known that the human body generates not only heat, but electricity and magnetism. Our body, a generator of diverse and

[122] ENRIQUE DE VINCENTE. *The Powers of the Mind.* América Ibérica S.A., Madrid, Spain 1995. p. 180.

complex radiations, emits electromagnetic waves and produces electrical currents which in circulation, creates electric and magnetic fields with their respective negative and positive charges. With respect to human magnetism, each being forms about itself fields of which have an extension and intensity that are proportional to all its mental, psychical, and emotional processes. Magnetic energy propagates following the direction of its own line of force fields, concentrating in the hands, which assume the function of electrical poles, and exteriorizes through the finger tips, these acting as hyper-sensitive terminals.

Comprehension of the healing effects of magnetism is facilitated when the human being is envisioned from a holistic and systemic perspective through which all its components reciprocally interact. From this viewpoint, illness is a manifestation wherein balance and harmony have been severed in relation to its parts. The action of magnetic energy consists in basically recovering this lost stability, exerting its influence over the subtle anatomy of the spirit, or that is to say, its perispirit, so that from there it can irradiate its effects that can alleviate or cure the physical body. Naturally, this is while counting on the patient's cooperation who should strive in favor of his or her recuperation through the harmonization of his or her thoughts, sentiments and channeling all this positive energy for overall well-being.

MAGNETISM and SPIRITISM

The magnetism of a magnet cannot be perceived by our physical senses, but that does not impede the force of its action in precise domains, and in fact, they are easy to verify. The limited sensory perceptions that characterize us are those that permit us to understand the world in a certain manner, but they do not reach the infinite possibilities of other dimensions of extraordinary richness. It would be necessary to wait for further scientific developments to understand that our five physical senses are only sensitive to extremely defined and narrow vibratory frequencies. For example, we cannot hear sounds in the infra and ultra sound levels, nonetheless, this does not constitute a valid reason to deny the existence of an array of sounds that can be found within levels that are unreachable due to our human limitations. A wide spectrum of information, energies, waves and vibrations exist that are unknown and imperceptible to us and of which our scientific instruments are still not yet able to register, however, there are some people with well developed psychic faculties that can capture them. One such is human magnetism, and where it is situated today; an imperceptible reality regarding its nature, yet verifiable by the effects produced over an organism or based on psychic phenomenon.

The concepts advanced by Mesmer during the eighteenth century and the development reached by the practice of magnetism during that century, and afterwards, opened a pathway towards the social and scientific recognition of the existence of psychic forces of a special nature. These studies concerning magnetism and som-nambulism (hypnotic state or trance) facilitated the emergence of Spiritism.

The educator RIVAIL occupied himself with the study and practice of mesmeric applications before concentrating himself on the basis and systematization of what would become known as the Spirit-ist doctrine. It was his friends involved in the study of magnetism that invited him to witness sessions in which spirits would manifest, estab-lishing in this manner an historical and ideological bridge between magnetism and Spiritism. Later on, writing while already known as ALLAN KARDEC, he conveyed this in the following statement:

"Magnetism prepared the road for Spiritism, and the rapid progress of this last doctrine is indisputably due to the popularization of the first. From the phenomenon of magnetism, of somnambulism, and of the excitement regarding spirit manifestations, it is but only one step away; its connection is to the point that, for it can be said in these terms, it is impossible to speak of one without the other. If we had stayed out of the science of magnetism, our picture would have been incomplete and we could be compared to a physics professor who refused to speak about light." [123]

In this article from his Society's Journal, Kardec presents recommendations about terminology and proposes that a difference should be made between the **magnetizer,** one who practices magnetism, and the **magnetist,** one who accepts the theory or philosophical principles of magnetism. He also clarifies that one could be a magnetist without being a magnetizer.

After the publication of *The Spirits'Book*, Kardec continued to occupy himself with all the workings of magnetism, combining wise and prudent considerations of its nature and properties, while conferring great value upon the effects that were derived in favor of recognition of the existence of the spirit, and denoting its healing applications within the ethical principles of the Spiritist doctrine. Note the importance of the response received by the spirits to the following question:

"Is it possible by means of timely help to restore the ties that were ready to break, and give back life to a person who, but for this help, would have definitely ceased to live?"
The spirits replied: "Yes, undoubtedly. Frequently, with magnetism, as in this case, can be a powerful resource because it restores to the body the vital fluids that it lacks, and of which, was not sufficient for the maintenance in the functioning of its organs." (Question 424) [124]

Examining the source from which magnetism emerges, Kardec reached the conclusion that it is a modification of the *cosmic universal fluid* and could originate from both disincarnated spirits the

---

[123] *Revue Spirite*. Magnetism and Spiritism. March of 1858.

[124] ALLAN KARDEC. *Libro de los Espíritus*. [*The Spirits' Book*], Second book, Chapter VIII: Emancipation of the Soul. No. 424. Ibid. p.177.

same as incarnated spirits, or as a result of the fluidic combination of both during the act of mediumship:

"Magnetic action can be accomplished in different ways:

1) By the fluid of the magnetizer; called *human magnetism*; its action is determined by its strength, but most of all, by the quality of the fluid;

2) By the fluid of the spirits that act directly and without an intermediary on an incarnated person, whether to heal or alleviate suffering, to initiate a spontaneous somnambulistic sleep or to exert a physical or moral influence. This is called *spiritual magnetism*, and its strength depends upon the qualities of the spirit; and,

3) By the fluids that the spirits project over a magnetizer, that serves as a conductor. This is called *mixed magnetism, semi-spiritual* or *human-spiritual*. The spiritual fluids combined with the fluid of a human, provide qualities that are lacking in the latter. The collaboration of spirits, in similar circumstances, is at times spontaneous, but is generally produced by an evocation by the magnetizer." [125]

These criteria are of great usefulness in definitively establishing the different processes that allow for the application of magnetism, and its relationship with the various beneficial objectives that may be pursued. This reaffirms that this field of study, with its theoretical and practical perspectives, are legitimately within the realm of Spiritism. Clearly, magnetism is a chapter within Spiritism.

THE AURA

All incarnated and disincarnated beings are surrounded by a luminous halo that constantly varies in its colors, in brightness, in its

---

[125] *Génesis [Genesis]* Chapter XIV. The Fluids. Ibid. page 236.

amplitude, and extension; and is generally known by the name of the **aura**. The aura is like a covering of electromagnetic forces through which all of our mental currents flow through. It is a fluidic mirror which reflects our psychic and spiritual fields; and our whole range of thoughts, emotions and feelings are projected onto it. It has been established that its constant fluctuations have a direct association with the psychological states that dominate the mind of each human being.

In ancient drawings and paintings, spiritual guides and masters are represented surrounded by luminous halos. In the same manner, pictures throughout Christian hagiographies, artists have placed an areola of light over saints' heads in recognition of their spirituality. In oriental traditions, the lighted halo does not have a symbolic meaning nor is it reserved for significant personalities, it represents the energetic force that surrounds each person.

Numerous investigators have attempted to demonstrate through various experiments the existence of the aura, of magnetism, and other psychic energies. The French physician HIPPOLYTE BARADUC (1850-1909) presented in 1895 to the Medical Academy a "memory" in his research in the field of psychic photography, through which he maintained to be capable of objectively registering an individual's aura and could measure the intensity of the magnetic fluids by using an apparatus of his invention call a Bio-meter. In 1911, a British physician, WALTER JOHN KILNER (1847-1920), a member of London's Royal College of Medicine, published his book, *The Human Atmosphere*, related to having experimentally demonstrated the visibility of the aura of any person, sensitive or not, while observing it through an alcohol solution combined with what he referred to as dicyanin. According to his observations, the aura exhibited numerous zones or bands differentiated among each other by density, color and size. In the Soviet Union, experiments developed by VALENTINA KIRLIAN (died approx. 1971) and SEMYON KIRLIAN (died approx. 1978) in the early 1940s provided an important experimental basis in favor of the existence of the aura by designing a photographic procedure that permits it to register on high frequency electrical generators the luminous energy fields that is emanated by living beings, different from the crown effect produced around physical objects.

The observation of the aura of a patient and its characteristics and variations can be of great help for a magnetizer, since it may offer valuable information regarding what is afflicting the patient and regarding the healing process. Many sensitive persons affirm that they are able to see the aura and they describe it as a force field that is in constant fluctuation. Due to its ultra sensitivity it reacts to the most minimal of influences in its surrounding, including thoughts, emotions, feelings of pleasures or affliction, while continuously varying in color, intensity, form and size. They maintain that by placing or moving hands over an ill person, a connection is developed between the two, to the point that during the process of the application of magnetism, it is as if both of their auras combine into one. Through the use of Kirlian photography, changes in the luminous halo have been observed in an individual that has been treated with magnetic applications and it has been verified that the individual's aura has been registered to have been fortified, reflecting itself to be more amplified, illuminated, more regular and continuous in all its extensions, and as if its energy had been recharged.

Regarding the colors of the aura and its diverse spectrum, the majority of researchers seem to agree that this corresponds to the particular emotional and physical states that dominate a person at that particular moment in the person's life.

From one of the best books, written by way of spirit communications and jointly received by Brazilian mediums FRANCISCO CANDIDO XAVIER and WALDO VIEIRA, below are provided some interesting concepts and information regarding the nature and properties of the aura that was expressed by a spirit that goes by the name of ANDRE LUIZ:

> *"All living beings, from the most rudimentary to the most complex, are clothed with a halo of energy that corresponds to each by their nature."*
>
> *"The psychic atmosphere, interlaced with dynamic elements, presents itself in a highly colored variety, according to the mental waves*

we emit, portraying all our thoughts in colors and images, which echo the objectives that we have chosen, be they ennobling or despicable."

And,

"Therefore, the aura is our basic omnipresent platform in all communication with another; it is the entrance to the spirit in all our activities of interchange with the life that surrounds us, of which we are observed and examined by the Superior Intelligences, felt and recognized by those similar to us, feared and hostile or loved and assisted by those that carry on in an inferior position to ours.

This is because we exteriorize, in a constant manner, a reflection of ourselves, in the contact of thought with thought, without the necessity of words for fundamental sympathies or repulsions.

It is due to that vibratory envelope, a type of fluidic cover, in which each consciousness constructs its ideal abode, in which began all acts of mediumship upon the earth. Mediumship is considered as an attribute of the incarnated being to communicate with beings freed of the physical body." [126]

CENTERS OF FORCE WITHIN THE PERISPIRIT

Located in diverse zones of the perispirit can be found a conjunction of different vortexes. They concentrate and distribute energy that originate from the spirit and are channeled throughout the physical organism.

These centers or disks have been known since ancient times, and have received the name of *chakras*, a term of Sanskrit origin meaning "wheel." And in reality, they are like wheels or disks of various dimensions within and surrounding each person, and are in

[126] FRANCISCO CANDIDO XAVIER and WALDO VIERA. *Evolución en dos mundos.* [*Evolution in Two Worlds*].Ch. XVII. Mediumship and the Spiritual Body.

a constant circular motion. They vary by size, thickness, brightness, color, and location; the same way they differ in the functions they fulfill. There are seven primary ones, and they correspond according to their position and interaction with the different parts that they regulate in an organism's system:

> **Psychic or Spiritual Centers of Force:** Crown (located at the top front and superior part of the head) and Frontal (in the front of the head, near the eyebrows).
> **Emotional Centers of Force:** Laryngeal (at the throat) and Cardiac (in the heart).
> **Vegetative Centers of Force:** Splenetic (at the level of the spleen), Gastric (located at the level of the stomach) and Genesic (located at the base of the spinal cord). [127]

The activation and harmonization of these centers of force can be achieved by way of psychic and magnetic exercises. The coronary center is directly related with the central nervous system, drives the intellectual functions and serves as the center of connection with the spirit. It coordinates and controls the functions of the other vital centers. The frontal center is associated with the functions of precognition and clairvoyance and because of this some authors speak symbolically of the "third eye" due to its location. The laryngeal center exerts control over respiration and speaking, as well as connected to the mechanisms of clairaudience and trance mediumship. The cardiac center influences the circulatory processes and directs emotions, corresponding to the ancient belief that associates the heart with feelings and emotions. The splenetic center is associated with the blood. The gastric center participates in the activities of the absorption and digestion of food. The genesic center stimulates and regulates the sexual and reproductive processes.

---

[127] The seven Chakras are commonly called: the Crown, the Brow, the Throat, the Heart, the Solar Plexus, the Navel, and Base Chakras. Also, keep in mind they have their original and specific Sanskrit names.

This knowledge can be important in the application of magnetism because it can help if one mentally focuses on the site of the problem to direct the fluidic emissions in a more concrete and precise direction.

PROCEDURES FOR THE APPLICATION OF MAGNETISM

In the administration of magnetic passes, what is essential is that we do it out of love, concentrating and mentally focusing on what we are doing, irradiating with a sincere desire in assisting a person to recuperate his or her physical and spiritual well-being. The different and various practices that are known regarding the procedures used in this process are not a primary factor of our concern here. *Whatever procedures are used, are of benefit, always and when, positive spiritual and moral values with a pure intent predominate.* To magnetize is an act of fraternal love, for it allows us to donate part of our own psychic resources for the benefit of someone else in need.

Magnetism may be applied using the following procedures:

Position of the Hands

The practice of placing one or both hands over a person originates from the most remote of times. It was practiced by the priests of numerous countries and cultures. Later on, it was considered a privilege reserved only to emperors and kings, in what became known as the "royal touch" to heal the sick. Jesus employed it with frequency and recommended its use among his disciples.

One or both hands can be applied. It is recommended placing the hands at a short distance from the superior part of the head of the recipient, and directing the magnetic energy towards the coronary center. For this application, the magnetizer should stand in front of the recipient, who should be comfortably seated, while the magnetizer extends the arms and places his or her open hands with slightly widened fingers over the recipient.

The time dedicated to the use of hands on each person will vary according to the circumstances needed as determined by the magnetizer. A general rule is to dedicate three or four minutes towards the process.

Passes

The term "Pass" is derived from the Latin and it means precisely "to pass" or "take from one place to another." It is the most applied terminology and procedure used among Spiritists, and also among magnetizers of other diverse schools, having as its essential goal to reestablish psychic and physical equilibrium. The pass, can be defined as a transfer of psychic energy from a donator to a recipient. Therefore, someone bestows, for the benefit of others who are in need, his or her own internal healthy resources, in an act of fraternal love.

There are several criteria in classifying passes. One of these takes into account the source from where the energy proceeds from, and this has served as a reference for Kardec to indicate the different ways in which the magnetic action can be confirmed as it was presented through his study of these fluids published in his book, *Genesis*. Therefore, in keeping with this line of thinking, magnetic passes can be classified as follows:

Magnetic Passes - These can be applied by any person that is disposed to voluntarily exteriorize their own magnetic resources in benefit of another human being.

Mediumistic Passes - These are those passes that apply when a medium (whether conscious, semi-conscious, or unconscious) is in harmony with a spirit that then applies passes to a person. The spirit enhances the medium's magnetic energy and primarily directs the process.

Spiritual Passes - These are energy passes projected directly by spirits from the spiritual world over incarnated beings without the need of the intermediary of a human being. Spirits can directly act over a specific person or over a group of persons.

In addition, one can also classify passes according to the overall direction of the movement of the hands and arms:

Transverse Pass – Passes are given while the arms and hands are in a crossed fashion. The palms of the hands are facing towards the recipient and the fingers are slightly tilted upwards. The arms are placed in front of the recipient in a way that they are crossed at the forearm, then are rapidly uncrossed and then crossed again, this continuing until such time is appropriate, moving back and forth every four to five minutes.

This pass is intended towards dispersion of energies which produces changes in the magnetic field of the recipient and functions as a psychic cleansing.

Longitudinal Pass - The hands are passed over the entire length of the body of the person who is receiving this action. These are passes of revitalization, to provide magnetic fortitude, which are applied from top (head) to bottom (feet) towards the subject that is placed in front of the magnetizer. These passes are applied by positioning the hands over the head, with the fingers slightly open. The hands descend down the length of the recipient, both on the left and right sides of the body, till the upper middle part of the abdomen is reached or towards the knees if the person is seated or even lower if the person is standing or laying on a bed.

The movements of the hands and arms should proceed slowly, continuously and without muscular tension. Each application of the pass should be approximately twenty to thirty seconds. The hands should be placed around ten centimeters from the recipient's body. Longitudinal passes can calm, relax, provide tranquility, and psychically comfort the individual.

Circular Passes - A hand is moved in a clockwise circular fashion, over a predetermined area of the person's body. In this manner, the energy is concentrated in a specific region of the body, associated with the corresponding centers of force in relation to the perispirit.

The majority of magnetizers use these circular movements to alleviate pain localized in a specific region of the body or to eliminate inflammation or tumors.

Magnetized Water

Water is an excellent accumulator and conductor of energy. Of all the elements of nature, it is the most capable in the absorption of psychical and magnetic radiations. Once water is permeated with these energies, and ingested, it acts as an efficient conductor of magnetism that can then disperse throughout the entire internal body of an organism, promoting the establishment of physical and psychic health.

The method is simple: hands are placed around a container of drinking water and then are slowly moved up and around it, allowing magnetism to flow in, as the will directs. This procedure may take two to three minutes. On certain occasions, spirits themselves may indicate that they will proceed to irradiate the water directly, without the participation of any incarnated person.

Other Procedures

In the application of magnetism there are many variations which are employed according to the experience and preference of the person. There are, among other procedures, the **pass at a distance** and the **self pass**. These can be helpful, as long as they are applied in an ethical and rational manner. However, those with exaggerated gesticulations or specific rituals should be avoided as they are unnecessary.

INDISPENSIBLE CONDITIONS FOR THE CORRECT APPLICATION OF MAGNETISM

Passes act as an transference of psychic-bio-energy; a fraternal and supportive act through which there is a personal displacement of the donor's magnetism, following the impulsion of his or her will, in the direction of a recipient, with the idea to help in the recuperation of his or her psychical-physical equilibrium. Magnetic forces are not a resource of exceptional beings or those endowed with magical powers. Any person is capable of exteriorizing their magnetism, and in fact, everyone does it on a routine basis without realizing it, during the different activities of his or her life. Naturally, a study regarding magnetism permits one to have a more comprehensive understanding of its practical and theoretical principles, especially for its final objectives, and a feel for its essential foundation in order to allow for a more proper and efficient application.

We have already stated magnetism is a chapter in the doctrine that is Spiritism, and its understanding and practice are highly valued within all Spiritist institutions, but this does not mean that all magnetizers are Spiritists or are orientated with the moral or technical guidelines that the Spiritist doctrine teaches.

It is also true that some people that identify themselves as Spiritists completely devote themselves to the practice of passes and similar procedures, lacking the proper Spiritist education. The actions of these other individuals may contribute towards the invention of absurd theories, the establishment of unnecessary ceremonies and rituals, and negatively complicate the exercise of magnetism with strange superstitious beliefs. The Spiritist practice of magnetism is simply a fraternal loving act.

Therefore, it is appropriate to precisely identify, based on knowledge of Spiritism, what the fundamental guidelines are and explain what the minimal conditions should be for those who wish to participate in Spiritist sessions in which magnetic passes are applied, whether in the capacity of the recipient, or as the magnetizer.

Conditions regarding the magnetizer

Spiritual equilibrium with physical, emotional and moral health - The magnetizer should be of good health to fulfill these activities, and if ill, should refrain from its practice till completely recovered. No one can transmit what they don't have, and if a person does not have good health, he or she is not in the proper condition to transmit beneficial irradiations.

Prior and during the fulfillment of their duties, and to achieve optimal results, the magnetizer should not have ingested alcoholic beverages, drugs, or excessive foods. Regarding their emotional state of being, they should be stable with internal peace and free from stress, anguish, depression, and any moral problems. Magnetizers should also be actively pursuing a morally correct path in life, practicing goodness and humility, emitting positive thoughts, and overcoming pride and selfishness. He or she should consistently strive to enrich their personal life, through study and taking advantage of the teachings of the Spiritism doctrine, and all else that would stimulate his or her moral and intellectual progress.

Knowledge and competency – If one wants to achieve good results in whatever discipline, constant study is a must. The magnetizer should educate him or herself regarding the overall scientific and technical aspects of magnetism; its origin, nature, and objectives. It is important to acquire some knowledge of human anatomy and physiology, the perispirit and its functions, and the different procedures that allow for the proper irradiation of magnetic energy.

Moderation and prudence - The magnetic pass is a natural resource that should be practiced in a simple manner, without any melodramatic behavior. The movement of the hands should not be confused with those of a random nature. The magnetizer should not give the impression that he or she is invested with "special powers" as if one were performing a magic trick. Simplicity is the best guaranty for passes that are serious, exactingly precise, and effective.

The time for each application should not extend for long periods. Experience suggests a duration that can vary between 5 to 30 minutes, depending on the specifics of each case. During this period of time, it is recommended that the two parties remain silent.

The physical and psychical capabilities of each person in donating magnetic energies has its limits, the same as in other matters, therefore the magnetizer should be observant and respectful to not compromise his or her own health. The magnetic pass should not be applied every day or at all hours. Once or twice a week, with rest periods of three to four days is considered reasonable.

Receipt of magnetic energy (either by magnetic passes or from irradiated water) does NOT replace professional medical care for any problems a person may have, and a person should always seek this help first. Also, if a person is already receiving medical treatments, he or she should continue these as long as is required. There are no contraindications regarding receiving the benefit of professional medical care along with the support offered by magnetism, and many times they can work in unison. The Spiritist magnetizer does not compete with, and is not a substitute for, medical professionals or other health care providers, and does not pretend to do so.

Conviction - The magnetizer should be calmly resolved and convinced about the existence of magnetic energy and the positive results obtained by its application. This conviction of will acts as an impulsion that drives the magnetic energy and conducts it towards the physical and spiritual areas that need to be reached. If the magnetizer has self-doubt about the effectiveness his or her powers, if skepticism and uncertainty prevail, and there is not a firm acknowledgement of the positive results that may be achieved, the magnetizer can block the projection of his or her own magnetism and not allow for the desired results. Those that find themselves in this mental state should not apply magnetism, since positive results will be difficult to obtain, and they may attribute failure to everything except to their own lack of conviction, which is the actual cause.

Will power is the force that mobilizes, shapes, and orientates the magnetic fluid, which is neutral in its natural state, but transforms into an active agent with the impulse of a person with a strong disposition and is sustained by a profound and honest conviction.

Concentration- Prior to the application of magnetic passes, the magnetizer should concentrate and try to obtain a state of calmness and mental serenity that distances him or herself from the distractions and preoccupations of daily life. Thoughts should solely be concentrated towards what is about to be executed and with an intense desire to offer fraternal love and support to the recipient. The magnetizer should mentally try to unite with the recipient so they can link together within the same psychic flow, until obtaining a maximum level of affinity between them. One should not begin the magnetic application process or other similar procedures until one has achieved this inner state of empathy. Once this level of concentration is obtained the magnetic energy can easily flow and converge over the recipient and splendid results may be obtained.

Appropriate Time, Location, and Atmosphere - The ideal place for the application of magnetism is at a Spiritist center, for it carries a most adequate psychic and spiritual atmosphere. Especially, if the focus of attention is to deal with the serious problems that may be associated with spiritual obsessions, due to the affinity of vibrations, there is a greater possibility for the establishment of cooperative participation of spirits assisting in a collaborative effort with the magnetizer, and in receiving inspiration on how to proceed with each case.

In those Spiritist centers that have adequate and/or large facilities, a specific place can be assigned for the exclusive practice of magnetism, where the best physical and psychic conditions can be met.

Although it is true that magnetic passes can be applied at any hour of the day or night; due to reasons of order and methodology, it is more convenient that regularity be established for its application for the benefit of both the recipient and the magnetizer, since all must fulfill family, social and work responsibilities.

Solicitation of spiritual assistance - It is not necessary that all who provide magnetic passes be mediums. It was Kardec himself who spoke of this and perfectly clarified the differences that exist regarding magnetic passes. First, there is the condition where the fluids are derived from an incarnated person; secondly, when the fluids are from the spirits through the intermediary of a medium; and finally, when spiritual fluids are projected in a form directly to incarnated individuals from the spiritual plane.

"Who says medium, is saying intermediary. The difference between the magnetizer, strictly speaking, and the healing medium, is that the first magnetizes with his own personal fluids, and the second with the fluids of the spirits, with the latter serving as a conductor. Magnetism where fluid is produced by a person is called human magnetism; on the other hand, the fluid that comes from the spirits is spiritual magnetism." [128]

However, when an incarnated person is applying a magnetic pass with the intent that the energy or fluids is to come from him or her personally, this does not restrict the participation and assistance of spirits that have an affinity with that person. Taking this possibility into account, it is appropriate then that the magnetizer, during his or her concentration in providing magnetic passes, should therefore request for spiritual assistance and protection. Continuing with what Kardec stated in the above cited text, by establishing this sort of affinity the effects of magnetism will multiply:

"Every magnetizer could become a healing medium if he has assistance of the good spirits. In this case, the spirits come to your aid,

---

[128] *Revue Spirite.* Regarding the healing Mediumship. September, 1865.

offering their own fluid, of which doubles or enhances a hundredfold the action of the fluids purely from the human."

It is very important that the magnetizer maintain an intuitively harmonious relationship with his or her spirit guides and spirit friends; those spirits that will always suggest to the magnetizer helpful ideas towards fulfillment of the act of magnetism and who will add of their own spiritual fluids as a further resource. There is much to be gained and nothing to be lost when one adds this practice, and, it is this which clearly marks a difference between a Spiritist magnetizer and a magnetizer under the original mesmeric tradition.

Give freely – In conformance with the principles of the Spiritist doctrine, the service of providing magnetic passes in all its applications is an act of fraternal love. It should be fulfilled absolutely without any monetary interest and guided by the noblest and sincerest of desires to help fellow human beings. This is in keeping with the teachings of Jesus who said, "…Give as freely, as you have received!" [129]

In the Spiritist practice, economically benefiting from the application of magnetic passes diminishes its efficacy and distances those elevated spirits that could assist. Spiritist magnetizers give with fraternal love their own psychic resources in benefit to others, acting as a spark to generate health and harmony without expectation of remuneration of any kind. They are simply willing to do good for the immense satisfaction of just doing good for its own sake.

For the person receiving magnetism (or magnetic passes):

The necessity of magnetism – There is no need to solicit or receive magnetism if there is no need. The magnetic pass is not to be done as a pastime or diversion. It is a serious restorative resource that can be applied to an individual that is experiencing problems of disequilibrium (whether of a moral, spiritual, or physical nature) that could benefit from it. It is not about receiving a certain "energy" or

---

[129] Matthew 10:8

"vitality" from a magnetizer to increase one's own. Yet, the habit of receiving magnetic passes without justification can, at times, constitute a mania that can be compared to the behavior of a hypochondriac who demands medical attention without truly having an illness. Many of those who ask for passes simply because they are in the habit of obtaining them, in reality, may only need more education in the Spiritist doctrine and its moral principles.

Mediums benefit greatly from the use of magnetic passes. In the initial stages of trance mediumship, if difficulties present themselves between the medium and a spirit communication, the application of magnetic passes is of great assistance throughout the entire process. Concluding a trance, it may also be appropriate to offer magnetic passes to the medium in order to fully recover his or her proper state of consciousness and control of the physical body. The application of magnetic passes is of tremendous utility for use in mediumship sessions specifically to assist persons with spirit obsessions. Frequently, it is precisely their very own spirit guides who irradiate the medium with their own magnetism, as well as the other participants at the session.

Receptivity - The person should adopt a positive mental attitude towards the process, accepting with gratitude the magnetism which is being offered and disregarding any skeptical, negative or defiant ideas, which may block the action. That is why one should have a firm conviction regarding the efficacy of magnetism and the benefit that can be reaped towards good physical and spiritual wellbeing.

In order to create an acceptable and comfortable rapport, the magnetizer should establish positive bonds with the recipient to establish mutual respect, trust, and confidence.

Relaxation – The recipient that is able to receive magnetic passes, whether standing up, sitting or laying down, should be comfortable. Regarding their attire, the only recommendation is that his or her clothing be slightly loose to not provoke discomfort.

The person should be invited by the magnetizer to physically and mentally relax. Breathing should be calmly maintained, without moans or irregular modifications, and all physiological rhythms should be functioning normally.

Physical contact is unnecessary - A magnetic pass should not be confused with a massage. The magnetizer should execute all hand movements, maintaining a prudent distance that can be from five to ten centimeters, without touching the recipient. At this distance, psychic interaction can take place without difficulty, both psychic connections interact, magnetic fields connect, and the fluids penetrate within the structure of the perispirit, and from there, exercises its action on the physical body. This physical separation has the virtue of preserving the relationship between the two parties from misunderstandings of any possible ethical transgressions, especially when this activity is performed between persons of different sexes.

In summary, we can say that magnetism, described by Leon Denis as "the medicine of the humble," is an authentic restorative process; a loving exchange from one soul to another of physical and spiritual resources. Knowledge of its process and application is of great importance, and it should not be done as an end in of itself. It should be viewed as a tool that serves for the better understanding of the great faculties of the human soul, and from this knowledge, for the expansion of consciousness and the conquest of new evolutionary states.

We reiterate that magnetism is only but a chapter in the book of Spiritism.

Chapter Nine

SPIRITISM AND PARAPSYCHOLOGY

> *"The ancient belief that we cannot know anything before it passes through the doors of known sensory organs, should follow the same pathway of Newton's mechanics in the face of the theory of relativity."*

Joseph Banks Rhine Pioneering American
Parapsychologist (1895-1980)

GENERAL AND HISTORICAL CONSIDERATIONS

The term *parapsychology* was first introduced in 1889 by MAX DESSOIR, a German psychologist of French ancestry. The Greek prefix *para* means "along side of" and consequently, in light of its etymology, parapsychology is a discipline that is situated as such in a particular relationship with psychology. In truth however, it is "along side of" but "not in" because the academic establishment in the field of psychology has yet to integrate the investigation of parapsychology, with its extensive world of the paranormal, into its studies and programs.

Metaphysics, a term which preceded it was coined by CHARLES RICHET, found great difficulties in being accepted by scientists in the first several decades of the twentieth century. The prefix *meta* was understood to involve knowledge that was "beyond" what was covered by psychology, and in addition, with the suggestion of the idea of the existence of something spiritually "beyond," numerous negative reactions burst forth among those in the scientific disciplines.

The reluctance of the scientific community, and in particular fields such as psychology, to study parapsychological phenomenon was a product of the cultural and scientific climate that predominated in Western society during the nineteenth century, for numerous discoveries and technological advances during that time imprinted a physical, tangible and materialistic influence among these scientists.

Psychology, by its own name, is the *Science of the Soul*. Yet, in its hurry to free itself from the tutelage of philosophy and metaphysics, it transformed into a science without a soul, even worse, into a science opposed to the very idea of a soul. Eventually, it became a biology of behavior with an environmental basis that promoted the study of the relationships that individuals established with their surroundings. Starting with the works of German experimentalists, like ERNEST HEINRICH WEBER (1795-1878) and GUSTAV THEODOR FECHNER (1801-1887), who were inclined to defend a psychophysiological parallel through the formulation of laws that numerically correlated physical variables (stimuli) and psychological variables (sensations), as well as WILHELM WUNDT (1832-1920), creator of the first laboratory of experimental psychology at the University of Leipzig, acquired a decidedly naturalistic orientation, which carried with it an anti-philosophical and anti-spiritualistic position.

The efforts to clearly establish a closer relationship between the mind and the body gave birth to *psychophysics*, and from there were produced the *gestalt* and the *psychoanalytical* schools, though they took different paths. The latter, it must be duly recognized, comes closer to the original sense of psychology by recognizing certain mental principles that are not totally dependent on the physiology of the brain.

It must not be forgotten that in spite of his reservations, FREUD was named an honorary member of the *American Society of Psychical Research* (1915) and of the *Society of Psychical Research* (1938). It is unlikely that he would have accepted such distinctions if he had totally rejected the existence of phenomenon of a paranormal nature since that is what constituted the reason for being of these institutions.

In 1921, in a work entitled *Dreams and Telepathy*, Freud wrote:

"It no longer appears possible to leave aside for a later time the study of what is called occult phenomena."

Later adding,

"It would not be the first time that psychoanalysis becomes the champion of dark but indestructible intuitions that sink their roots within common sense, against professed intellectual knowledge."

In a letter sent to his collaborator MAX EITINGTON, dated February 4, 1921, thanking him for having sent him books on the subject of parapsychology, he wrote:

"The thought of that bitter apple makes me shudder, but there is no way to avoid the need to bite into it."

As is well known, CARL GUSTAV JUNG, initially a follower of Freud but later opposed him and developed his own theories, penetrated so profoundly into the knowledge and acknowledgement of occult phenomena, that he established a bridge of communication between psychoanalysis and parapsychology.

Sadly, the behaviorist movements that dominated twentieth century psychology spearheaded primarily by JOHN BRODUS WATSON (1878-1958), IVAN PERTOVICH PAVLOV (1849-1936) and BURRHUS FREDERICK SKINNER (1904-1990), reduced the study of psychology to the observable behavior of individuals in their interaction with the world around them. They considered psychic processes as epiphenomena derived of the physiology of the nervous system. They also placed the human being and its learning and adaptation processes within a stimulus-response equation, whether it is within the Pavlovian schematic that emphasizes reflex activity or giving more weight to the spontaneously elicited response, which decreases or increases its frequency rate if it is punished or reinforced, according to the conditioning model in place. In the behavior-based schools, any sort of mental activity that does not have its origin in the brain is inadmissible. Because of this, parapsychology encounters so many difficulties when it acknowledges the existence of psychic functions that are extra-physical in nature.

In opposition to this, a new movement which came to be known as transpersonal psychology began to gain momentum. Introduced as a "fourth force" within the field of psychology, it is dedicated to the study of the human being and its behavior within a holistic and spiritual perspective. It was different from the positivist or behaviorist theories ("first force"), as well as from the humanist psychology ("third force"). The transpersonal movement is a collective one and does not have a particular leader, but it includes the contributions of learned academics like CHARLES TART, STANSLISLAV GROF, ROBERTO ASSAGIOLI, KEN WILBER and DANIEL GOLEMAN. This vision gave considerable importance to the transcendence of self, acknowledges the scientific legitimacy of the study of various aspects of personality and behavior in different areas, such as: unitive consciousness, mystical experiences, altered states of consciousness, transcendental dreams, mediumship, reincarnation and other manifestations relative to afterlife survival, as well as a wide range of other paranormal phenomenon. Other schools had relegated this phenomenon as incidental or had totally rejected them. Therefore, the transpersonal movement became the link that was needed to connect psychology with parapsychology and facilitate the long awaited integration of the latter with the former.

In its most general meaning, parapsychology is the discipline that undertakes the scientific study of paranormal phenomena, also known as extrasensory or supra-normal. It is important to note that paranormal does not mean supernatural, which is a non-scientific term that is generally used in religious circles.

Paranormal is also not abnormal, for it does not deal with events that have pathological implications. An appropriate definition of parapsychology would be that which involves the scientific study of all phenomenon in relation to man with its biological, psychological and social surroundings, wherein no known sensory ranges intervene or no known type of physical energy is initiated. The following are definitions along the same lines, provided by experts:

> *"Parapsychology is the branch of psychology that deals with those personal acts or of conduct that are demonstrated not to be physical, that is, that do not fall within the limits of physical principles."* JOSEPH BANKS RHINE and JOSEPH GAITHER PRATT [130]

> *"In its strictest sense, parapsychology is the proof and experimental study of psychic functions that have yet to be incorporated into the scientific psychology system, with the finality of incorporating them into this named system, thereby broadening and completing it."* ROBERT AMADOU [131]

> *"It is the science whose object is to study physical or psychological phenomena produced by forces that appear to be intelligent or by faculties unknown by the mind. "* RENE SUDRE [132]

> *"Parapsychology is the branch of psychology that is occupied with psychic acts that appear to be beyond the realm, at the present, of what are recognized as normal laws."* JOSE RICARDO MUSSO [133]

---

[130] Parapsicología [Parapsychology]. Troquel Editorial. Buenos Aires. 1967, p. 220.

[131] La Parapsicología [Parapsychology]. Paidós Editorial. Buenos Aires. 1971, p. 60.

[132] Tratado de parasicología [Treatments of Parapsychology]. Siglo Viente Editorial, Buenos Aires, 1970, p. 49

[133] En los límites de parasicología [At the Edge of Psychology]. Paidós Editorial., Buenos Aires, 1965, p. 41

"The object of parapsychology is the verification and study of the psychic functions of a paranormal nature, commonly designated as: telepathy, clairvoyance, pre-and post-cognition and psychokinesis. From that standpoint, it aspires to join itself to psychology, being practically its continuation." HERNANI GUIMARAES ANDRADE [134]

Parapsychology is a new scientific attempt to comprehend certain unusual human psychic manifestations. It comes to substitute the preceding English "psychic research" and the French *"metaphysics,"* but it is important to recognize that in previous times to what has been mentioned here, there had already existed research as an to attempt to understand and explain this phenomena.

The French physician CHARLES RICHET, Nobel Prize winner of physiology in 1913, presented his distinguished *Being a Treatise on Metaphysics*, in which he outlined the evolution of parapsychological knowledge into the following four great stages:

Mythical period: It extends from antiquity to the eighteenth century. Prevalent are historical accounts, empirical observations and explanations from a magical or mythological perspective concerning events that suggest their paranormal nature.

Magnetic period: It ranges from the eighteen century to the middle of the next century. It owes its name to the interest aroused by Mesmer's theories of animal magnetism and their therapeutic applications.

Spiritist Period: It begins with the mediumship phenomena at Hydesville in which the Fox sisters played the main role, and acquires greater dimension with the work of Allan Kardec and the development of the Spiritualist/Spiritist movements in the USA and Europe.

Scientific period: It developed at the start of 1870 with the experimental work of WILLIAM CROOKES; the English movement known

---

[134] *Parasicología Experimental* [*Experimental Parapsychology*]. Edicao Calvario Publishing, Sao Paulo, 1967, pg. 24

as psychical research, and all of the subsequent advances made after the birth of metaphysics.

CLASSIFICATION OF PARANORMAL PHENOMENA

After RHINE'S initial proposition in classifying paranormal phenomena within two basic concepts: extra-sensory perception (ESP) and psychokinesis (PK), the field of study of parapsychology has been widening markedly in recent decades. That is why it has been necessary to adopt certain criteria that are uniform and coherent, so that the phenomena are classified in accordance to the relationship and similarity between them. The following outline serves to provide a panoramic view of the wide spectrum of paranormal phenomena with the understanding that it is not a final or definitive classification, for many of these phenomena can be placed under many groups simultaneously, depending on their nature and source. These are the four groups:

Parapsychic phenomena – They are also known as extra-sensory perception (ESP), Psi-Gamma, or Subjective. They refer to paranormal events that are connected with cognitive processes.

Paraphysical phenomena – They are also known as psychokinesis (PK), Psi-kappa or objective. They refer to the PSI function with aspects of action or movement and include all the paranormal influences that exercise tangible effects on physical reality.

Parabiological phenomena – These comprise (psychic and physical) or mixed paranormal manifestations exercised over living beings, independent of their level of evolutionary development within the phylogenetic scale, and which trigger modifications in their constitution or functioning.

Parathanatic phenomena - They are also called Psi-Theta. These include certain unusual events that are purportedly provoked by beings that are already dead, in other words, by disincarnate spirits or theta agents. In general, they refer to any episode that involves any form of life after death, be it of a subjective (theta-psi gamma) or objective (theta-psi kappa) nature.

PARAPSYCHIC PHEOMENA

Telepathy – Mental communication. Transmission of thought at a distance. Extra-sensory reception of another person's mental content.

Clairvoyance – Remote-viewing. Extra-sensory perception of knowledge of persons, material objects or of actual events. Synonymous terms are metagnomy and cryptesthesia. There are other varieties such as:

Clairaudience - Paranormal hearing. Extra-sensory perception of sounds incapable of being heard within normal physiological parameters.

Clairsentience – Awareness, sensing or feeling of other realities outside the normal physiological boundaries.

Crystallomancy – Extra-sensory reception of images reflected in crystals or in a liquid or any type of reflecting surface.

Psychometry – Extra-sensory reception of images or information obtained by a person by touching or feeling an object, and who functions as a psychic conductor. Also known as *tactile metagnomy* or *pragmatic cryptesthesia*.

Autoscopy – Paranormal health diagnosis. The sensitive person sees an image of his or her body as if an outside observer. Internal view of the body is called *internal autoscopy*; the subject visualizes the interior of the bodies of others. In these cases the sensitive usually formulates diagnoses or prognoses of one or several illnesses without conducting physical examinations.

Radiasthesia - Collection of radiations emitted by persons or objects through instruments like a pendulum or of a dowsing rod. It is frequently used to locate sources of wells, springs, buried objects, missing persons, cadavers, etc.

Precognition – Paranormal perception of a future event that is unable to be rationally inferred from currently known facts. A variety of this is *retrocognition*, which is the knowledge of events that have already taken place, recently or long ago, and which were unknown to the sensitive person.

Bi-location or Out-of Body Experience or Astral Projection – Paranormal phenomena that happen spontaneously or can be induced at will. It consists of a psychic or spiritual projection outside of corporeal (physical) limits. It can lead to an experience where there is an appearance of a person appearing in two different locations simultaneously. These experiences are that one is viewing the world and especially one's own body from a position outside the physical body. Kardec used the word *bi-corporeality*.

PARAPHYSICAL PHENOMENA

Psychokinesis – the force exercised by a person over something physical and tangible without the means of instruments or known physical energies. When the action is done remotely it is known as *telekinesis.*

Levitation – Suspending objects or living persons in the air, apparently defying the laws of gravity, without utilizing any known physical energy.

Apports – The materialization of objects within a closed space without the involvement of any visible physical forces. Abnormal apparition and displacement of an object in a closed space.

Poltergeist – A psychokinetic manifestation characterized by noises or displacement of objects, regularly linked with the energy released by a person acting as the epicenter of the phenomena. The actions appear to be focused in an intelligent manner; their aim is to attract attention, perturb or cause harm. When manifestations appear to be linked to one place no matter any of its inhabitants, it is referred to as a *haunting* or *haunted house.* If stones are hurled, the phenomena is known as *paralithogenia*; if there is movement or tremors it is known as *parasysmogenia*; and if fire appears, it is referred to as *parapyrogenia.* The collective poltergeist phenomenon is also known as *Recurrent Spontaneous Psychokinesis* (RSPK).

Paranormal Electronic Voices – Electronic voice phenomena (EVP) or instrumental transcommunication (ITC). These involve recordings of human voices, music and/or a myriad of sounds of a paranormal nature that are produced on unrecorded tapes of recording devices or through other electronic equipment.

Psychic photography or spirit photography – Paranormal photography that registers mental images triggered by a psychokinetic action on unexposed film. A variety of these phenomena is of an experience involving mediumship in which disincarnate spirits are photographed.

Kirliangraphy or Kirlian photography - Phenomena that are bio-energetic in nature, which registers the structural variations, intensity, magnitude and hue of the luminous emanations observed in living things when they are exposed to special frequency and high voltage cameras. Through Kirlian photography it is possible to examine the aura of persons and consider their current physical and psychic state.

PARABIOLOGICAL PHENOMENA

Hyperesthesia – States of exacerbation of sensitivity in special circumstances, which allow a subject to pick up physical stimuli that are not able to be perceived by most people. Hyperesthesia include a wide range of sensory alterations, such as: *Hyperacusia* (auditory sensitivity), *hyperosmia* (hypersensitive sense of smell), *hypergeusia* ((hypersensitive to taste), hyperaphia (tactile hypersensitivity), *hyperoptics* (visual hypersensitivity), *hypermnesia* (hypersensitive memory), and *hyperalgsia* (hypersensitivity to pain).

Dermo Optical Perception **(DOP)** – Ability to see shapes, written texts or colors with bandaged eyes, through epidermal contact with the object to be deciphered, with the fingertips most of the time. In some texts, it is also referred to as *extra-retinal vision*.

Cenesthesia – Strange sensations that an individual feels with regards to his or her own body, as if movements or alterations were taking place in the internal organs. Cenesthsia effects can be provoked in a subject through hypnosis.

Bio-pause – Domination and neutralization of organic functions at will. Included in this group are the effects produced by those such as fakirs when they are not deceptive or fraudulent. Also included in this group are those who can control pain and go without food and water for exceptionally long periods of time.

Dermography – Scribbles, signs, and drawings that are etched on the skin of a sensitive subject as a result of a paranormal action. Stigmata appear in the form of wounds or ulcers.

Pyrovasia – Paranormally fireproof. Normally in the action of walking on fire without burning oneself or feeling any pain. It is also called *absefalesia* and *apyropathy*.

Transfiguration - Spontaneous modifications of facial features or bodily dimensions that appear quite different from normal. Generally, this phenomenon is associated with mediums, trances, where there is a change in the outer appearance of the medium, which resembles the spirit that is being manifested through him or her.

Prasopopesis – Abrupt, spontaneous or provoked change that is produced in a subject's psychological make-up within a trance state producing of the emergence of two or more personalities. They can happen by way of suggestion, due to psychological and/or pathological reasons or in certain mediumship experiences.

Paranormal Healing Therapies – They include the wide spectrum of healing derived by many means, like magnetic applications, healing by thought, and the many types of healing due to psychic and mediumship phenomena.

An-psi or Animal parapsychology – Paranormal phenomena of various types that happen around animals, whether individually or in groups. They also include those that are paranormally related that can take place between animals and humans.

Phyto-psi or Plant parapsychology – Paranormal phenomena that are produced in the plant kingdom within the interaction between human beings and plants. *Phytometarchy* is when effects are provoked that brings about the growth and improvement in the quality of plant life, as a result of a psychic paranormal action. Pschothanatosis is that same activity, but directed to cause harm or death in plants.

PARATHANATIC PHENOMENA

Extra-cerebral memories or past life memories – Spontaneous or induced (generally by hypnosis and/or past life regression) memories that appear to come from one or more previous lives. It is associated with all research relating to *reincarnation.*

Life After death – Wide array of manifestations that offer evidence of the survival of the soul or the personality, after physical death. The most important studies in this field are near death experiences (NDE's) also known as *reversible clinical death.*

Mediumship - Communications with disembodied spirits through mediums. It includes all interactions between living and non-living beings.

SPIRITISM AND PARAPSYCHOLOGY

There exist relationships, analogies and differences between Spiritism and parapsychology. In its broadest definition, Spiritism is a doctrine, in as much as parapsychology aspires to be recognized as a science. Spiritism is highly interested in research and experiments with regards to the vast domain of psychic phenomena; however, it is also concerned and cares about the design and the laying of the foundations of a philosophical theory that decisively contributes to the expansion of human consciousness and its moral transformation. Psychology concentrates its interest in demonstrating the existence of special faculties of the human psyche that are manifested on the boundaries of the physiological resources which defy the limits of the physical categories of time and space. In the parapsychological field, philosophical subjects are of little interest and with moral issues even less.

Spiritism supports a spiritualist interpretation of psychic phenomena that considers them to be manifestations of the spirit, in other words, from a Being that is able to surpass the sensory limitations of its physical organism as well as transcend it after death, preserving its ability to continue generating, from that other world dimension, other psychic phenomena. Taking into consideration the origin of those manifestations, Spiritism recognizes that they are divided into two categories: some that have their source within the mental processes of living beings (psychical) and those that are produced by disincarnate beings (especially via mediumship).

Parapsychology is occupied in the gathering of evidence that demonstrates the objective reality of paranormal phenomena; and, does not convey any interpretation concerning its nature, whether of a materialist or spiritualist type.

When interpretations have been presented that affirmatively supported any of these theories, it must be remembered that these are made individually and is not subscribed as a whole to that discipline. Spiritism respects the neutrality of parapsychology and considers it a prudent and reasonable attitude, for the bottom line is that the object of science is not to certify that materialism or spiritualism is right, but to seek truth with the supreme mission to expand knowledge of humanity about itself, about life, and the universe.

It is important to point out that there is no demonstration of parapsychology that contradicts or renders taboo any of the principles upheld by Spiritism; quite the contrary. The theories that are essentially accepted by the majority of the parapsychologists of the world were declared by ALLAN KARDEC and his followers more than a century ago. It must be kept in mind that the codifier of the information contained in what is known as Spiritism presents solid arguments aimed to prove the existence of psychic functions, extra-physiological and extra-physical in nature, in all human beings. He divided it into two categories: one having to do with *intelligent effects*; the other with *physical effects*. RICHET followed this outline when he separated metaphysical phenomena into *subjective* and *objective*, and so did RHINE when he established that paranormal phenomena are expressed following these guidelines: those that have to do with *extra-sensory perception* (ESP) and those that have to do with *psychokinesis* (PK).

All that parapsychology has been studying and proving in the wrongfully termed field of the supernatural, every power of the mind that it is making evident, all that in ancient times was considered "impossible" and that is now being presented as reality with the backing of a considerable amount of empirical proof, is day-by-day consolidating the foundations upon which the Spiritist doctrine rests. It is also confirming that the vast psychic phenomenology which manifests upon mankind is more clearly and rationally explained by the teachings of the Spiritist school than by any other doctrine. In *The Mediums' Book*, KARDEC presented a meticulous description of the phenomena of mediumship and also those that would later be labeled as paranormal. In that work, he also recognized that knowledge of psychic events that had their origins in the mind of the very same subject, without the participation of disincarnated spirits, and this is highly important to the understanding of those that are mediumship-related. He succeeded in establishing a rigorously scientific methodology to determine the origin of each phenomenon, suggesting that the Spiritist interpretation be the last hypothesis and not the first, in order to investigate every possible explanation that would dispense with or omit spirit intervention:

"Studies teach us to separate that which is true from that which is false or exaggerated, insofar as phenomena that we cannot explain. If an unusual effect is produced, be it a noise, a movement, even an

apparition, etc. the first thing we must think is that it is of a totally natural cause because that is what is most probable.

Therefore, we must look with all caution for that cause and solely admit the intervention of the spirits when there is full knowledge of it. This is the only way not to be deceived." [135]

This attitude makes the connection between parapsychologists and Spiritists, within one experimental program, easier for them to honestly and without preconceptions discover the true nature of psychic phenomena until they are enlightened as to their source and the laws that govern them. RENE SUDRE rightly wrote, around 1920, that "contemporary psychology was at an impasse without the support of metaphysics." Paraphrasing this well known French scholar, we can say that it is through its identification with Spiritism that parapsychology will be able to resolve this impasse.

The difference that has traditionally separated Spiritists and the original parapsychologists lies in the controversy of the spirit and its continuation beyond death. Meanwhile, for the former it is an undeniable point of doctrine, the latter have only solely arrived in considering it as a hypothesis still subject to be proven. Fortunately, the evolution of parapsychological studies very clearly points towards recognizing the existence of a spiritual factor, which will allow thinking towards a quick and definitive improvement regarding that divergence.

The opening of a new chapter within parapsychological studies, called *parathantic* or *Psi-theta*, proposed by the respected U.S. researcher JOSEPH GAITHER PRATT (1910-1979), signified a great step forward on the road leading to obtaining of the proof to certify spiritual survival (survival of consciousness) and established a direct link to spiritual science, which had already been proven in the past century. One must not forget that the first objective that RHINE undertook at Duke University was the search of such elements of proof,

---

[135] Second part, Ch. V, Spontaneous manifestations, No. 91. Ibid. pg. 95.

which towards the end of his lifetime and that of his wife, they were inclined to recognize.

The progress achieved in contemporary science, particularly in the field of physics, is propelling in a spiritualistic direction. Notable researchers like, EINSTEIN, PLANCK, EDDINGTON, JEAN CHARON and other physicists of the twentieth century, have contributed theories and demonstrations that eliminated the false belief in the absolute independence between space and time, between matter and energy, fusing these notions into one concept that goes beyond that which is tri-dimensional and that is expressed through mathematical symbols or intuitions that are not bound to concrete forms of logical rationalist thinking. Never seen particles and anti-particles, gravitational fields, space-time *continuum*, anti-matter, *quanta*, and parallel universes are terms that form a part of a unique language that is light years apart from mechanistic materialism. EINSTEIN, with good reason was right, when he ironically stated, "materialism died of asphyxia…due to lack of matter."

No one can deny the extraordinary contributions made by prominent scholars of Spiritism to the establishment and development of the disciplines that undertake a study of the paranormal. No matter if the discussion is about psychical research, metaphysics, of para-psychology, psychophysiology or of biophysics, presented within, is the names of those fundamental to the Spiritist school. The founder of metaphysics, with all due respect, made this honest acknowledge-ment of the work of KARDEC:

> *"He always relies on research, in such a way that his work not is merely a grandiose and homogenous theory, but also an imposing depository of facts. "* [136]

If we find useful indeed the outline presented by RICHET, in order to show how the evolution of the study of physics has devel-oped, it does not seem right to separate the Spiritist stage from the sci-

---

[136] CHARLES RICHET, *Traité de Métapsychique* [*Treatise on Metaphysics*], Librairie Felix Alcan, Paris, 1923, p. 33.

entific one, for the work of KARDEC represents the true beginning of the scientific era within the history of the study of the paranormal and that which is spiritual. It can be confidently shown that a substantial percentage of researchers that have delved in this field, finally opted to accept precepts of Spiritism: the work of WILLIAM CROOKES and his experiences with mediumship that followed strict laboratory procedures; cases like that of LOMBROSO who relented in light of the evidence produced by spirit materializations; and, of RICHET himself, confessing to BOZZANO that he had finally arrived at the conclusion that "death is the door to the other life," have repeatedly occurred thousands of times. Such is the history of Spiritism; incredulousness was vanquished and defeated by the weight of the facts. It suffices to cite scientists with Spiritist tendencies such as, WILLIAM FLETCHER BARRETT, ALFRED RUSSEL WALLACE, OLIVER LODGE, FREDERICK MYERS, W.J.CRAWFORD, GUSTAVE GELEY, PAUL GIBIER, CAMILLE FLAMMARION, JOHANN F. K. ZOLLNER, WILLIAM JAMES, ALEXANDER AKSAKOF, KARL DU PREL, RICHARD HODGSON, JAMES HYSLOP, to acknowledge that they, with their methodical studies and experiments regarding psychic phenomena, laid the foundation of metaphysics and present day parapsychology.

To set the foundation for the establishment of an adequate relationship between Spiritists and parapsychologists has been of great concern to many Spiritists in the Americas and Europe. In one of his inspired works, the distinguished Argentine writer HUMBERTO MARIOTTI (1905-1982), expressed it precisely:

> "Spiritism as an integral science stands firm before Parapsychology, for it, directly as well as indirectly, does nothing but reaffirm its teaching principles. Spiritism, as it is known, is the more advanced spiritual reality in all its phases and ideas that have faced materialism; consequently, Parapsychology, although it persists in its anti-Spiritist posture, will always remain a science

with spiritual tendencies for its results will never be favorable to the materialist interpretation of man and of life.

Spiritism when confronted with Parapsychology represents a scientific advance, being that the body of its doctrine not only attends to the supernormal field of the psychological, but transcends it by penetrating into the live and real world of the spirits. Therefore, its ideological force will always remain undamaged and steadfast, giving the timid and the remiss the luminous truths of the future. " [137]

In conclusion, Spiritism supports and promotes the development of parapsychology and confidently awaits its confirmations and advancement with the certainty that this science will ultimately accept, that it is not before a "mind" or a "brain" when it confronts paranormal phenomenon, for in reality it is a *spiritual entity*, pre-existing, surviving, and hence reincarnating, and it is that agent which is responsible for all manifestations. When parapsychology returns to psychology and its "lost objective," it is then when it will finally open itself up to acknowledgement of the immortal soul.

---

[137] La Parapsicología a la luz de la Filosofía Espirita [Parapsychology in the light of Spiritism].Constancia. Buenos Aires, 1975.

Chapter Ten

THE SPIRITIST PARADIGM

> *"Spiritism, in enabling us to know the invisible world that surrounds us and whose center we live, the laws that govern it, its relationships with the visible world, the nature and state of the beings that inhabit it, and consequently, the destiny of mankind after death, is an authentic revelation in the scientific sense of the word."*
>
> ***Allan Kardec***

The greatest obstacle to acceptance of the existence of the spirit does not come from lack of evidence, but rather the belief that its existence is impossible. Numerous eminent researchers of the paranormal have drawn attention to this phenomenon of a psychological nature, yet it is with great consternation that they have come to the realization that it is *they* who have propagated it.

The case of Professor CHARLES RICHET, who as we already know, was a highly regarded physiologist and Nobel Prize winner, and distinguished himself as a critic, skeptic and persistent researcher of the paranormal and of mediumship, illustrates a classic example of the behavior that was typically prejudicial and highly influenced by the opinions of his peers. After having accomplished a series of

meticulous sessions with the medium EUSEPIA PALADINO, he
wrote the following:

> *"But at this point, one notices a curious psychological phenomenon.
> We note that they are witnessed events, but notwithstanding every-
> thing, they are absurd, that they are in contradiction with every day
> observational events, and which are denied, not only by science, but
> by all mankind; events that are quick and fleeting, that take place in
> semi-darkness, and almost by surprise, with no other proof than the
> testimony of our senses and we know that these are often fallible.
> After having witnessed these events, everything helps to cast doubts
> upon them. Well now, when these events take place they seem true
> to us and we are ready to state so, but when we reconsider, when all
> of our friends laugh at our gullibility, we almost feel disarmed and
> we begin to doubt. Could it all have been an illusion? Was I perhaps
> bamboozled? Then, when the moment of the experiment becomes
> more and more remote in time, that experiment which once seemed
> so conclusive becomes more and more uncertain, and we end up
> being persuaded to think that we were the victim of trickery."* [138]

The belief in the impossibility of psychic and paranormal
phenomena was forged foremost as a result of the successes obtained
in the nineteenth century in the scientific field of physiochemistry
built upon the foundation of the principles of motion established by
ISAAC NEWTON (1642-1727). One of the most outstanding scientific achievements of the century was the prediction of the existence
of the planet Neptune on the basis of its gravitational effects, before
it was discovered by telescope. Science arrived at a more amplified
understanding of a variety of natural phenomena integrating it into,
seemingly universal, of the physical world in a great number of fields
until then considered separately, such as: heat, light, electricity, and
magnetism. The appealing equations presented by JAMES CLERK
MAXWELL (1831-1879) afforded the explanation concerning the

---

[138] *Traité de Métapsychique*, Ibid. p. 651

propagation of the electromagnetic field that would consequently lead to the invention of the radio. In its technological applications, the increasing use that mankind made of its knowledge resulted in the construction of bridges, ships, factories, and railroads, which also demonstrated its firm foundation of its power over nature. Already towards the end of the nineteenth century, some scientists had concluded by saying that their only fear was that there appeared to be few, so as not to say any, areas left of ignorance yet to be explored…

Most knowledgeable people, within that climate, believed that space, time, and mass, the atom, energy and other ideas were already clear and under the complete control of science. In its ultimate extreme, everybody was made up of solid atoms, analogous to billiard balls. Spatial coordinates could be described, and upon the introduction of Newtonian concepts of time, velocity could be expressed with complete exactitude. Matter was indestructible; its shape could change from solid to liquid or to gas, but it could never disappear. In addition, energy was indestructible, although its form could change as well.

It also seemed that the vital functions of plants and animals could also be reduced in the end to physical and chemical processes. In addition, humans began to be understood within these reductionist parameters. Physiologists and neurologists affirmed the direct relationship between the mind and the brain. Deficiencies of personality or mental functions, caused by different kinds of brain lesions, even led to the belief that the concept of "mind" was superfluous. At every turn researchers were more compelled to adhere to "epiphenomenalism," in other words, the theory that asserts that mental processes are merely a secondary effect of brain activity, so that it sufficed to understand brain physiology in order to comprehend psychological or mental functions.

Insofar as the spirit was concerned, that concept was rejected and labeled as outdated and unscientific. Formally, there was continued respect for religious tradition with respect to the soul, but death was considered to be the final extinction of life.

It was no wonder, therefore, that in such an atmosphere of materialistic euphoria there was no room or attention given to the supposed phenomena that were studied by Spiritists and paranormal researchers. Telepathy, clairvoyance, precognition, psychokinesis, and other manifestations of paranormality ended up left unexplained according to the world model that was present in the nineteenth century. And, what was to be said about spirits, mediumship communications, or reincarnation? All of these things were impossible according to the official scientific community of experts; the great majority of them ignored or scorned the phenomena. Generalizations were made about alleged erroneous reports or fraud or they were even attributed to human gullibility.

That skeptical and condemning climate would prevail for many decades and would experience significant changes that would allow an accumulative and unresolved process that continued throughout the twentieth century, but would eventually lead science to liberate itself from this mechanistic hold. FRITJOF CAPRA, a physicist, researcher, and writer at Berkeley University in California, wrote in 1982 in his book *The Turning Point*:

> *"One of the most important lessons that physicists had to learn in this century was the fact that all the concepts and theories that we use to describe nature are limited...."*

The new climate of opinion was due, in great part, to the conviction that the image of the universe that was prevalent in the nineteenth century was no longer valid. And, it is precisely in the field of physics wherein the most radical transformations came from. In the 1900s, the German physicist MAX PLANCK (1858-1947) formulated the hypothesis of the discontinuity of energy (energy does not vary continuously), creating quantum theory, and founding modern physics. A *quantum* is the fundamental and indivisible unit of energy. A short time later, ALBERT EINSTEIN (1879-1955) introduced his theory of relativity which modified Newton's laws of mechanics, and introduced the equivalence of mass and energy. The sub-atomic entities of the Universe elude ever day concepts and are interrelated by a network of mathematical probabilities whose rules adapt to the laws of relativity and quantum theory. The physicists of the twentieth century have demolished the old structure, and in its place have theorized a model that is no longer three-dimensional; one that is endowed with properties that are so incredible, that the paranormal field by comparison, might be considered as something commonplace.

The principle of complementarity imposed itself upon theoretical physicists as a direct consequence of the dual nature of sub-atomic particles: sometimes they behave like particles, other times like waves. It is from this uncertainty that important consequences in the paranormal field may be derived. The uncertainty principle that was introduced in 1927, by the physicist WERNER HEISENBERG (1901-1976), points out that it is not possible to simultaneously or accurately measure the location and speed of a particle at the basic particle level. In other words, when the magnitudes being worked with are quantum in nature, classic determinism is lost. The no-localization principle yields that links between particles or events separated by great distances are produced simultaneously without actions of an intermediary system. The most diverse psychic phenomenon may reside within the realm of relativity and quantum physics.

Different schools of thought have been developed in order to describe and interpret quantum relationships. One of them, out of the "Copenhagen School" of theories by the Danish physicist NIELS BOHR (1885-1962), suggests that the factor that prompts the deadlock of an indeterminate quantum system in solely one state is the *act of observation* undertaken by a *conscious observer*. If measures were to be taken by some type of non-conscious machine, even then each of the possible states would be present until a conscious human being would make an observation of the system. In this manner, the Copenhagen interpretation introduces the human consciousness within the heart of physics, by granting the observer the role of giving a definite form to the chaos of an indeterminate quantum state. To consider the observer capable of forcing the quantum system towards a definite shape, to asking the observer if he or she could or not decide in which specific state the system could be when observed, is just a step away. United within there, may be actions tied to telepathy, clairvoyance, precognition, and psychokinesis!

And, it is surprisingly beautiful that the declarations of physicists, regarding the nature of reality and of the world of the senses, appear to be each time more similar to the notions maintained in the most diverse esoteric and spiritualistic traditions. Just these few quotes are sufficient to confirm this:

> *ARTHUR EDDINGTON (1882-1944) English astronomer, expressed: "It is difficult for the matter of fact physicist to accept the view that the substratum of everything is of mental character."*

> LOUIS DE BROGLIE (1892-1987), French physicist, creator of the field of wave mechanics and Nobel Prize winner in physics in 1929, said: *"In space-time, all that for one of us constitutes the past, the present and the future, appears in one block."*

> JEAN CHARON, modern physicist, notes in the preface of his brilliant work *The Unknown Spirit*: *"In order to perceive in a mode that is complete and satisfactory the structure and the properties of certain elementary particles, the intervention of a particular space-time is necessary, presenting all the characteristics of a space-time of the spirit, accompanied with that of gross matter."*

Keeping in close relationship with quantum physicists, the new psychologists are inviting us to a change of attitudes so that we can open our minds to other realities. Probably, KARL GUSTAV JUNG represents to the world of psychology the same revolutionary experience, as significant as PLANCK and EINSTEIN had on physics, when he laid down the groundwork for a spiritualist interpretation of mankind that would grant privilege to its transcendental nature. He would be followed by ABRAHAM MASLOW, with his humanist proposition; ROBERTO ASSAGIOLI, the founder of psycho synthesis; STANISLAV GROF, who developed holotrophic breathing techniques; CHARLES TART, KEN WILBER, DANIEL GOLEMAN, and ROBERT ORNSTEN, pioneers of transpersonal psychology; RAYMOND MOODY, MORRIS NETHERTON, EDITH FIORE, and HELEN WAMBACH, forging the way with studies of near-death experiences and past life regressions.

In this new vision of reality, which shows the universe and mankind in a new light, it no longer seems impossible for the spirit world to reconcile itself with science.

By closely observing the evolution of knowledge in history, it is evident that civilization finds itself before the presence of a new scientific paradigm that shows mankind different perspectives and horizons.

Paradigm is a term used by the U.S. born historian and philosopher of science THOMAS KUHN (1922-1996) in his book *The Structure of Scientific Revolutions*, which alludes to the conceptual systems that dominate the thinking of scientific communities during specific periods in the evolution of science. Therefore, examples of ancient and modern paradigms include Aristotelian logic, heliocentric theory, Cartesian dualism, Darwin's theory of evolution, Newtonian mechanics, Einstein's theory of relativity, etc. Kuhn proposed a division between *normal* science, that which is created by the scientific community and founded upon a paradigm that serves as a foundation for advances to come, and *abnormal* science which is produced as a consequence of the collapse of the current paradigm due to the emergence or appearance of anomalies that cannot be satisfactory explained. That crisis situation is finally resolved with the substitution of one paradigm by a new one.

The new concepts that are being derived from modern physics, psychology, or parapsychology undoubtedly will constitute a new paradigm that will substantially transform the vision of mankind and the world. Nonetheless, what is still lacking here is a central element that explicitly should be at the center of this paradigm: the HUMAN SPIRIT, the dynamic factor of life, pre-existent at birth and surviving death, which progresses indefinitely, in multiple existences, following the infinite trajectory of its cosmic evolution.

And, it is Spiritism, a school of thought that encompasses the study of the spirit in a more complete manner, and facilitates the comprehension of the principles and laws that guide it. In having a man of science and profound thinker as Allan Kardec as its founder and codifier, who assumed completely his historic and spiritual mission, one can affirm simply that Spiritism is an authentic scientific paradigm. The culture and educational training of Kardec is completely evident in all his work, in building an admirable and coherent model that is compatible with the developments of science, in which Spiritism adopts a receptive attitude to incorporate its new discoveries.

According to the Kuhn's vision, Spiritism has identified legitimate scientific problems relating to "the study of the origin, the nature and the destiny of the spirit and its relationship with the corporeal world." It introduces a methodology that allows for scientific research supported by interchange with spirits by mediumship and through a vast range of psychic phenomenology. It also explains a most adequate criterion by which to evaluate the data obtained, guided by logical and rational analysis.

Approximations towards the knowledge of spiritual reality that are gleaned from quantum physics, transpersonal psychology, parapsychology, and the esoteric schools of thought are valuable and important, but they shall remain incomplete until they incorporate the Spiritist Paradigm, which is the natural and legitimate foundation of the Science of the Spirit.

With definitive acknowledgement of Spiritist principles, the process of substituting the old reductionist - materialist and dogmatic- religious paradigm that has prevailed during thousands of years of our history will come to an end, and the world will welcome the new scientific-spiritualistic paradigm, which can already be seen on the horizon of the third millennium. It is a paradigm that reunites science and consciousness, that shines by its ecological disposition regarding the respect and the preservation of life and of nature by its holistic vision, and in which a human being is conceived to be a dynamic and integrated entity with psycho-socio-spiritual components. And, because of the force it brings towards altruistic behavior, solidarity and fraternity, aimed to building a beautiful, free, just, egalitarian and loving world, the one always thought and dreamed of by humans, that with their light, example, and efforts they will have fostered the transformation of our humanity.

When all this occurs, the mission of Spiritism will have been fulfilled!

author has only a 99% (or less)
grasp of English
gets distracting at times

also — author is gullible

poor English ~~thoughout~~ +
poor proofreading of that

— morality —
intuitive — positive

o/w — too much room for self-delusion
+ rationalization

(Eileen Garrett wasn't sure about
her perceptions?)

Made in the USA
Lexington, KY
21 March 2014